The European Encounter with Hinduism in India

Currents of Encounter

STUDIES IN INTERRELIGIOUS AND INTERCULTURAL RELATIONS

Editor in Chief

Marianne Moyaert (*Vrije Universiteit Amsterdam, the Netherlands*)

Editorial Board

Catherine Cornille (*Boston College, USA*) – Marion Grau (*MF Norwegian School of Theology, Norway*) – Paul Hedges (*NTU, Singapore*) – Henry Jansen (*Vrije Universiteit Amsterdam, the Netherlands*) – Bagus Laksana (*Sanata Dharma University in Yogyakarta, Indonesia*) – Willie L. van der Merwe (*Vrije Universiteit Amsterdam, the Netherlands*) – Jonathan Tan (*Case Western Reserve University, USA*)

Founding Editors

Jerald D. Gort
Hendrik M. Vroom (†)

Advisory Board

Gavin d'Costa (*University of Bristol, Department of Religion and Theology*)
Lejla Demiri (*University of Tubingen, Center for Islamic Theology*)
Nelly van Doorn- Harder (*Wake Forest University School of Divinity*)
Jim Heisig (*Nanzan Institute for Religion & Culture*)
Mechteld Jansen (*Protestant Theological University, Amsterdam*)
Edward Kessler (*Woolf Institute and Fellow of St Edmund's College, Cambridge*)
Oddbjorn Leirvik (*University of Oslo, Faculty of Theology*)
Hugh Nicholson (*Loyola University Chicago, Department of Theology*)
Anant Rambachan (*St. Olaf College, Northfield, USA*)
John Sheveland (*Gonzaga University*)
Mona Siddiqui (*University of Edingburgh, School of Divinity*)
Pim Valkenberg (*Catholic University of America*)
Michelle Voss Roberts (*Wake Forest University School of Divinity*)
Ulrich Winkler (*University of Salzburg, Center for Intercultural Theology and the Study of Religions*)

VOLUME 62

The titles published in this series are listed at *brill.com/coe*

The European Encounter with Hinduism in India

By

Jan Peter Schouten

Translated by

Henry Jansen

BRILL
RODOPI

LEIDEN | BOSTON

This work was originally published in Dutch as *Aangenaam kennis te maken. De ontmoeting van Europeanen met het hindoeïsme in India* by Uitgeverij Damon, Eindhoven.

This publication in English has been made possible thanks to the financial support of the Van Coeverden Adriani Stichting, the Stichting Van Eijkfonds, the Stichting Zonneweelde, and the J.E. Juriaanse Stichting.

Cover illustration: Philippus Baldaeus with servant in Sri Lanka. Painting by Jean de la Rocquette (Rijksmuseum, Amsterdam).

The Library of Congress Cataloging-in-Publication Data is available online at http://catalog.loc.gov
LC record available at http://lccn.loc.gov/19054317

Typeface for the Latin, Greek, and Cyrillic scripts: "Brill". See and download: brill.com/brill-typeface.

ISSN 0923-6201
ISBN 978-90-04-42006-9 (paperback)
ISBN 978-90-04-42007-6 (e-book)

This book is printed on acid-free paper and produced in a sustainable manner.

Contents

Acknowledgements IX
List of Illustrations XI

Introduction 1
1 A Functioning Temple 1
2 A Long History of Encounter 2
3 The Prehistory of Dialogue 2
4 Terminological Relativisation 4

1 The First Visitors: Marco Polo and the Franciscan Friars 7
1 Beyond Byzantium 7
2 The Mongol Advance 7
3 Marco Polo 9
4 People with Dog's Heads 10
5 A Strange Culture 13
6 A Separate Caste 14
7 The Friars Speak 17
8 Odoric 18
9 Another Civilisation in View 20

2 Knowledge is Power: Nicolò de' Conti and Jan Huygen van Linschoten 24
1 Traders Make their Way to India 24
2 A Penitent Apostate 24
3 A Corporate Spy in Action 25
4 A Humanistic Work 26
5 Feasts 28
6 Shocking Religious Phenomena 29
7 A Dutchman in a Portuguese City 30
8 Caste Hierarchy 32
9 Religious Customs and Religious Faith 34
10 Monotheism 36
11 An Unknown World 37

3 A Foreign Culture Baptised: The Jesuits Roberto de Nobili and Thomas Stephens 40
1 Travels to Asia 40
2 Jesuits in Mission 40

3 A Promising Young Man 41
4 In the Capital 42
5 A Christian *Sannyāsī* 43
6 De Nobili's Appeal for Brahmins 45
7 Opposition from the Church 46
8 Local Customs 47
9 Conversion and *Accomodatio* 49
10 Affinity with Hinduism? 51
11 Caste as a Stumbling Block 52
12 De Nobili as an Example? 53
13 Thomas Stephens in Goa 54
14 The *Purāṇa* 55

4 Dutch Ministers in the VOC: Rogerius and Baldaeus 60
1 The Oldest Manual 60
2 Pastor and Missionary 60
3 Rogerius' Career in the East 61
4 Study on Hinduism 64
5 Sources 64
6 An Honest Report 66
7 The Structure of the Book 68
8 An Appealing Book 70
9 Baldaeus and Mythology 72
10 Sources 74
11 Refutation 75
12 Other Ministers 77

5 A Pietistic Preacher in Danish Territory: Bartholomäus Ziegenbalg 82
1 A Danish Undertaking 82
2 Pietistic Germans 83
3 Preaching in Tamil 84
4 Sources of Language and Religion 85
5 The "Malabar Correspondence" 88
6 On the Path to Salvation? 91
7 Systematic Work 92

6 A Disappointed Missionary: Abbé Dubois 99
1 Reading for the Curious 99
2 A Costly Manuscript 100

3 Missionaries in Turbulent Times 101
4 A Hindu among the Hindus 103
5 Mission Impossible? 105
6 A Manual 107
7 Inclusion of the Lower Castes 108
8 Contamination 110
9 Reincarnation 111

7 **British Government Officials: John Muir and Nascent Indology** 114
1 The East Indian Company 114
2 An Influential Translation 114
3 A Learned Society 116
4 The Serampore Trio 118
5 'Little Britain' in a Foreign Society 119
6 The Christian Faith Disseminated 120
7 Writing in Sanskrit 121
8 Divine Properties 122
9 Hindus Respond to the Challenge 125
10 Other Research into Hinduism 127

8 **The Image of the East in the West: Nineteenth-century British India in Fiction and Travel Reports** 130
1 Romantic Orientalism 130
2 The First Detective Novel 133
3 Emily Eden: A Lady Travelling in a Strange Land 135
4 Mary Carpenter: A Visitor in Search of Renewal 137
5 D.C. Steyn Parvé: Fear of Rebellion in the Colonies 139
6 Willam Urwick: A Reflective Tour 140
7 A Princely Picture of India: Prince Bojidar 142

9 **Missionaries from Switzerland: The Basel Mission in South India** 147
1 A Minister Honoured 147
2 On the Road in a Mission Field 147
3 A New Beginning 150
4 Church in India—An Indian Church? 151
5 Mapping a Language 153
6 Examining the *Liṅgāyats* 153
7 In Search of a Point of Contact 154
8 An Exceptional French Swiss 156

Acknowledgements

Whoever writes a book on such a broad theme as this one is very much indebted to the assistance of others. I am very grateful for the contact I have had with experts in different areas of this extensive history. Bit by bit, more and more details were added to the story of the encounter of the Europeans with Hinduism. Gradually, the survey offered by this book thus emerged, and some lines began to take clear shape.

Some of the material on which this history is based is already old. That is of course the case with regard to the sources: travel accounts and reflections by those who visited this distant country in earlier centuries. But there were also many researchers working in this area in the past. For me, this meant that I—in addition to the books in my own library—had to get access to many older works. The staff at Leiden University Library proved once again to be very helpful, just as they were when I was working on my earlier book, *Jesus as Guru*, and managed to locate many works that turned out to be treasures for me. I am also grateful to the staff at the library of the Rijksmuseum in Amsterdam for their extensive assistance.

Not all the material I needed to consult had been published, however. My search into the past therefore also led me to various archival institutions. The two large European mission archives provided indispensable material. The Frankesche Stiftungen in Halle made valuable writings digitally accessible, and the staff at the Basler Mission archives offered their ready assistance with documents that clarified the course their missionaries took in India.

In some areas, I needed special assistance. Drs Corstiaan J.G. van der Burg, who once upon a time initiated me into Sanskrit at the Vrije Universiteit Amsterdam, was also willing to help me now with some difficult texts in that language. And in an entirely different area, Mr and Mrs Max and Sigrid Jansen in Naarden in the Netherlands helped me with reading some archival documents in the old German Suetterlin script.

I am happy that this book can also be published in the series Currents of Encounter, just as my previous work *Jesus as Guru* was. And, just as he did for that work, Dr. Henry Jansen once again took on the task of translating this book into English. I am deeply indebted to him for the work and care he devoted to this task.

Some foundations were willing to contribute to the costs of this publication: the Van Coeverden Adriani Stichting, the Stichting Van Eijkfonds, the Stichting Zonneweelde, and the J.E. Jurriaanse Stichting. I am very grateful for this financial support.

I am very happy that this book, which I have wanted to write for so many years, is now complete. It was written with a great deal of pleasure, and I hope that it will also be read with pleasure.

Jan Peter Schouten
Naarden, the Netherlands

Illustrations

1 Indian men with dogs' heads. Illustration in Livre des merveilles. Manuscrit français 2810 (Bibliothèque nationale de France) 12
2 Two kinds of Brahmanical life: traders in secular circumstances and naked ascetics in the forest. Illustration in Livre des merveilles. Manuscrit français 2810 (Bibliothèque nationale de France) 16
3 Jan Brandes, Image, temple, and tower in Negapatna, 1733 (Rijksmuseum) 20
4 Pagode en Mesquita (Temple and Mosque). Illustration in Van Linschoten's Itinerario. (Rijksmuseum) 35
5 Roberto de Nobili as a sannyāsī (Baltasar da Costa, 1661). (Portuguese Academy of Sciences) 44
6 Illustrated title page of Rogerius' De Open-Deure Tot het Verborgen Heydendom, 1651 (University Library, Leiden University) 71
7 Philippus Baldaeus with servant in Sri Lanka. Painting by Jean de la Rocquette, 1668 (Rijksmuseum) 76
8 Ziegenbalg in conversation with Aleppa Kuru. Frontispiece of Ost-Indisches Gespräch: In dem Reiche der Todten (University Library, Leiden University) 87
9 Monument to Ziegenbalg in Tharangambadi (Photo: Michael Gäbler) 96
10 Abbé Dubois in Indian clothing. Portrait: Thomas Hickey, 1820 (British Library) 104
11 Title page of the final edition of Muir's Mataparīkṣā (1852) (British Library) 123
12 A Hindu ascetic. Drawing by Emily Eden (British Library) 136
13 A Brahmin preparing for his pūjā; illustration in Urwick, Indian Pictures, 1885 142
14 The statue of Ferdinand Kittel in Bengaluru, decorated for Karnataka State Formation Day 2017 (Photo: Bernhard Dinkelaker) 148
15 Ferdinand and Julie Kittel-Eyth (Basel Mission Archives) 151
16 Auguste Bourquin in 1871 (Basel Mission Archives) 158
17 Bourquin's Grave in Fairmount Cemetery in Denver (Photo: 'Find a Grave' employee, Valerie R.) 160

Introduction

The first time I came face to face with Hinduism in real life was not the most pleasant experience. I had arrived in New Delhi the day before, and I was now ready for my first visit to a Hindu temple. That was an entirely new experience because there were no Hindu sacred places in Europe at all at that time (1976). There would be many temples to see in India, and it was simply a matter of walking out of the hotel and starting with the first one just around the corner.

1 A Functioning Temple

The temple complex was certainly impressive as far as size was concerned.[1] High, brightly coloured temple towers drew my attention immediately, and a number of halls were linked together in an immense, labyrinthine whole. This holy place had been built by a very rich industrialist shortly before the war, and it was evident that he had spared neither expense nor pain. But a jumble of pillars, balustrades, and various kinds of ornamentation gave the impression more of 'kitsch' than of 'art.' That was just the outside. What took place inside this flashy edifice impressed me even less.

There were few people in the temple. An older woman came with a few offerings and turned to a priest behind a kind of counter. He accepted the offerings of fruit and flowers and rang a temple bell before laying the offerings down in front of an image. That was all. The apparent lack of interest on the part of both the priest and the woman was striking. The priest appeared to be downright drowsy and performed his tasks in a mechanical, robotic way. The woman who brought the gifts did not exactly radiate devotion either. She did what apparently had to be done but did not display any piety or personal engagement in it.

I still remember my reaction to this interaction: "It's going to take a lot to understand all this." I had acquired a reasonable amount of knowledge: history and sociology of religion, Sanskrit, and some Tamil. But all that only seemed to be of limited help. It was not that difficult to dig into the myths and legends behind the images of gods and saints. And I also had some knowledge of the theology behind some of the rituals. I just couldn't *feel* it. I couldn't sense what the priest and the believer were experiencing. It was only when I returned to the Netherlands, just under half a year later, that the world of Hinduism opened

1 The Laxmi Narayan Birla Temple in New Delhi, built in 1938.

 | DOI:10.1163/9789004420076_002

up for me a bit. Thanks to visits to a great many temples and holy places, seeing rituals, and talking with people about their religion, I did learn to sense what this religion meant to its adherents.

2 A Long History of Encounter

My first encounter with Hindu religious life in New Delhi also made me realise something else. This was not only my personal acquaintance with a foreign world—a European tourist who was observing something of actual Hinduism for the first time in his life. In that confrontation, I realised I was also participating in a centuries-long history of encounter. Did Western travellers not ask the same questions again and again over the course of history: What kind of religion is this? What do the people experience in it? How is this religion related to our own Christian tradition?

I often wondered during my first trip through India—and during many later trips—how people from outside India had experienced and interpreted these religious phenomena for the first time. The difficulty that I myself experienced in understanding this religion of others, is, however, certainly inherent to the encounter with a strange religious world. When did people first gain some true understanding of that other religion? Who actually learned the languages of the other culture? And who was the first to take a few steps further into the world of Hinduism?

These questions are inseparably connected with questions from a different angle. If Hinduism is experienced by people in India as the ultimate truth, how is this religion related to the other religions in the world? And for visitors from Europe, certainly missionaries, the question was focused of course on their own worldview: How can Hinduism be assessed from a Christian perspective? Where can this religion find a place in the structure of Christian theology? From a missionary perspective, those were—and are—not non-committal, academic questions. Those who embark on a mission to spread the Gospel are forced to ask themselves what their message adds to what those they are addressing already have in a religious sense.

3 The Prehistory of Dialogue

Over the years I have collected a wide variety of books that were the basis for such knowledge and evaluation. There are old travel reports that were striking in their awkwardness in describing something of the strange and attempting to understand it. There were pious treatises intended to clarify to the European public why a forceful missionary movement was necessary to "defeat heathenism." I acquired essays that were meant to explain systematically for the first time what Hinduism actually was and how this other religious culture was expressed in ritual and practice. And I obtained the first, careful attempts to begin a dialogue with the adherents of Hinduism.

Writing this book gave me a good opportunity to go through all those old works again and to read, with great interest, the enthusiastic discoveries written by travellers in an earlier time. And one book led to another. To this list we could add many other works in libraries and archives. And thus, a history slowly and gradually started to take shape: the development of knowledge of the Hindu world.

This history could be characterised as a reception history. After all, it sketches how Hinduism was slowly mapped. At the same time, it also shows how the evaluation of this strange religion developed. The medieval figures who stand at the beginning of this history assumed the existence of an amorphous 'heathenism' that was manifested in more or less the same form throughout the whole world, alongside the revealed religions of Judaism, Christianity, and Islam. As the knowledge of the culture and religion of India increased, so the understanding grew that this was a unique religion that also had overlappings with Christianity. From this point on, we can speak of a nascent dialogue between Hindus and Christians.

The theme of this book can thus best be described as 'the prehistory of dialogue.'[2] In tandem with the increasing knowledge of the strange world of Hinduism, an initial awareness arose of the possibilities of Hindus and Christians asking each other about the attribution of meaning and morality. It was, after all, Christians from Europe who visited India, primarily as missionaries. And by far, most of the written sources that were preserved were written by Christians. The trips that people took compelled them to reflect on what this religion presented as true and how they could assess it from their own background. It is too bad that hardly anything has been preserved from the centuries prior to the nineteenth of what the responses of Hindus were to this encounter between two cultures or religions. But there was always an implicit response by the Hindus: they had to choose between accepting and rejecting the missionaries' message. The encounter with the visiting Europeans likely also gave rise to a sense of how people judged their culture and religion. For the time being, however, we will limit ourselves to the contribution made by Christians in the initial phase of this dialogical encounter.

---

2 Analogous to Sweetman's approach in Sweetman 2004.

4 Terminological Relativisation

This study describes how Westerners, particularly visitors to India, looked at Hinduism from the thirteenth century up until the beginning of a genuine Hindu-Christian dialogue at the end of the nineteenth century. The question will perhaps arise as to whether we can speak in general of something called 'Hinduism' over such a long period. In recent years, it has often been emphasised that 'Hinduism' is a social construct that arose in a certain period under certain social conditions.

Following the publication of Said's controversial book, whose main focus was not—for that matter—South Asia, a debate arose among Indologists about the interests and power positions that had a determinative influence on their academic activity.[3] The post-colonial theorisation that originated in this debate led to the view that 'Hinduism' had been a British invention developed around the year 1800 which principally served colonial purposes. 'Hinduism' was construed as an all-inclusive category under which quite divergent religious phenomena were grouped in one system that, in actuality, was very arbitrary.

In that debate, the deconstructionists met with resistance from various sides. It was obvious that they needed to re-examine the central place of the Vedic scriptures, which had always been regarded as authoritative in all those varying schools of thought in India. But the way in which Hindus referred to themselves religiously throughout history was also pointed out. Even though the word 'Hinduism' is not found in Sanskrit literature (which generally uses the term *dharma* or *sanātana dharma* [eternal teaching]), the term was used in their vernacular languages, as Lorenzen has convincingly shown.[4] Since the coming of Islam, Hindus were well aware that they were not Muslims. Already in the late Middle Ages, they were using the term 'Hindu' to characterise their own religiosity.

Many examples of writers who distinguished their religious beliefs from Islam can be found especially in the poetic texts of the Bhakti movements.[5] There the term 'Hindu' appears to function as a general term that groups quite different forms of religion together. A paradoxical argument is that precisely the resistance of mystical poets to dividing people into Muslims and Hindus confirms the existence of both groups. For example, Kabīr writes:

3 Said 1978. For this debate see especially Llewellyn 2014.
4 Lorenzen 2014.
5 On the Bhakti movements, see Schouten 1996.

> Hindu and Turk—where did those two come from?
> Who had shown them the way?[6]

In the current state of the academic debate, therefore, it seems completely justified to use the word 'Hinduism.' Following the centuries-long use of this term in India and elsewhere, it can certainly be used to refer to the multiform religious phenomena in India.[7] But the passionate debate among the Indologists has left us with a permanent warning: when describing Hinduism, we should always keep in mind the interests that have influenced the establishment of certain elements. Colonial interests are also a part of this. But not only that: the position of power the Brahman upper crust held in comparison to the lower castes they thought to be unclean cannot remain ignored and left unremarked either. And—as this study will show—it is generally true that in India the religion of one is not the same as the religion of another and that various forms of this religion can be seen at various times and places.

The use of the term 'India' for the venue where this beginning dialogue takes place can also be seen as problematic. The Republic of India was of course not founded until 1947, and the names for this subcontinent in all periods previous are legion. For the sake of convenience and readability, we will nevertheless speak in general of 'India' when referring to the area of the Indian subcontinent. That is the country where Hinduism belongs and where the encounter between Christians and Hindus slowly—over the course of many centuries—took shape.

Bibliography

Brockington, J.L. (1993). *The Sacred Thread: Hinduism in its Continuity and Diversity*. 4th ed. Edinburgh: Edinburgh University Press.

Gispert-Sauch, George (2012). "Hinduism and Christianity." In: Knut A. Jacobsen (ed.). *Brill's Encyclopedia of Hinduism IV*. Leiden/Boston: Brill. Pp. 505–20.

Llewellyn, J.E. (ed.) (2014). *Defining Hinduism: A Reader*. London /New York: Routledge.

Lorenzen, David N. (2014). "Who Invented Hinduism?" In: J.E. Llewellyn (ed.) *Defining Hinduism: A Reader*. London/New York: Routledge. Pp. 52–80.

Said, Edward W. (1978). *Orientalism*. New York: Pantheon Books.

6 Turk = Muslim; Vaudeville 1993:227.

7 Brockington 1993:1: "a definite, and definable, entity." Brockington looks for the definition, in all extreme plurality, in a common history going back to the Vedas. See also Sweetman 2003:9–13.

Schouten, Jan Peter (1996). *Goddelijke vergezichten: Mystiek uit India voor westerse lezers*. Baarn: Ten Have.

Sweetman, Will (2004). "The Prehistory of Orientalism: Colonialism and the Textual Basis for Bartholomäus Ziegenbalg's Account of Hinduism." *New Zealand Journal of Asian Studies* 6: 12–38.

Sweetman, Will (2003). *Mapping Hinduism: 'Hinduism' and the Study of Indian Religions, 1600–1776*. Neue Hallesche Berichte 4. Halle: Verlag der Franckeschen Stiftungen.

Vaudeville, Charlotte (1993). *A Weaver Named Kabir: Selected Verses, With a Detailed Biographical and Historical Introduction*. Delhi: Oxford University Press.

CHAPTER 1

The First Visitors: Marco Polo and the Franciscan Friars

1 Beyond Byzantium

In the year 1200, Constantinople was the edge of the world for most Europeans. The Byzantine Empire was well known—people had become even more aware of it in the centuries prior because the armies of the Crusaders had travelled through it. And people were of course familiar with the state of the Holy Land, alternately attacked by the armies of Islamic rulers and the troops of the Western Crusaders. That an entire continent lay beyond those regions, larger and more culturally varied than Europe was almost unimaginable.

Some individuals who had some acquaintance with the classical literature from antiquity on geography and history likely had some idea of countries like Persia and India that Herodotus, Pliny the Elder, and others had written about. And whoever was involved in international trade knew the stories of luxury goods like ivory and silk that occasionally reached Europe from distant Eastern countries. But in general, Asia was *terra incognita*: there was no knowledge of what lay beyond the eastern border of the Byzantine Empire, and that world played no role in the Western experience of current events.

2 The Mongol Advance

This view shifted radically over the course of the thirteenth century. Via the Christian communities in the Levant came ominous reports of a ruler in distant Mongolia who was conquering one region after another, founding a mighty empire. The fame of this new world leader, Genghis Khan (1162–1227), spread quickly in Europe, and the accompanying stories of his military dominance and cruelty led to a great deal of commotion and excitement. Not only were people frightened of the Mongol troops, but they also saw an opportunity: the Mongols could be the ideal ally against the Islamic archenemy. Many a European leader shared that view, including the pope (Lach 1965: 31).

Another side of the Mongolian empire emerged after some time. Countries like Poland, Silesia, and Moravia were the victims of raids by the Mongolian hordes, but while the invading Mongols did not immediately annex these East

 | DOI:10.1163/9789004420076_003

European countries for the time being, they left a staggering trail of destruction behind when they withdrew. It would not be that easy to turn Genghis Khan and his successors into allies.

Nevertheless, Europeans made various attempts to approach the ruler of the Mongol Empire. The khan was in any case not a Muslim, and the belief grew that he was particularly positive with respect to Christianity. The latter, however, is questionable. Clergy and spiritual leaders from all persuasions were welcome at the Mongolian court. Obviously, the khan assumed that every contribution by a religious community would help him and promote stability in his empire (Reichert in Odoric 1987:10). It was a pragmatic approach that Islamic rulers would certainly not have chosen. It did, however, make it possible for Christian missionaries to find a place at the court of the Mongolian ruler.

The court of the Great Khan in Beijing thus became the main destination for many European visitors. It was primarily Franciscan monks who were sent there. The founder of the order, Francis of Assisi (1181/2–1226), had already given a missionary example by seeking a dialogue with the sultan of Egypt (Hoeberichts 1994:passim). In the thirteenth century as well, the Franciscans were the ones who had the greatest motivation to cross borders to go on dangerous expeditions among non-Christian people. The first to go was John of Plano Carpini, an Italian Franciscan, who was sent in 1245 to the Mongolian ruler by the pope. This diplomat was the first to write down his experiences after his mission was over and thus gave Europeans insight into the society and culture of the Mongols.

Many followed in the footsteps of this first visitor. They were often monks whose goal was to spread the Christian faith, and sometimes this missionary activity was carried out in combination with a diplomatic mission of the Church or rulers. In the middle of the thirteenth century, the Flemish Franciscan William of Rubruck was sent by the French king to the court of the Great Khan. His Italian confrater, John of Montecorvino, had a more ecclesiastical mission. He arrived in Beijing in 1294, where he became the first Roman Catholic bishop. About 20 years later, Odoric of Pordenone, also a Franciscan from Italy, travelled to China, where he—according to a pious tradition—baptised 20,000 heathens.[1] But it was not only monks who made the grand trip to that distant country: the most famous were the members of the Polo family, merchants from Venice, who travelled more than once to the Mongolian court and travelled around East Asia for 20 years.

The letters and travel reports that all these visitors wrote attracted much attention. There was, apparently, an enormous desire among the European

1 According to a saint's life from the fourteenth century; see Odoric 1987:150.

intelligentsia to know something about the wondrous world of Asian cultures. There was not a great deal of difference between the reports by the monks and those by merchants in this respect. The servants of the Church did sometimes give some insight into their specific work for the Church, such as preaching, building churches, and caring for the relics of martyrs, but they also liked to tell their compatriots about the products of the distant country, noteworthy plants and animals, and in particular the morals and customs of these barbaric peoples. On the other hand, the merchants from Venice were certainly not only interested in goods but also in the fantastic rich court life in Beijing and the almost incredible wonders they saw on their travels.

The goal of these early world travellers was always the court of the Great Khan in Beijing and his summer residence, Shangdu. Anything we come across in the travel reports about India is 'by-catch.' There was no powerful, central state on the Indian subcontinent at that time: in any case, a trip to that country did not serve any political purpose. For merchants as well, it was less interesting than the Mongolian court, for there was no large-scale industry or trade. In addition, the country was less accessible: any form of missionising was a risky undertaking in the parts under Muslim control, and the indigenous Hindu population was also not especially inclined to share its culture and religion with outsiders. On the way there and back, the visitors probably only passed through a small piece of the large subcontinent. In any case, the many marvellous things that the Europeans encountered did stimulate the imagination.

3 Marco Polo

The most famous writer is certainly Marco Polo (1254–1324). As a 17-year old boy, he was allowed to accompany his father and his uncle, who had already visited the court of the Great Khan earlier. The trip had a diplomatic aspect. During their previous visit, the Mongol ruler had, namely, given the brothers a letter for the pope, and he was expecting an answer. When they returned, moreover, the khan was expecting a special religious gift, namely, a pitcher containing the oil that was burned at the site of Jesus' resurrection at the Church of the Holy Sepulchre in Jerusalem. Of course, the Venetian merchants were also set on engaging in trade and exploring the innumerable new possibilities of economic contacts. In 1271, the company left Venice for Beijing, where the powerful Kublai Khan (1215–1294) ruled his extensive empire.

After their arrival, they were conscripted into the khan's civil service, and the khan made ready use of the knowledge and skills of his foreign visitors. The young Marco especially appeared to make an impression on the ruler. He was quickly put in charge of carrying out all kinds of inspections at the ruler's order, and for a few years he had an appointment as the governor of a provincial city. In this way, the Venetian visitors gained ample opportunity to explore the country, but it was not an easy matter to leave the ruler's service. After 20 years, they were finally given permission to leave. Back in Venice, the Polos were praised for their fantastic stories about the distant country and the impressive and very luxurious court life of the Great Khan.

By sheer luck, Marco Polo came into contact with someone who could write it all down for him. He was taken prisoner after a sea battle between Venice and its major competitor Genoa, and in the Genoan prison he became acquainted with Rustichello da Pisa, a writer of knightly romances. Da Pisa wrote down the stories of this world traveller in the language of the elite: French.[2] The book was called *Divisament dou monde* (Description of the World), but it slowly became known by Marco Polo's nickname (Il Milione, i.e., 'The Man from Emilia') (Polo 1994:xi).

Even though Marco Polo's book was primarily about China and the government and court life of the Mongol ruler, it also looks at some aspects of the culture and religion of India. On their return journey, the Polos had also sailed along the coast of the Indian subcontinent. They were therefore among the first Europeans who were able to say something first-hand about this entirely unknown, wondrous country. Marco Polo's literary style was not very restrained, and in his enthusiasm he often let himself be led into exaggeration. For example, he once described "a not very large" city in China, where he saw no less than 15,000 ships docked (Polo 1994:§ 143). And he calculated the income from taxes that he, as governor, handed over to the Great Khan to be billions of units of gold (Polo 1994:§ 149). On the other hand, he also punched holes in fables and described the rhinoceros, which had been imagined as a graceful unicorn, to be "a very ugly animal" (Polo 1994:§ 162) that would certainly not allow itself to be captured by a virgin.

4 People with Dog's Heads

What picture did Marco Polo paint of India, a region about which antiquity had already come up with various fantastic fabrications? His account of the famous 'dogs' heads' in India is typical. On the basis of the not very authoritative Ctesias of Cnidus (circa 400 BCE), it was said that there were people in India

2 In the Middle Ages, books were generally dictated and not written by the author himself. See Yule in Polo 1903–1920:I, 430.

who had dogs' heads instead of human heads and, instead of speaking in human language, barked and howled. They were called *cynocephali* (κυνοκεφαλοι) (Nichols 2011:53–54). This story was part of the narrow common knowledge about India in medieval Europe. The first European who lived for a year in South India in the thirteenth century, John of Montecorvino, wrote in a letter that he had asked many times about people who had a different appearance and also tried to find them. But he never saw one.[3]

In his account, Marco Polo claims that he did see the people with dogs' heads! When he sailed from China to India, he passed the Adaman Islands, an island group between Burma and the Indian subcontinent. Even today, the population of these islands, even though they belong to the Republic of India, are hardly part of pan-Indian culture. That was even less the case in Polo's time, when the naked black tribes on these islands were viewed as extremely uncivilised.[4] Marco Polo wrote that they "were like wild beasts." Their appearance contributed to his characterisation of them: "Everyone on the island has a head like a dog's head and teeth and a nose like a large dog'."[5] The comment here seems to be more metaphorical than a reference to an actual physical feature.

The commonsensical way in which Marco Polo here deals with the classical tradition of the *cynocephali* does not reflect the view of many of his contemporaries, however. They did not expect barbaric people who acted like fierce wild dogs but an actual subspecies of the *genus humana*. This can be clearly seen in the illustration accompanying this passage in the finest and most renowned manuscript of Polo's book. This *Livre des merveilles* was prepared in 1412, commissioned by the Burgundian duke John the Fearless (1371–1419) (Bibliothèque nationale de France, Paris, manuscrit français 2810).[6] This volume contains a number of travel reports: in addition to Polo's, including—among others—the report by Brother Odoric of Pordenone and the fantastic, probably fictitious, travel experiences of John Mandeville. The manuscript is illustrated with 265 miniatures of very high quality.

The illustrator did not depict the *cynocephali* as wild, frightening barbaric people but as a human subspecies (Bibliothèque nationale de France, Paris, manuscrit français 2810, fol. 76f.). The natives are well dressed and standing around, chatting about the quality of their goods just as ordinary European

---

3 John of Montecorvino, *Epistola I*, § 8; in Yule and Cordier 1913–1916:III, 58–70.

4 Yule (in Polo 1903–1920:II, 779) characterises the population in his time (around 1900) also as "Oriental negroes in the lowest state of barbarism."

5 Polo 1994:§ 168: "la capo come di cane e denti e naso come di grandi mastini."

6 See the fine edition by De Klerk and Wijsman 2008, which contains all illustrations from the section on Marco Polo. Cf. Wittkower 1957.

FIGURE 1 Indian men with dogs' heads
Illustration in Livre des Merveilles. Manuscrit français 2810

citizens would do, with the only difference being that they have dogs' heads. Marco's analogy was here turned into a communication of pure fact (see Wittkower 1957:160). Other writers did in words what the miniaturist did in his depiction. Odoric of Portenone also claims to have seen the dogs' heads on islands in the Bay of Bengal, but he places them on the Nicobar Islands. His description, however, has a much different character than Marco Polo's. Although Odoric also describes the *cynocephali* as warlike and cruel, he does depict their culture as a refined, religious one. These people, he writes, worship cows as gods, and therefore everyone wears a gold or silver image depicting a cow on their foreheads (Odoric 1929:Ch. XVI). This description does not exactly fit the image of primitive, uncivilised island dwellers. Characteristically, we do come across this story of the images on foreheads in some versions of Marco Polo's book as well, but then in his description of Maabar, on the southeastern coast of India, what is now Tamil Nadu, or in Gujarat.[7] It fits better there. This report stems perhaps from a meeting with the Liṅgāyatas, a people who had a deep reverence for the divine bull Nandī and wore the sacred *liṅga* symbol on their

7 Polo 1994:§ 173: "Brahmins in Gujarat (Lar), many of whom wore a metal image on their foreheads." Cf. Van den Wyngaert in Odoric 1929:452, n. 3: "a Marco Polo pro Maabar narratur."

neck or forehead (Yule in Polo 1903–1920:II, 921–22).[8] In any case, however, they were not found on the Andaman or Nicobar Islands.

5 A Strange Culture

Marco Polo's description of the mainland of India conveys more about the culture and the religions he saw there. He first describes the coast of the Tamil area, which at that time was simply called Maabar, speaking highly of this region: "This is the best India there is" (Polo 1994:§ 170). The merchant was impressed by the products he saw there, especially the precious stones and pearls. He gives a detailed account of the divers who retrieved the pearl oysters from the sea floor and also reports a striking aspect of Indian religiosity: every time the divers went down, the divers hired Brahmanical magicians (*incantatori*) to keep the sharks at a distance by magical means.

What kind of religion did the inhabitants of this country actually practise? Marco Polo characterises it by the words he used as a refrain in his description of innumerable northern regions: "These people worship idols" (*Questa gente adorano l'idole*). Thus, he found himself again in pagan territory. He does specify, however, the nature of the heathen religion he found in the region: most of the people there worshipped cows. As a result, no one ate beef and no one wanted to kill a cow. He relativised this immediately: slaughter was unacceptable, but there were some people who did eat beef from a cow that had died a natural death. He calls these people *Gavi*. The *Gavis* of course constituted one of the castes at the bottom of the population pyramid; it has been suggested that it is an old term for *Paṟaiyar* (pariahs) (Yule in Polo 1903–1920:II, 875).

Apparently, this deep awareness of ritual purity made a profound impression on this European visitor. Polo reports how the population, both men and women, followed the purity laws very closely. Thus, people bathed twice a day, once in the morning and once in the evening, and they never ate or drank without having bathed. The writer explains to Western readers that those who did not do this were viewed as heretics (just like the Patarenes in the West).[9]

The various types of suicide receive a great deal of attention. He first describes the *satī*, the ritual suicide of the widow after the death of her husband. European visitors have always shown a fascination down through the centuries

---

8 For the Liṅgāyatas, see Schouten 1991:6.

9 Polo 1994:§ 170: "come sono tra noi i paterini." The Patarenes formed a religious movement that arose in Italy in the twelfth century and were similar to the Cathars. See Bernard Hamilton in Eteriano 2004:1–13.

with this remarkable custom. Polo describes how the widow cast herself into the fire at her husband's cremation so that she could burn with him. He adds: "Women who do this are praised very highly, and many women do it." A less well-known phenomenon is related to this. We read how a criminal who had been condemned to death could choose to kill himself as a sacrifice to a specific divinity. Just like the *satī*, the most striking point is that whoever performs this act is greatly honoured. Polo concludes that such a holy suicide would be buried by his relatives with great reverence.

Religious and magical representations dominate all of life in this country. Marco Polo makes that clear by laying the stress on the role of apparently unimportant portents. He even asserts that nowhere else in the world is so much value attached to signs that could reveal something about the course events would take. Hearing someone sneeze would be enough to abort a trip that had already begun. It is obvious that great value was also attached to what was written in the stars. When a child was born, the time and place of his or her birth, as well as the position of the stars at that time, was carefully noted.

There are, however, also places where religion and ritual in particular were experienced intensely. Polo mentions the monasteries (*monasteri d'idole*) where there were also many children, especially girls, who had been handed over by the parents for service in the temple. He describes the religious feasts in which they offered sacrificial food to the gods and the girls in particular danced. The institution of the *devadāsīs* seems to have had a long history in Tamil Nadu.[10]

6 A Separate Caste

Polo devotes a special chapter to the caste of the Brahmins as he encountered them in the region of Lar (Gujarat). Precisely in this part of the book we are given special insight into what he understood as the religion of India (Polo 1994:§ 173).[11] This chapter also, however, contains a number of serious errors and misunderstandings. It is certainly not true, as Polo claims, that the Brahmins all came from Gujarat. Even worse, Polo describes the Brahmins as a group of merchants. This shows that the religious position of this highest caste escaped the author completely, even though he had already introduced them

10 On the *devadāsīs*, see Kersenboom 1984.

11 It is certainly quite remarkable that an indisputable authority like K.A. Nilakanta Sastri almost completely ignores this chapter: Nilakanta Sastri 1957:119.

earlier on the Pearl Coast as conjurers who used magic against sharks. But these errors are compensated by the fact that Polo gives us a wide range of information on the way of life of this segment of the population.

That Polo became acquainted with the Brahmins as merchants is not remarkable as such. The priestly function of this caste was less apparent to outsiders. Trade, which was Polo's primary interest, was certainly practised by the Brahmins, particularly trade in pearls and precious stones. Polo describes the Brahmins as "the best and most reliable merchants of the world." He characterises them as a group with a high morality: they are said to never lie or cheat their competitors. Their way of life was also entirely healthy: because of their strict diet, they lived longer than other people. Moreover, Polo observed how they chewed betel leaves, and he thinks that this was the reason for their strong teeth.

According to Polo, Brahmins could be recognised by the sacred thread that they wore over their naked upper bodies. The so-called *yajñopavīta*, which up until today characterises the highest caste, was striking already then. Most striking, however, is that Marco Polo relates that there were two different ways of life practised by the Brahmins. On the one hand there were merchants who took part in society, engaged in trade, and were occupied with worldly affairs. On the other hand, however, there were Brahmins who were ascetics (Polo calls them *uomini regolati*), who led an entirely different sort of life. They fasted in accordance with strict guidelines and called themselves *coniugati*, 'bound ones.' The word *yogī* can probably be detected here. They had broken all contact with worldly life, and that is why they wore no clothing. They themselves knew no shame because they did not commit any sin with their sexual organs as a whole. Their lives were, for the rest, lived in many respects in accordance with the strictest rules. Thus, they would not kill at all, not even insects.

What Marco Polo describes here are two of the four phases of the classical doctrine of *varṇāśramadharma*: the position of the householder (*gṛhastha*) and that of the ascetic (*sannyāsī*). Indeed, these were the two most striking phases of Brahman life; the preparatory period of the student and the intermediary phase of the forest dweller (*vanaprastha*) are, as to be expected, left out. In the model life of the Brahmin, the absolute contradiction between the man who lived in the midst of society and the ascetic who had broken with all worldly concerns is striking.

The phenomenon of the Brahmanical world renouncers was not entirely unknown in the West. A few references to that can already be found in writings from antiquity, including those by Christian authors. Thus, Tertullian objected to his contemporaries accusing Christians of being otherworldly in these words: "We are not Indian Brahmins or Gymnosophists, who dwell in woods

FIGURE 2 Two kinds of Brahmanical life: traders in secular circumstances and naked ascetics in the forest
Illustration in Livre des Merveilles. Manuscrit français 2810

and exile themselves from ordinary human life."[12] What Polo adds to our knowledge about the Brahmins, however, is, that he tells his European contemporaries how both ways of life were found next to each other in the Brahmanical community: worldly traders and withdrawn ascetics.

Polo accentuates the difference by depicting the *sannyāsīs* in the most radical form. They walked around completely naked and only covered parts of their bodies with the powder of burned cow manure, "just as Christians do with holy water" (Polo 1994:§ 173).[13] Heavy emphasis is laid on the fact that ascetics renounced sexuality completely. Polo gives a detailed description of how

12 Tertullian 1952:Ch. XLII: "Neque enim Brahmanae aut Indorum gymnosophistae sumus …."

13 The comparison of holy ashes (*vibhūti*) with holy water is very apropos: it underscores the religious aspect of this use.

the ascetics proved their chastity in the monasteries: the girls who were dedicated to serve the gods, i.e., the *devadāsīs* stimulated the men by lying with them and fondling them. Only those who did not have an erection were allowed to remain in the monastery. There is a long tradition of proving one's sexual abstinence (*brahmacarya*): we know that Mahatma Gandhi, in the middle of the twentieth century, regularly shared his bed with naked girls from the circle of his family or followers to test his control over his sexuality (Mehta 1982:190–202).

Thanks to Marco Polo's writings, the double lifestyle of the high castes from India had become well known among the Europeans. Illustrators have also contributed to the notion. The dichotomy of Brahmins 'in' and 'outside' the world is very nicely illustrated in John the Fearless' famous *Livre des merveilles* (Bibliothèque nationale de France, Paris, manuscrit français 2810, fol. 83r). On the left, we see a few well-dressed Brahmins engaging in trade, obviously offering their wares to the king (who, according to Polo, gladly bought pearls and precious stones). On the right, we see another group of Brahmins, who have withdrawn into the woods, barely clothed or completely naked, depicted as a counterculture alongside the urban milieu of trade. Among the ascetics are men and women; two of them even appear to be husband and wife. But the most striking thing is that those in the woods are still depicted with trade goods (cotton or perhaps sago)—once a merchant, always a merchant. That notion would have appealed to Marco Polo.

7 The Friars Speak

The Franciscan friars did not have much to add to the extensive account provided by this Venetian merchant. We often find the same descriptions in them and, in general, their reports are much more concise. But a few times they do, understandably, show some more attention for what was specifically religious, in which they focused on the difference from or perhaps similarity to their own Christian background.

The earliest writer in this category is, at least as far as India itself is concerned, John of Montecorvino. Before traveling to Beijing—his ultimate destination—he stayed for a year on the Coromandel Coast (Tamil Nadu). Modern Indologists and historians are certainly not impressed by his descriptions of the culture there. He has been judged harshly in part: it is said he did not understand the culture at all in which he lived for such a long time (Filliozat, 1953:82–83; Lach 1965:39–40). He does go too far when he claims that there was no literature or lawbooks; writing was only used for business purposes.

This also primarily shows that there was a whole world of scholarship that remained completely closed to him as a stranger.

Montecorvino did, however, explore the world around him. He visited temples: houses with images of gods. And he saw how the cultus was organised. People did not go to the temple on fixed days or at fixed hours; there was no common worship service: everyone went whenever he or she felt called and then performed whatever religious acts were required. The same obtained for fasts and expressions of joy: there were no fixed times for fasting; there was no holy day in the week, i.e., no Sunday (John of Montecorvino 1929:§ 9). Although this is not a spectacular point, Montecorvino does indicate here a characteristic difference between the regulated and communal Christian practice of devotion and the much more individual relation with the sacred in India. This Franciscan friar also gives evidence of sound observation with respect to human emotions. He describes the cremation rituals that were accompanied by a great deal of music and dance, but he also notes that this did not mean that the people were not sad (John of Montecorvino 1929:§ 11).

8 Odoric

The Franciscan friar who wrote the most extensively about India was Odoric of Pordenone († 1331). He travelled to Thana, near Mumbai, at the beginning of the fourteenth century. Muslims had killed four brothers of this order there in a gruesome way. Odoric brought the bones of the martyrs to China where they were given an honourable funeral. Odoric subsequently remained for a few years with the small Franciscan community in Beijing, which had close connections with the court of the Great Khan. In 1330 he was back in Italy. His provincial instructed him to produce a travel report, and he dictated his experiences to his fellow mendicant, William of Solagna, who was apparently more familiar with the art of writing.

What is striking in Odoric's account is that he, more than Marco Polo, was interested in the religion of the foreign peoples in Asia. People practised idolatry in this country—that much was immediately clear.[14] He added immediately what it was they celebrated: the fire, the snake, and the trees. Here Odoric followed the classical image that Europeans had of pagans: just as in antiquity, this included the veneration of natural forces. For the rest, Odoric had certainly got it right: for the European visitors, the sacred trees and, below them, the stones with images of snakes were and are the first symbols of Hindu

14 Odoric 1929:Ch. VII: "Huius terre populus ydolatrat."

religiosity. And the central place of fire in many Hindu rituals is certainly unmistakable, although it remains a question as to whether fire itself is worshiped or is only an instrument in the worship.

In addition to the generally widespread worship of natural forces, Odoric also saw specific Hindu elements. During his stay in Quilon (Kerala), he was struck by the worship of the sacred cow, which involved everyone, including the local royal couple. He describes how the king and queen spread the urine and excrement of the sacred cow on their bodies. The purifying power of the cow's products has been an important belief in India throughout the ages. Even the damage wrought by the greatest sin can be countered by the *pañcagavya*, a mixture of the five products of the cow: milk, buttermilk, butter, urine, and excrement (Muusses 1920:64–65).

And then there are the images. Odoric describes an image in Quilon that was part human and part cow. This is probably a man-lion, which is certainly a depiction of the fourth incarnation of Viṣṇu, *Narasiṃha*. More than likely, this has to do with a particularly gruesome cultus, for, according to Odoric, child sacrifices were regularly made to this image (Odoric 1929:Ch. x).

One image found in Maabar, now Tamil Nadu received a great deal of attention (Odoric 1929:Ch. x–xi).[15] The image was huge ("as large as Saint Christopher is usually painted") and was made entirely of gold and draped with expensive precious stones. Many pilgrims travelled here. Odoric describes extensively what the pilgrims would all do for this journey. Some walked tied to a rope; others carried a board on their neck, still others even stuck a knife in their arm. On the journey, people imposed all kinds of restrictions on themselves: for example, there were those who threw themselves fully stretched out on the ground at every fourth step. Others attempted to hold a scale with burning incense during the whole journey. These are phenomena that can still be observed today, both in India as well as among Hindus in the diaspora.

Most remarkable, however, were the events during the yearly feast in the temple, on the anniversary of the inauguration of the image of the god. The image was placed on a large, handsome wagon. The people then followed the wagon in a procession through the city. According to Odoric, every year five hundred pilgrims threw themselves under the enormous wheels of the temple wagon and were crushed. They were considered holy because of their vow to die for the divinity. This story immediately calls to mind the Jagannātha temple

15 Hunink and Nieuwenhuis, who translated Odoric's travel account into Dutch (Odoric 2008), incorrectly write "Malabar" (the west coast of South India). But it is 'Mobar,' from the Arabic 'Maʿbar,' which indicates precisely the east coast of South India. See Odoric 2008:25–26.

FIGURE 3 Jan Brandes, Image, temple, and tower in Negapatna, 1733

in Puri (not in Tamil Nadu but much further north, in Orissa), which has become well known because of a similar history of ritual suicide.[16] In earlier centuries, this happened in several places. One could also think here of Nagapattinam (Negapatna), which is in Tamil Nadu and where, moreover, an enormous image had been erected.

Marco Polo and the Franciscan friars shared a fascination with the culture and religion of India, even though their primary interest was in the northern empires of Mongolia and China. They also saw various opportunities for trade in southern India, however. Agriculture and fishing attracted their attention, and the cultivation of spices, especially pepper, would continue to attract Europeans. And there also appeared to be many opportunities to easily acquire the most expensive trade goods, both precious stones and luxury textiles.

9 Another Civilisation in View

The countries on the Indian subcontinent constituted a strange world, and the writings of the European visitors bore witness to that, page after page. We do in

16 Yule and Burnell 1986, ad "Juggurnaut." On the temple in Puri, see Starža-Majewski 1983.

any case find the first attempts to chart that other civilisation—however awkwardly—in those writings. For the visitors, as tourists *avant la lettre*, it was also a journey of discovery, spending some time outside the sphere of influence of Christianity and Islam. Here they saw actual paganism—something they had previously known only from reports dating from antiquity. That the judgment about this "idolatry" could not be anything else than negative is obvious. It was not without some degree of pleasure that people sometimes seemed willing and eager to get to the descriptions of the cruelty and squalor that they encountered in the religious world around them. They were surprised by the fact that people who were so cut off from the Christian revelation could nonetheless live extremely virtuous lives and proved to be trustworthy in their business dealings, as Polo observed with amazement among the Brahmins of Gujarat.

The stories, teachings, and piety that were behind these strange religious customs remained concealed for the time being. On the one hand, the worship of natural phenomena, heavenly bodies, and patterns could be easily recognised—it had been no different in antiquity. On the other hand, the very extensive and refined mythology and wisdom tradition of India was completely closed to the visitors. John of Montecorvino would not be the only one who could not imagine that such literature existed. The tip of the iceberg gradually came into view in later centuries. But even in the seventeenth century, the scholar Hugo Grotius (Hugo de Groot) wrote a manual for the traveller headed for distant places, in which he swept all cultures and religions outside Europe into one heap as an endless repetition of what had already been asserted in antiquity.[17] With respect to that, in any event, both Marco Polo and the Franciscan friars made a better attempt to understand what was unique about India.

Bibliography

Text Editions and Translations

John of Montecorvino (Johannes de Monte Corvino) (1929). "Epistolae." In: Anastasius van den Wyngaert (ed.). *Itinera et relationes fratrum minorum saeculi XIII et XIV*. Vol. 1. Ad Claras Aquas Quaracchi-Firenze: apud Collegium S. Bonaventurae. Pp. 333–55.

Polo, Marco (2008). *De wonderen van de Oriënt: Il Milione*. Transl. Anton Haakman. 2nd ed. Amsterdam: Athenaeum-Polak & Van Gennep.

Polo, Marco (1994). *Milione: Versione toscana del Trecento*. Ed. Valeria Bertolucci Pizzorusso and Giorgio R. Cardona. Milano: Adelphi.

17 De Groot, *Bewys van den Waren Godsdienst*, especially the Vierde Boeck.

Polo, Marco (1993). *The Travels of Marco Polo: The Complete Yule-Cordier Edition, including the Unabridged Third Edition (1903) of Henry Yule's Annotated Translation, as Revised by Henri Cordier, Together with Cordier's Later Volume of Notes and Addenda (1920)*. Two Volumes. New York: Dover Publications.

Odoric of Pordenone (Odoric of Friuli) (2008). *Mijn reis naar het verre oosten: Een verslag uit het begin van de veertiende eeuw*. Transl. Vincent Hunink and Mark Nieuwenhuis. Amsterdam: Athenaeum-Polak & Van Gennep.

(Odorich von Pordenone) (1987). *Die Reise des seligen Odorich von Pordenone nach Indien und China (1314/18–1330)*. Transl. Folker Reichert. Heidelberg: Manutius Verlag.

(Odoricus de Portu Naonis) (1929). "Relatio." In: Anastasius van den Wyngaert (ed.). *Itinera et relationes fratrum minorum saeculi XIII et XIV*. Vol. I. Ad Claras Aquas Quaracchi-Firenze: apud Collegium S. Bonaventurae. Pp. 379–495.

Secondary Literature

Eteriano, Hugh (2004). *Contra Patarenos*. Ed. Bernard Hamilton et al. The Medieval Mediterranean 55. Leiden/Boston: Brill.

Filliozat, Jean (1953). "Les premières étapes de l'indianisme." *Bulletin de l'Association Guillaume Budé* 3/3: 80–96.

Gispert-Sauch, George (2012). "Hinduism and Christianity." In: Knut A. Jacobsen (ed.). *Brill's Encyclopedia of Hinduism IV*. Leiden/Boston: Brill. Pp. 505–20.

Groot, Hugo de (1622). *Bewys van den Waren Godsdienst*. S.l.

Hoeberichts, J. (1994). *Franciscus en de Islam*. Scripta Franciscana 1. Assen: Van Gorcum.

Kersenboom, Saskia Cornelia (1984). *Nityasumaṅgalī: Towards the Semiosis of the Devadasi Tradition of South India*. Utrecht: Rijksuniversiteit.

Klerk, Jan de, and Hanno Wijsman (2008). *Marco Polo's boek over de wonderen van de wereld: Toelichtingen bij de miniaturen, de tekst en de historische achtergronden aan de hand van 86 folio's van het handschrift van het Livre des merveilles van Marco Polo bewaard in de Bibliothèque nationale de France te Parijs (manuscrit français 2810)*. 's-Hertogenbosch: Stichting Erasmus Festival.

Lach, Donald F. (1965). *Asia in the Making of Europe*. Vol. I. Book 1. Chicago/London: University of Chicago Press.

Mehta, Ved (1982). *Mahatma Gandhi and His Apostles*. Harmondsworth: Penguin Books.

Muusses, Martha Adriana (1920). *Koecultus bij de Hindoes*. Purmerend: J. Muusses.

Nichols, Andrew (2011). *Ctesias: On India, and Fragments of his Minor Work: Introduction, Translation and Commentary*. London: Bristol Classical Press.

Nilakanta Sastri, K.A. (1957). "Marco Polo on India." In: É. Balazs et al. (eds.). *Oriente Poliano: Studi e conferenze tenute all'Is. M.E.O. in occasione del VII centenario della nascita di Marco Polo (1254–1954)*. Rome: Istituto Italiano per il Medio ed Estremo Oriente. Pp. 111–20.

Phillips, Kim M. (2014). *Before Orientalism: Asian Peoples and Cultures in European Travel Writing, 1245–1510*. The Middle Ages Series. Philadelphia: University of Pennsylvania Press.

Ristuccia, Nathan J. (2013). "Eastern Religions and the West: The Making of an Image." *History of Religions* 53: 170–204.

Schouten, Jan Peter (1991). *Revolution of the Mystics: On the Social Aspects of Vīraśaivism*. Kampen: Kok Pharos.

Starža-Majewski, Olgierd Maria Ludwik (1983). *The Jagannātha Temple at Puri and its Deities*. Amsterdam: University of Amsterdam.

Tertullian (1952). *Apologeticum: Verteidigung des Christentums*. Ed. Carl Becker. Munich: Kösel-Verlag.

Yule, Henry, and Henri Cordier (1913–1916). *Cathay and the Way Thither: Being a Collection of Medieval Notices of China*. New ed. Four volumes. London: Hakluyt Society.

Yule, Henry, and A.C. Burnell (1986). *Hobson-Jobson: A Glossary of Colloquial Anglo-Indian Words and Phrases*. 2nd ed. London/New York: Routledge & Kegan Paul.

Wittkower, R. (1957). "Marco Polo and the Pictorial Tradition of the Marvels of the East." In: É. Balazs et al. (eds.). *Oriente Poliano: Studi e conferenze tenute all'Is. M.E.O. in occasione del VII centenario della nascita di Marco Polo (1254–1954)*. Rome: Istituto Italiano per il Medio ed Estremo Oriente. Pp. 155–72.

CHAPTER 2

Knowledge is Power: Nicolò de' Conti and Jan Huygen van Linschoten

1 Traders Make their Way to India

In the succeeding centuries, many traders went to Asia, following in Marco Polo's footsteps. The famous court of the Mongol rulers, with its extraordinary wealth, remained an important goal, but the Indian subcontinent became an attractive destination for many as well. The extensive cultivation of spices, especially pepper in South India, as well as the pearls, gemstones, and other treasures drew many European traders. Only seldom did the visitors in the fifteenth and sixteenth centuries compile written reports of their experiences. They were always driven more by trade than by the desire to expand their knowledge or to entertain a literate population.

2 A Penitent Apostate

Sometimes, visitors to India had special reasons for sharing their adventures. Especially curious is the occasion that led the Venetian trader Nicolò de' Conti (1395–1469) to write a report of his major trip through India, a trip that lasted dozens of years. At the beginning of the fifteenth century, he left Damascus with a caravan on a major trade expedition. He crossed the whole Indian subcontinent and arrived in areas where no other European had ever been. He married a native Indian woman, and they had three children. His return journey, however, was one of great hardship. When passing by Mecca he and his whole family were taken prisoner and all of them were threatened with death on the grounds of heresy. To escape execution by fire, he and his family converted to Islam. He could continue on his journey, but the plague had broken out in Egypt and claimed the lives of his wife and one of his children. He finally reached Italy and applied to the pope to be received into the Church again as an apostate. The pope was willing to grant him absolution, but he did require him to be interrogated extensively by the papal secretary about his travels.

It is to this secretary, the well-known humanist Poggio Bracciolini (1380–1459) that we owe the beautifully written account of the adventures of this Venetian trader. The papal secretary was obviously deeply impressed by the

 | DOI:10.1163/9789004420076_004

stories De' Conti told him about India. He was very well acquainted with the classical writers and was eager to hear facts that the authoritative writers from antiquity had not been aware of.

In addition to this literary account of high quality in polished Latin, we also have the notes of a Spanish aristocrat who travelled to the Middle East purely out of interest. He had met De' Conti in St. Catherine's Monastery in the Desert of Sinai, which was apparently a meeting point for European travellers. This Spanish aristocrat's name was Pedro Tafur (ca. 1410–1484), and he was certainly the opposite of the papal secretary. His writing style was awkward, and he was not hampered by wide geographical knowledge—he thought that the Indus and the Nile were the same river. In contrast to Bracciolini, however, he wrote in a direct and personal way about his meeting De' Conti. They became friends apparently, and De' Conti succeeded in convincing his Spanish friend that it was far too risky to make the dangerous trip to India.

3 A Corporate Spy in Action

Completely different in character is the travel account by the Dutch adventurer, Jan Huygen van Linschoten (1562/63–1611). Towards the end of the sixteenth century, from 1583 to 1588, he lived in the Portuguese settlement of Goa, as the clerk for the archbishop. At that time, Goa was the capital of *Asia Portuguesa*, and all lines from the Portuguese government and the trade with Europe converged there. Van Linschoten was on a good footing with his powerful employer, and his career in those few years was impressive. When the archbishop left for Europe on a business trip, Van Linschoten was appointed steward in order to keep the considerable archdiocesan business running. In addition to his work for the Portuguese, however, he also had his own agenda. In a few years he actually collected all information available about the Portuguese policy, their trade with various areas of India, the sea routes and military reinforcements, the nature and culture of the marvellous world in which he found himself. The Portuguese had been careful to keep their dealings in India fundamentally protected from the eyes of others. The descriptions of sea routes (*roteiros*), which had been kept very accurately up to date and contained information provided by generations of sailors on meteorological facts and strategic peculiarities, were limited to a very small circle, as state secrets. Van Linschoten managed to gain access to all those sources. When he got into difficulty because of political intrigues involving his superior, he succeeded handily in finding a berth on one of the returning pepper ships, taking with him all his notes, sketches, and the natural products he had collected. In retrospect, it boggles the mind as to why the Portuguese authorities let him leave with his "thorough and extensive knowledge of all aspects of that wonderland wrapped in mysteries, which he would reveal to his compatriots, to their great advantage" (McKew Parr 1964:116).

After returning to the Netherlands, the knowledge he had collected was published, and the great advantage of the Dutch could begin. The first to be published was his *Reysgheschrift* (1595), which would become the route description *par excellence* for sailors of all nationalities sailing to Asia. His *Itinerario* appeared a year later, which was a treasure trove of information on nature and culture, trade and lifestyles in the closed countries of India. Like a perfect corporate spy, Jan Huygen van Linschoten revealed all the Portuguese secrets, and the Portuguese supremacy was broken for good.

It was not only the sixteenth-century Dutchman who showed that trade gained an advantage with such knowledge, but the travel account that the pope's secretary drew out of Nicolò de' Conti more than a century earlier also had a business aspect. The papal order to prepare a travel account did not emerge from pastoral concern or from the need to provide good reading material. In a time in which the Muslim world was tightening its grip on the trade routes to the East, it seemed to be of great importance to chart both the sailing routes and the balance of power.[1] There was a consideration of another kind as well. The growing circle of humanist scholars felt a great need for new, up-to-date information about the geography, nature, and culture of other continents. Up until that time, all knowledge was based on the information derived from the ancient authors. However much authority they still had, people were beginning to come to the realisation that there was more to discover (Rubiés 2000:85–88). The papal secretary Poggio Bracciolini was one of those who gladly sought new information.

4 A Humanistic Work

Nicolò de' Conti was the ideal source for Bracciolini. This interviewing process entrusted to a papal jurist convinced him of the reliability and expertise of the apostate Venetian traveller. He received De' Conti in official meetings with other scholars and privately at his home as well. The information he heard he wrote down in an extensive report, which is certainly influenced by the literary style of the humanists. He wrote as he was taught to write—following the

1 This importance is brought to the fore primarily by Geneviève Bouchon in her introduction to Ménard and Amilhat-Szary 2004; see especially p. 29.

example of the ancient writers. The part in which he gives an overview of the geography of India begins with the sentence: "The whole of India is divided into three sections," a direct borrowing from the then already well-known opening sentence of Caesar's *De bello gallico*.[2] Incidentally, to entertain his readers, the papal secretary also added striking details, such as the custom in south Burma whereby men had small metal bells placed under their foreskin: "I report this just for fun."[3]

Bracciolini gives a detailed overview of travel routes, geographical peculiarities, and natural products. He also, however, provides a picture of the way of life of the various peoples in Asia and their religion. What is striking in his travel account from the middle of the fifteenth century is its extensive detail and that he also looks for overlappings and similarities between these foreign cultures and his own European civilisation. And that was new. For the writers a century and a half previously, all Hindus were simply idolaters, and thus the content of their religion was no longer interesting. Their religion as a whole was shoved aside. In De' Conti's report, the recognition in cultural and religious fields was limited as well, but not everything appeared to come across as foreign to him. Characteristic here is what De' Conti says about the worship of divinities in temples: "Gods are worshiped everywhere in India, temples are built for them that look very much like ours."[4] The (sometimes metres high) images are described, as is the way the Hindus prayed and sacrificed, which showed great variety. Adherents went to the temple mornings and evenings, after first washing themselves. There was no ringing of church bells, but people banged copper bowls together to achieve the same effect. A kind of incense was offered by burning herbs and fragrant wood for the gods. And there was a custom that was also present in Europe during its pagan antiquity: feasts were organised in which food was distributed to the poor.[5] Indeed, it was possible to observe similarities even in the content of the worship. In a famous passage—unfortunately difficult to place geographically—De' Conti describes the religion of a certain people in East India, possibly Indochina. They did worship idols, but every day, when they got up, they faced the east and prayed with folded hands: "Triune God, and his law, protect us!"[6] De' Conti's suggestion (or that of the writer) is that, behind the various cults of 'idols,' all shared the

2 Bracciolini 1723:IV, 139: "Indiam omnem in tres divisam partes." Cf. Julius Caesar 1958:Ch. 1: "Gallia est omnis divisa in partes tres."

3 Bracciolini 1723:IV, 132: "quam joci gratia scripsi." See Teensma 1991.

4 Bracciolini 1723:IV, 143: "Per universam Indiam Dii coluntur, quibus templa simillima nostris fiunt."

5 Bracciolini 1723:IV, 144: "Gentilium priscorum more."

6 Bracciolini 1723:IV, 133: "Deus trinus, et lex ejus eadem, nos tuere."

orientation to the one God, none other than the Christian one. Today, the call to a 'triune God' that De' Conti heard is usually connected with the notion of the Trimūrti, the combination of Brahmā, Viṣṇu, and Śiva (Ménard and Amilhard-Szary 2004:148, n. 99/1; Ristuccia 2013:196, n. 115).

What people actually stand out in the religious culture of India? These are, obviously, the Brahmins; De' Conti clearly came to know them as the religious leaders of the people. Just like Marco Polo, he distinguishes between those who led a normal worldly life and the ascetics who had withdrawn from the ordinary world (Bracciolini 1723:IV, 142; cf. Rubiés 2000:106). He called the former *bachali*; they functioned as priests during worship and at cremations. De' Conti attributed to them an active role in particular in the burning of widows. He described the homeless ascetics as philosophers of a kind (*philosophorum genus*) who devoted themselves primarily to astronomy and predicting the future. They led holy lives and occupied themselves solely with honourable activities. The healthy lifestyle of the Brahmins also comes to the fore when De' Conti reports that he met an ascetic who was three hundred years old.

5 Feasts

An exciting part of De' Conti's travel report is his account of the feasts of the Hindus. If earlier travellers had made only general remarks about religious feasts, here an attempt is made for the first time to sketch the yearly cycle. In Bracciolini's account, this section links up directly with a few remarks about the city Vijayanagar (Bracciolini 1723:IV, 144–45). De' Conti seems to have stayed here for a longer period of time, and it is also obvious that he described feasts that took place in this city as well. Vijayanagar was a powerful, rich city in the middle of the fifteenth century, the capital of the Hindu kingdom that ruled over a large part of South India. It was a first-rate place to be a participant observer of the religious life of the Hindus! In the four feasts that De' Conti describes, there is first of all one in which men and women bathed in the water of the river, put on new clothes and then spent three days in festival activities, dancing, singing, and eating. It has been suggested that this was a local New Year's feast (Sewell 1900:85). That is certainly not impossible, but, given that De' Conti says he will focus on feasts that were celebrated generally, it is more obvious to think of *Mahāśivarātri*, which is viewed everywhere as one of the most prominent Hindu feasts. The feast begins with a day of fasting, after which a bath in the river and putting on new clothes are the start of a lively community feast. In any case, the second feast De' Conti describes is unmistakable, a feast in which an innumerable quantity of small lamps with sesame oil are placed on the outside and roofs of the temples that burn day and night. This is of course *Dīvālī*, the feast of lights in honour of the goddess Lakṣmī, which is still the most popular Hindu feast, right up to the present. Then De' Conti describes a feast that lasted nine days and in which decorated poles were set up in the street. Devout people were also placed on them and let themselves be pelted with fruit by the public while remaining unflappable. This is certainly a description of *Navarātri*, a feast in honour of Devī, the great goddess. The devout are certainly no longer pelted with fruit today while they are praying, but it was probably a local custom in the fifteenth century. The feast is still celebrated in the area around the earlier Vijayanagar. The cultural capital of the area especially, Maisuru (Mysore), is known for its impressive grand processions on the final day of the feast, *Dasahrā* (Sivapriyananda 1995:passim). Finally, De' Conti described a three-day feast in which people splashed each other with saffron water. Even the king and queen did not leave during this activity, and the event caused general hilarity. Obviously, this is the joyful spring feast of *Holī*.

6 Shocking Religious Phenomena

De' Conti does not only report on recognisable, attractive aspects of religious life in in India. He also writes about things that European travellers were always surprised and shocked about. The first one he wrote about was of course the ritual suicide of widows with their husbands, *satī*. He describes how the woman jumped into the fire at the priest's invitation. It was not always a spontaneous act on her part, however: he emphasised that women often recoiled from this step and were then thrown into the fire by the onlookers.[7] Another remarkable phenomenon was the self-chosen death of someone who sacrificed his life out of devotion to a divinity. An apparatus had been invented by which one could chop off one's own head, a kind of guillotine one could operate by oneself. De' Conti describes this device in detail and sensationally, and it can also be found in the travel account written by Pero Tafur. This anecdote was apparently a favourite of De' Conti's (Bracciolini, 1723:IV, 144; Tafur 1874:101).

It was no surprise that De' Conti also wrote about the large processions with the temple wagons, whereby devout spectators let themselves be crushed under the immense wheels of the wagon on which the image of the god was transported. He also related that a procession like this took place in Vijayanagar, with many casualties, giving the impression that he himself had been an

7 Bracciolini 1723:IV, 141: "saepe reluctari videntur." Cf. Tafur 1874:104–05.

eyewitness (Bracciolini 1723:IV, 144). He added something, however, that we have not yet found in other sources: he writes that some people had the flesh on their back perforated and a rope pulled through the perforations so that they could be raised up and thus show their devotion by hanging from the temple wagon. There are commentators who doubt the truth of these stories (so Ménard and Amilhard-Szary 2004:152, n. 115/1). We do, however, have various later reports of such ritual self-flagellation, known in the colonial period as 'hook swinging.' It still occurs today, if only sporadically. The custom is forbidden in India, but the traditional back hooks were used in an Indian procession in Den Helder, in the Netherlands, on 28 June 2015.

7 A Dutchman in a Portuguese City

In Vijayanagar, De' Conti found himself in the ideal environment for acquainting himself with Hinduism. As the capital city of a Hindu kingdom, it offered the opportunity to regularly observe rituals and events. With respect to that, Jan Huygen van Linschoten found himself in a less privileged environment. In the Portuguese settlement of Goa, he could observe Hinduism only from the sidelines. Goa was (and is) a city of churches, not temples. Life was dominated by the Portuguese managers and merchants and their Christian, European culture. On the other hand, the native culture was never far away. Crossing the river that surrounded the Portuguese settlement brought one into authentic Indian surroundings. And in the city as well, the majority of the population consisted of Indians. Goa was one of the greatest cities of the world; with a population of 225,000, it rivalled Antwerp and London (McKew Parr 1964:80). The Portuguese rulers did impose rules for life in the city, but it was impossible to mould the activity of such a large, non-European majority to their wishes.

Jan Huygen van Linschoten has described this multicultural society with a great deal of insight, basing what he wrote both on what he saw around him and what he heard from other Europeans. He also made short trips into the interior to immerse himself in native culture. Moreover, Goa was the centre of all Portuguese Asia, and his employer, the archbishop, stood at the head of all church activity in the whole continent. Already because of his job alone, Van Linschoten had access to a constant stream of information from the whole continent and far beyond. After all, a papal decision in 1494 had given the entire heathen area that lay east of the Atlantic Ocean to Portugal, whereas Spain was given the countries west of that ocean to exploit.

From Van Linschoten's report on life in Goa, his distance from the culture of Portuguese is as clear as day. He did not feel too much at ease in the ostentatious display of status and wealth of the Portuguese citizens and the meticulous etiquette that were linked to them. Irritated, he writes in particular about the Portuguese women who spent all their time in idleness and were exclusively focused on amorous relationships. Adultery and incest were, apparently, quite common, and illicit relationships led regularly to murder and manslaughter. To a certain extent, there is good reason to speak here of "Linschoten's heavily exaggerated observations" (Van den Boogaart 2000:22). In any case, it appears that Van Linschoten did not feel part of the cultural circle of Portuguese citizens, despite his position with the archbishop. Making the numerous secrets of the Portuguese rulers public after his return was certainly not a matter of treason to a society he had belonged to for a period in his life. Rather, it was the result of his feeling excluded from that society and ignored for years.

What did Van Linschoten think of the Indian society he was exposed to in Goa? While he did in any case share the same religion as the Portuguese (he was undoubtedly still Roman Catholic at that time), he nevertheless found examples of inspiring moral behaviour among the "heathens." That obtains first of all for the highest caste among the Hindus, the Brahmins (Van Linschoten 1596:Ch. 36). He called them the most honest and most esteemed group among the heathens. He was impressed by the way in which they occupied the highest posts and were held in high regard among the people. He described the particularities of their way of life, the sacred thread they wore, their turbans, and long loose hair, and their strict vegetarian diet. He also told of their practice of child marriage: children married when the boy was nine years old and the girl seven, though they did not actually start to live together until later. He also knew about the ritual suicide of the widow at her husband's cremation, *satī*, but relativised its universality: if a woman did not want to die, she was shorn and had to remove her jewellery. It is interesting to see that he provides an argument for this cruel custom of burning widows with their dead husbands. According to him, this was done because women previously often killed their husbands when they had enough of them—the fear of being burned alive would deter that practice!

Ambivalence emerges as well with respect to the religious function of the Brahmins, They did not assume their religious convictions lightly, as could be seen from their strict observance of certain rules, in particular fasting. But, over against that, they also served in the temple (*menistren van de pagoden* [ministers of the pagodas]) and devoted themselves to the service of the "devilish idols." They convinced the people of all kinds of marvellous "nonsense and fables" and were believed by the people as if they were prophets. Van Linschoten was not very interested in the mythology (*wondere historiën ende mirakelen* [strange stories and miracles]), but he also spoke with appreciation of a fundamental notion in Hindu faith, i.e., that they believed that there was a supreme God who governed everything and that the human being had an immortal soul. It was believed that the soul—both animal and human—moved from one body to another. Van Linschoten heard an echo of Pythagoras in this belief, and that link brought this far Eastern belief into European waters, which made it a somewhat acceptable and safe notion.

8 Caste Hierarchy

What is particularly special about Jan Huygen van Linschoten's work is that he not only describes the Brahmins but other castes as well. For the first time, he gives us a picture of the stratified society in which all people are included in a strict, hierarchically arranged caste structure. After the Brahmins came the *Gujarātīs* (*Gusuratten*) and the *Baniyās* (*Banyans*) (Van Linschoten 1596:Ch. 37). These groups originally came from Gujarat, which was further north. They were typical merchant castes, whose members were characterised by a sound knowledge of goods and were very precise in bookkeeping and administration, in which they were also better than the Portuguese. Especially striking is their strict vegetarian practice: they ate no meat, not even eggs, and also attempted to convince others to cease slaughtering animals. Thus, they sometimes bought birds and other animals from Christians that were destined for the table and set them free. They also had animal shelters where they cared for sick animals. Even the smallest animals could count on their protection: they did not kill lice and fleas either. The worst thing one could do to them was to kill an animal in their presence. They adhered very closely to caste boundaries, never taking food from other castes and certainly not from Christians. If they went on a sea voyage with an insufficient amount of food, they would fast until they died of hunger.

The next two castes, the *Kanaras* (*Canaras*) and the *Dakṣiṇās* (*Decanijns*), were from a different area (Van Linschoten 1596:Ch. 38): they came from the high Deccan Plateau, east of Goa; just like the previous castes, they stood considerably high in the hierarchy and earned their living primarily as traders. Their specialty was buying and selling material for clothes. They were not strict vegetarians, but they did not eat any beef, pork, or fish. Their love for the cow was proverbial: they loved to feed and pet the animal and kept it in the home as a member of the family. Their rituals and observances were the same as those of the Brahmins, to whom they were related like laity to the clergy. They also leased the tolls from both the Portuguese and the native rulers. They could acquit themselves well in judicial matters and were completely trustworthy under oath, for they did not commit perjury.

The following two castes in Van Linschoten's account represent a lower level in society: the *Kannaḍiyans* (*Canarijns*) and the *Kuṭumbīs* (*Corumbijns*) were distinctly lower castes (Van Linschoten 1596:Ch. 39). The *Kannaḍiyans* were the small farmers and fishermen in the area, but some also practised the lowly esteemed occupations of washer and messenger. Van Linschoten characterises them as "the most despised and miserable of the Indians." They lived in small reed huts, and all lived in poverty. They were originally Hindu, just like the previous two castes, but many of them had already been baptised as Christians.

Van Linschoten devotes a separate chapter to the groups from the Malabar coast (currently Kerala) who came to live in Goa (Van Linschoten 1596:Ch. 42). This is all the more interesting because the castes from this area were quite distinct. Two groups can be distinguished: the *Nāyars* (*Nayros*) and the *Puliyar* (*Polyas*). The *Nāyars* were a caste of warriors who carried weapons in service to kings. They had a high position—only the Brahmins were above them. The *Puliyar*, in contrast, were the lowest caste from this area. The *Nāyars* considered them to be untouchable. Van Linschoten appeared to be well informed about the relationships between the castes. He describes the *Nāyars* as military men who always had their weapons with them, and he used a term for them that one would not readily expect from a Dutchman: "noble." His description is in line with older reports on this caste. Already at the beginning of the sixteenth century, the Portuguese government official Duarte Barbosa had reported on the relationships between the castes on the Malabar coast. It is highly probable that Van Linschoten read and used this text. Barbosa had depicted the *Nāyars* as nobility (*fidalgos*), whose only task in society was to conduct war (Barbosa 1946:138–39; Barbosa 1867:124). This shows how well the Dutch clerk of the archbishop was informed; he made ready use of the undoubtedly large library of his patron.

In addition, Van Linschoten also relied a great deal on his own observations. He certainly saw the fearsome *Nāyars* walking on the street, their weapons clattering, and calling out loudly so that the unclean lower castes could move out of the way on time. And he had certainly heard the curious stories about the sex relations within the warrior caste, which always fascinated Europeans. The *Nāyars* did not marry. Because of their military duties, the men could not lead a normal family life. But they could enter into casual relationships, and the women were free to have relationships with several men if they were from the same or a higher caste. This polyandry started at a young age, and it was said that girls had sexual relations from the age of seven or eight. One can easily understand why Van Linschoten described them in accordance with the usual judgment of the Europeans as "the most luxurious and unchaste nation that could be found in the whole of the Orient."[8]

9 Religious Customs and Religious Faith

Van Linschoten's description of religion also displays a curious combination of older written sources, his own observations, and generally shared European ideas. In his chapter on the 'pagodas,' he copied a passage written by an earlier Portuguese writer,[9] which did not always promote clarity about his subject. For example, he used the word 'pagoda' to refer not only to Hindu temples but also to figures and images of gods. This habit led to confusing phrases like "the most prominent pagodas (or temples, but more like caverns in which the pagodas are found)."[10] He added original information in stories about his own experiences as well as engravings that were based on his own drawings. In both word and image, we regularly see the influence of Christian schemas.

This becomes quite clear in his discussion of divine images and the cultus in the temples. For Van Linschoten and his environment, the worship of the gods remained a matter that was difficult to deal with. They could not feel much respect for the remarkable images that had more than two arms, strange features, and a horrifying ambience. Van Linschoten's report of a little trip to the continent that he made with some Portuguese is characteristic and somewhat shameful (Van Linschoten 1596:Ch. 44). When visiting a village, they went to view a temple, and, as a joke, one of the Europeans sat astride an image of Nandī in the shrine, pretending to ride it like a horse. The temple priest was profoundly shocked and called for the men of the village to come. Only soothing words and apologies prevented a violent riot from occurring. The visitors then pressured the priest into opening the closed internal area of the temple for them. What they detected in this holiest of spaces (*garbhagṛha*) was not able to charm them either. The evening ritual of laying the image of the god to rest, after a circumlocution and a ritual bath in the temple pond invoked nothing more than a lack of understanding and mockery.

---

8 For the *Nāyars*, see Thurston and Rangachari 1975:V, 283–413.

9 Van Linschoten 1596:Ch. 44. See the note in the edition by Kern and Terpstra (Van Linschoten 1955–1957); this concerns a passage from *Coloquios* by Garcia de Orta (1563) (1895).

10 Van Linschoten 1596:Ch. 44. Cf. De Orta (1895:II, 340), who correctly describes 'pagodas' as "casas de idolatria" (houses of idolatry).

FIGURE 4 Pagode en Mesquita (Temple and Mosque)
Illustration in Van Linschoten's Itinerario

The illustration that is included in the book with this passage helps clarify matters. Van Linschoten boasted that his drawings, which were later made into engravings by the Van Doetechum brothers, were strictly 'true to life.' That was certainly true of landscapes, trees, and fruit. The depictions of various types of people are also quite lifelike, though not always as artistic. The engraving of the religions of the country seems, however, to be primarily symbolic in nature. It contains a message.

Van Linschoten himself gives a description of this illustration in his book: "And so that its demonic, idolatrous figures can be better understood, I have added here the likeness of such things in public on roads, mountains, rocks, and caves, with a stone cow or calf, likewise the church, which they call a mesquita, of the Mahomedans" (Van Linschoten 1596:Ch. 44).[11] The attention thus falls primarily on the Hindus' images of gods and the mosques, which did not

11 Kern and Terpstra incorrectly read *kop* (head) instead of *koy* (cow).

have much to see, did not serve as much more than a contrast to the shocking world of heathenism. The depiction of the temple does not, however, come across as very true to life. It is fortunate that the caption says that it is a stone image of a cow, for the print suggests more of a live cow. It should be an image, and the words "cow or calf" are very suggestive: just like the Israelites worshipped a golden calf during their wanderings in the desert, these people were also committing a terrible idolatry (Exodus 32). Also very suggestive is the idol in the niche at the back. That is not really what an Indian image of a god looks like; it looks more like the depiction of a demonic beast like those found in biblical apocalyptic literature. Van Linschoten explicitly referred to that in his description of the village temple he had visited: "many horns and long teeth that came out of his mouth and over his chin, and under the navel and belly an animal face with many horns and intestines ... in sum, it seemed to be a monster from the Apocalypse" (Van Linschoten 1596:Ch. 44).[12] That was how people imagined idols in Europe: "Terrifying images of the Indian gods" was printed below the engraving, to leave no question about that. And Van Linschoten, who uses few pious words in his book, ends this chapter with a prayer of thanks to God for not letting "us" be born among such heathens. And he calls his readers to join in prayer for these people that God would redeem them with "us" and give them salvation. Uncharacteristically for him, this section ends with "Amen."

10 Monotheism

This massive rejection of idolatrous religion is very much at odds with a different view that Van Linschoten has of the religion of India. More than once he says that the Hindus all confess that there is one God who has created all things and governs them, which also obtains for those who also worship the sun and moon. And Van Linschoten holds that they share the universal belief that there is another life after this one in which people are rewarded according to their works (Van Linschoten 1596:chs. 33 and 36). Apparently, a fundamental idea about a supreme divinity did not stand in the way of worshipping all other forms. It is certainly remarkable to find this notion of a monotheistic basis, which is so important for modern Hindus, already in this work from the sixteenth century. It is easily conceivable that the old monistic beliefs from the Upaniṣads were already used then as an argument against the Christian accusations of idolatry.

12 See Revelation 13:1, 2; cf. Mitter 1977:21–22.

It is precisely when Van Linschoten discusses the views of the Brahmins that these religious ideas come to the fore (Van Linschoten 1596:Ch. 36). Fundamentally, according to Van Linschoten, the Brahmins believed that there was one supreme God who ruled everything. To reach the supreme divinity, however, intermediaries were needed who argued and pleaded on behalf of the believers. And this was the function of the images of the gods that were worshipped in the temples. These 'idols,' according to the Brahmins who served them, were previously ordinary people, and it was because of their holy lives and good works, that they became holy, as was clear from the various miracles they performed. Now, they were 'advocates' who interceded before God for the people. This was the basis of the temple service that the Brahmins led. Whenever he talked about the ritual side of religion, Van Linschoten uses terms like "demonic superstitions." In his view, it is thus also through the instigation of the devil that the people had been ordered to make such ugly and gruesome images to worship idols.

What Van Linschoten continues to assess positively, however, are the perseverance and dedication that the believers, especially the Brahmins, showed (Van Linschoten 1596:Ch. 33). They followed the rituals "very closely" and would never go on a journey without first saying their prayers. And they also lived in accordance with many prescriptions regarding their external behaviour as well. He praised their regular bathing and purity rules that were both religious and hygienic in nature. Their reliability in trade was a great good. The moneychangers who were regularly needed could be trusted with no reservations whatsoever.

The terrain of the temple service, however, remained foreign territory. As one of the first visitors, Van Linschoten writes about the temple in Goa in which girls offered their virginity before their marriage: they let themselves be penetrated by an idol that was equipped with an ivory peg for this purpose. This remarkable tradition later attracted the interest of many in Europe. References to this can be found in Karl Marx' notes and in the works of the Marquis de Sade (Van Linschoten 1596:33).

11 An Unknown World

Jan Huygen van Linschoten was one of the first to give a detailed, reliable description of life on the Indian subcontinent. His book is the fruit of a stay of only five years in India and then in the Portuguese city that was only partly stamped by Indian culture. His achievement is indicative of his inquisitiveness and entrepreneurial spirit. He was driven by a great interest in what belonged to an unknown world. In an endearing way, he defended his undertaking in 1584 in a letter that he sent to his parents from Goa: "My heart does not think of anything else night and day than seeing foreign countries. That way, I will have something to talk about when I'm old." (quoted in Van Linschoten 1955–1957:xvii–xviii). When he returned to Enkhuizen, he did indeed have a great deal to tell about the unknown world of India. The tragedy of his life is that he did not live to be an old man. Jan Huygen van Linschoten died already in 1611, at the age of 48.

Bibliography

Text Editions and Translations

Bracciolini, Poggio (1723). *Historiae de varietate fortunae.* Vol. IV. Lutetiae Parisiorum: Typis Antonii Urbani Coustelier. Pp. 126–52.

Linschoten, Jan Huygen van (1955–1957). *Itinerario: Voyage ofte schipvaert van Jan Huygen van Linschoten naer Oost ofte Portugaels* Indien. Ed. H. Kern and H. Terpstra. 2nd ed. Three parts. 's-Gravenhage: Martinus Nijhoff.

Linschoten, Jan Huygen van (1596). *Itinerario: Voyage ofte Schipvaert van Jan Huygen van Linschoten naer Oost ofte Portugaels Indien.* Amstelredam (Amsterdam): Cornelis Claesz.

Ménard, Diane, and Anne-Laure Amilhat-Szary (2004). *Le voyage aux Indes de Nicolò de' Conti (1414–1439).* Collection magellane. Paris: Éditions Chandeigne.

Tafur, Pero (1874). *Andanças é viajes de Pero Tafur por diversas partes del mundo avidos (1435–1439).* Madrid: Ginesta.

Winter Jones, J. (1857). "The Travels of Nicolò Conti in the East in the Early Part of the Fifteenth Century." In: R.H. Major (ed.). *India in the Fifteenth Century.* London: Hakluyt Society.

Secondary Literature

Barbosa, Duarte (1946). *Livro em que dá relação do que viu e ouviu no Oriente.* Ed. Augusto Reis Machado. Lisbon: Agência Geral das Colónias.

Barbosa, Duarte (1866). *A Description of the Coasts of East Africa and Malabar in the Beginning of the Sixteenth Century.* Transl. Henry E.J. Stanley. London: Hakluyt Society.

Boogaart, Ernst van den(2000). *Het verheven en verdorven Azië: Woord en beeld in het* Itinerario *en de* Icones *van Jan Huygen van Linschoten.* Amsterdam/Leiden: Het Spinhuis/KITLV Uitgeverij.

Caesar, Gaius Iulius (1958). *Commentarii de bello gallico.* Ed. P.K. Huibregtse. Groningen: J.B. Wolters.

Gelder, Roelof van, Jan Parmentier, and Vibeke Roeper (eds.) (1998). *Souffrir pour parvenir: De wereld van Jan Huygen van Linschoten*. Haarlem: Uitgeverij Arcadia.

Koeman, C. (1985). "Jan Huygen van Linschoten." *Revista da Universidade de Coimbra* XXXII: 27–47.

Lach, Donald F. (1965). *Asia in the Making of Europe*. Vol. I. Chicago/London: University of Chicago Press.

Lee, Ton van der(2016). *Jan Huygen: Het gedroomde leven van de grondlegger van de VOC*. Amsterdam: Uitgeverij Balans.

McKew Parr, Charles (1964). *Jan van Linschoten: The Dutch Marco Polo*. New York: Crowell.

Mitter, Partha (1977). *Much Maligned Monsters: A History of European Reactions to Indian Art*. Oxford: Clarendon Press.

Orta, Garcia de(1895). *Coloquios dos simples e drogas da India*. Vol. II. Ed. Conde de Ficalho. Lisbon: Imprensa Nacional.

Phillips, Kim M. (2014). *Before Orientalism: Asian Peoples and Cultures in European Travel Writing, 1245–1510*. The Middle Ages Series. Philadelphia: University of Pennsylvania Press.

Ristuccia, Nathan J. (2013). "Eastern Religions and the West: The Making of an Image." *History of Religions* 53: 170–204.

Rubiés, Joan-Pau (2000). *Travel and Ethnology in the Renaissance: South India through European Eyes, 1250–1625*. Cambridge: Cambridge University Press.

Sewell, Robert (1900). *A Forgotten Empire (Vijayanagar): A Contribution to the History of India*. London: Swan Sonnenschein.

Sivapriyananda, Swami (1995). *Mysore Royal Dasara*. New Delhi: Abhinav Publications.

Thurston, Edgar, and K. Rangachari (1975). *Castes and Tribes of Southern India*. Seven volumes. Delhi: Cosmo Publications.

Xavier, Ângela Barreto, and Ines G. Županov (2015). *Catholic Orientalism: Portuguese Empire, Indian Knowledge (16th–18th Centuries)*. New Delhi: Oxford University Press.

CHAPTER 3

A Foreign Culture Baptised: The Jesuits Roberto de Nobili and Thomas Stephens

1 Travels to Asia*

Portugal invested a great deal in the patronage the pope had granted it over Asia. This *padroado* included the expansion of the Christian religion in particular, and, right from the start, religious initiatives went in hand in hand with commercial enterprises. In 1498 the Portuguese explorer Vasco da Gama (1460/1469–1524) reached the southwest coast of India in an impressive display of power. According to a well-known story, he was met by two North African traders who spoke Spanish and aggressively demanded, on behalf of the local population, to know why Da Gama had come. The Portuguese captain's answer was: "We have come to seek Christians and spices" (Fernando and Gispert-Sauch 2004:72–73).

The purpose of Da Gama's voyage was to break through the monopoly the Muslims held on the spice trade: the Portuguese wanted to buy spices in Asia without any middlemen. And, as it was also generally believed in Europe at that time, they felt they could build up better commercial contacts with fellow believers given that they thought there was a Christian kingdom located somewhere in the Orient under the leadership of the legendary 'Prester John.' But no such Christian state was ever found, and, as far as Christian believers were concerned, there were only small communities of Syrian Orthodox who had little influence. But, even if there were no Christians to be found, one could always make them. Da Gama was usually cited later as saying: "We have come to seek souls and spices" or—even more cleverly—in German 'Pfeffer und Seelen' (souls and pepper).[1]

2 Jesuits in Mission

About the middle of the fifteenth century, the conversion of 'heathens' became an important goal in Portuguese colonial politics. The new order of the Jesuits,

* An earlier version of this chapter was published under the title 'A Foreign Culture Baptised: Roberto de Nobili and the Jesuits,' in: *Exchange* 47 (2018), 183–198.'

1 Cf. the title of Plattner 1955: *Pfeffer und Seelen.*

 | DOI:10.1163/9789004420076_005

founded in 1534, provided workers for this important task, and many hundreds of Jesuits left for the Indian subcontinent to preach the message of the Gospel and to baptise new believers. The work of the Spanish Jesuit Francis Xavier (1506–1552) is especially important. He owed his later nickname 'Apostle of India' to, among other things, his missionary work among the fishermen of the Parava caste on the Pearl Coast. When he arrived, he found a number of people who had been baptised previously by the Portuguese but discovered that they had received no instruction at all in the faith. He thus made it his goal in the three years that he stayed with them to teach them. That was by no means a simple task, for the population spoke only Tamil and did not even understand Portuguese, whereas Francis spoke only Spanish.[2] The missionary was thus completely dependent on interpreters. Nonetheless, he was successful in converting the populations of entire villages to Christianity and baptising them.

The Jesuits quickly began to understand that mastering the language of the population was indispensable for missionary work. Furthermore, people were becoming more aware of the great cultural differences between them and the Asian peoples. Thus, at the beginning of the seventeenth century, the Jesuits began a new approach. Some Jesuits in both China and India mastered the local language thoroughly and also adapted their clothes and habits to those of the elite of the local scholars. Matteo Ricci (1552–1610) is well known for his activities in China: he attached himself to Confucian scholars and attempted to win them to the Christian faith. The idea was that the other strata of the population would follow if their leaders adopted the new faith. The proclamation of the Christian faith went hand in hand with a great tolerance for cultural customs that were important for the population. Thus, ancestor worship and paying homage to Confucius could continue during the transition to Christianity. The same approach was taken in India by a Jesuit of equal intellectual capacity, Roberto de Nobili (1577–1656).

3 A Promising Young Man

Born in Rome into an aristocratic and wealthy family, Roberto de Nobili had many opportunities to acquire a position of standing in society. A career in the Church was certainly possible, for he was, after all, named after an uncle who had been made a cardinal at a very young age. A combination of a career in the Church with the advancement of his social position as a large, aristocratic landowner would certainly be appreciated by his family. But the young Roberto

2 He wrote to the Jesuit order in Rome: "We could not understand one another, as I spoke Castilian and they Malabar." See Coleridge 1881:151.

had different plans. When he was 17 years old he became fascinated by the mission work of the Jesuits and was ready to give up his ancestral heritage with its attendant privileges to be part of that. This was met with strong resistance by his family, and Roberto then fled and crossed the border into the nearby kingdom of Naples. He found refuge with an aristocratic woman who was sympathetic to his idealism.

After two years, his family managed to trace him and tried to get him to toe the line. His powerful patroness, however, managed to make a convincing argument for his spiritual calling, and the young refugee was given permission by his family to enter the Jesuit order and to prepare himself for a future as a missionary. Because of the *padroado*, the king of Portugal was also responsible for the missionisation of India, and he also paid the missionaries' salaries. De Nobili thus left for Portugal, was accepted for service in Portuguese India, and ultimately travelled to Goa, where he arrived in 1605.

The 28-year-old missionary was sent to the Pearl Coast, where the work of Francis Xavier had resulted in a number of Christian fishing villages. The people of these villages belonged to the Parava caste, one of the lowest. Other than these people, the Indian population did not appear to be open to the Christian preachers. It was in this environment that De Nobili learned the local language, Tamil, in half a year. This was a major achievement, given that this difficult Dravidian language is not related to European languages in any way.

4 In the Capital

The provincial superior of the Jesuits, Alberto Laerzio (1557–1630), however, had a different place in mind for De Nobili once he had learned the language. Laerzio transferred him to a small mission post in Madurai, the capital of the kingdom. An older Portuguese priest, Gonçalo Fernandez (1541–1619), had worked there for more than 10 years without producing one single convert (Cronin 1959:39).

De Nobili attempted to understand what held the local population back from being open to the missionaries. He slowly came to understand that the unwillingness to listen to the European missionaries was due not to their message as such but to their way of life. The missionaries were exponents of a strange culture that did not link up with any of their local norms and values in any way. The locals called them *paraṅgi*, a word that had entered their language via Arabic and was derived from 'Frank.' The Franks were not only foreigners but enemies by definition and represented everything that was opprobrious and unclean. *Paraṅgis* ate meat, even that of the sacred cow, drank alcohol, and showed no respect at all for the meticulous purity rules of the

Hindus. The boorish behaviour of many of the Portuguese soldiers and sailors reinforced this negative judgment.

Worst of all, the Portuguese themselves were proud of their status as *paraṅgi*. They invited Hindus from all classes and castes, even the most despised castes, to join them and to break with their own backgrounds and dignity. Notably, Father Fernandez referred to his own religion by the term *paraṅgi mārkkam*, 'the religion of the foreigners.' That such a religion held a certain attraction for low-caste fishermen or even completely impure pariahs was understandable. But at the same time that was another reason for those in the higher castes to keep a good distance from a religion of this kind.

Nevertheless, De Nobili aimed precisely at the higher caste people. Like his fellow Jesuits in China, he wanted to reach the spiritual leaders in India with the aim of getting the whole population to follow them. De Nobili thus focused his attention on the Brahmins. He was thus in the right place in Madurai: the city was dominated by one of the largest and holiest temples and there were many Brahmanical educational institutions. To gain access to the Brahmins, De Nobili adapted his lifestyle to the Hindu environment. He switched to a vegetarian diet and bathed at set times in accordance with Indian custom. He firmly denied that he was a *paraṅgi* and presented himself as a member of the *Kṣatriya* division of castes. His background would have been the equivalent of the *Rājā* caste: the fact that he was descended from Emperor Otto III (980–1002) gave his claim weight. The '*rājā* from Rome' was from a different order than the Portuguese, whose company he kept as little as possible after that.

5 A Christian *Sannyāsī*

De Nobili did attract the attention of the Brahmins with his new way of life, and discussions arose about religion and philosophy. He emphatically denied that he had come to proclaim the religion of the *paraṅgis* and from that point on referred to the Christian faith by the charming Indian term *cattiyavētam* (*satyaveda*), true knowledge. There were, however, Brahmins who continued to be bothered by his clothing, for the black soutane he wore was, in their view, inseparably associated with the *paraṅgis*. The church authorities had not given him permission to wear anything else, but he now asked the provincial superior of the Jesuit order to be allowed to wear different clothes. He did have the strong argument that the Brahmins themselves had asked him to wear appropriate clothing. Permission was given, with emphatic reference to the clothing of the Jesuits in China who had adapted their clothing to that of the scholars there (Bachmann 1972:67; Rajamanickam 1972a:19).

FIGURE 5 Roberto de Nobili as a sannyāsī (Baltasar da costa, 1661)

From that time on, De Nobili wore the *kāvi*, the garment of the Hindu ascetic, the *sannyāsī*. He went around dressed in three pieces of ochre-coloured cloth, wore wooden sandals, and shaved his head bald, except for the traditional Brahmanical lock of hair on the top of his head. He had his ears pierced so that he could wear earrings and also used sandalwood powder to mark his forehead with a rectangular figure, a custom of Brahmin gurus. And to emphasise his connection with the higher castes, he also wore the Brahmin's sacred thread (*yajñopavīta*), although he did add a small crucifix to it. The latter was not a choice he had thought about deeply. This sacred thread was worn by members of the higher castes, but *sannyāsīs* took it off when they embarked on a mendicant life. Only later did De Nobili see how the sacred thread was incompatible with his monastic way of life, and he then stopped wearing it.

This Christian *sannyāsī* lived in a traditional mud house with a thatched roof in the Brahmin district of Madurai. He hired Brahmanical personnel to cook for him and to do his laundry. Most of the time, he remained indoors to avoid becoming impure by looking at women. Whoever wanted to visit him had to go to a great deal of trouble to do so: he had visitors return time and again before he received them. His primary activity was, after all, to study and contemplate. In addition to his house, which was usually called—in accordance with Hindu custom, *maṭha*, holy place—he had a simple church built in the Indian style. Already within a short period, he succeeded in building up a small community of Brahmins. After dressing like a *sannyāsī* for half a year, he had baptised more than 50 Brahmins (Cronin 1959:129).

6 De Nobili's Appeal for Brahmins

What attracted the Brahmins from Madurai to this remarkable preacher from the West? The primary factor was De Nobili's extensive ability with languages. His contemporaries testified that he spoke Tamil so well after a few years that it seemed as if it was his native language (Rajamanickam 1972a:26). In addition, he had also mastered Telugu, the language of the court and the civil servants. Moreover, one of his Brahmanical converts taught him Sanskrit and acquainted him with the old sacred books of the Vedas—a very extraordinary undertaking, given that Brahmins were expressly forbidden to familiarise people outside their caste with this sacred literature. The lessons thus had to be conducted in the strictest secrecy. There was great danger, for the traditional punishment was to have the eyes of both the teacher and the student plucked out. Gradually, the Brahmins also became used to the fact that this 'different' teacher had also mastered Sanskrit. De Nobili was now the first European to master the sacred language and to become acquainted with the most sacred books of Hinduism (Caland 1924; Bachmann 1972:73–75; Cronin 1959:85–87).

He knew a great deal of the literature in Tamil and Sanskrit that the Brahmins held to be authoritative. In line with Oriental custom, he had also memorised a great deal of it so that he could illustrate his explanations with suitable passages, learning and adopting the style of education in the Indian tradition. He was rightly called an *aiyar*, a teacher, by the Brahmins.

He led an extremely simple life, eating only once a day and then only food that had been prepared by his own Brahmanical cook. No meat or alcohol, for which the *paraṅgis* were notorious, was found in his house. He ate his meals in Indian fashion: sitting cross-legged on a plank on the floor, with a banana leaf as plate, eating with the fingers of his right hand. This adaptation to Indian customs seems overdone, but, for the meticulous Brahmins, it was the only way that contact with him was possible. This Western teacher also knew how to act. Brahmins—who followed the purification rules of their caste extremely meticulously—had no difficulty visiting him.

De Nobili went quite far in his adaptations. When the malicious rumour spread that he was actually nothing more than a *paraṅgi*, he wrote a statement in Tamil on a palm leaf that he had nailed to a tree in front of his house. In this statement, he denied under oath that he was a *paraṅgi*: "I am not a Parangi. I was not born in the land of the Parangis, nor was I ever connected with their race …" (cited in Rajamanickam 1972a:31; cf. Cronin 1959:136–38 and Bachmann 1972:113.). He then declared that he was from an aristocratic family in Rome and had become a *sannyāsī* already when he was quite young. He wrote that he proclaimed service to "the true God—whoever says that it is the teaching of the *parangis*, commits a very great sin. To follow the true God was do nothing dishonourable or against his caste, and he who dares say the contrary will be deserving of the punishment of hell" (Rajamanickam 1972a:31).

This emotional statement shows how far De Nobili was willing to go to maintain good relations with the Brahmins. If being a *paraṅgi* is equated with being 'Portuguese,' he was correct, strictly speaking. He was, after all, from Italy. But, for convenience's sake, he completely ignores the fact that he was sent there by the Portuguese king and was paid by him. And in the eyes of the Indians, Italians were just as much *paraṅgi* as the Portuguese. That he expressly denied—with curses and all—his connection to his own order and other fellow Christians is extremely disputable.

7 Opposition from the Church

The opposition that he invoked from the Hindus came and ebbed away again. He was confronted a few times after that with gossip and backbiting. He appeared to be in a vulnerable position when there were political shifts, and he was briefly imprisoned twice. More dangerous for the continuation of his mission in Madurai, however, was opposition by the Church. In particular, it was his predecessor, the old Portuguese priest Fernandez, who let no opportunity slip to discredit the Christian *sannyāsī*. Initially, De Nobili had a faithful patron in the provincial superior of the Jesuits, Aberto Laerzio. But when the latter was succeeded by a new superior, Pero Francisco (1564–1615), De Nobili found himself even more in the line of fire.

A major conflict broke out that is known as the Malabar Rites Controversy.[3] It was hotly debated in various places: in Madurai, on the Pearl Coast, the centre of Roman Catholic Christianity in South India as well as in Goa where the archbishop resided, and in Rome. In 1623 Pope Gregory XV issued an apostolic constitution in which a number of the customs De Nobili had introduced were approved.[4] But that was at the end of a long and difficult road.

8 Local Customs

The first question that arose was whether the Church could offer room for local customs that were very important to converts. Brahmins who considered becoming Christians did not want to abandon their caste in any way. They wanted to remain Brahmins and not become *paraṅgi*. That is why they wanted to continue to emphasise their separate status. They wanted to remain recognisable externally and in behaviour as members of the highest caste.

For classical missionaries under Father Fernandez' leading, this was out of the question. Whoever converted to Christianity broke with all heathen customs and became a *paraṅgi*. In the eyes of the Portuguese, this was something to be proud of. But De Nobili understood the sensitivity of the Brahmins and wanted to meet them halfway on precisely this issue. He wrote extensively about this in his works.

Thus, already in 1610, he wrote an extensive defence against the charges of Fernandez and others, known as the *Apologia*.[5] A few years later he went into the topic even more deeply and systematically in a work called *Informatio*.[6] His primary argument was that the contested behavioural rules that his converted Brahmins were allowed to continue to follow were nothing more than social customs and had nothing to do with their former 'heathen' religion. This had to do specifically with wearing the sacred thread (*yajñopavīta*), growing the lock of hair on the top of one's head (*kuḍumi* or *cūḍā*), and decorating one's forehead with a figure in sandalwood powder (*tilaka*). Moreover, the Brahmins

3 This is most extensively described in Županov 2001; see also Xavier and Županov 2015:148–57.

4 This was the papal bull, *Romanae sedis antistes*, issued 31 January 1623. The text can be found in Dahmen 1931:186–89.

5 The text can be found in Dahmen 1931.

6 The text is found in Rajamanickam 1972b.

wanted to hold on to their customary baths. De Nobili wrote passionately about all of this, feeling that only in this way could the spiritual leaders of the country be won for the Gospel.

He made his case in both works in a very detailed way and with a great number of quotes from the sacred books of the Hindus. If there is one thing that De Nobili showed convincingly in his discussions, it is that he was actually very much at home in the literature that was normative for the Brahmins. Understandably, he makes generous use of the lawbook of Manu, the oldest and most authoritative guide for Brahmin life. But he also quotes from all kinds of other literature. Of course, the laws and rules in the *dharmaśāstras* attracted his attention, for it was here that the ethical principles of the Brahmins are worked out but he regularly quotes various *purāṇas* (mythological narrations), as well as the *Yajurveda*, one of the four sacred revealed texts (Arokiasamy 1985:105). His *Informatio* consists of eight theses on the non-religious character of Brahmanical customs. De Nobili had these theses confirmed by a number of non-Christian Brahmanical scholars, who endorsed this presentation of their tradition as correct by signing it (Rajamanickam 1972b:156–68 [Latin]). That he invited the holy number of 108 Brahmins for this shows how sensitive he was to the culture he lived in.

In connection with these very emphatic arguments, we should remember that no one in the Christian world could check whether De Nobili was right on any of these issues. He was, after all, the only one in ecclesiastical circles who had access to this knowledge. There was no way for others to repudiate any of his arguments. This was certainly true for his arch-rival Father Fernandez, a former soldier in the Portuguese colonial army. One could even wonder if Fernandez actually knew Latin and more of the Tamil language beyond the simple dialect of those living in the fishing villages (Županov 2001:49). This simple Portuguese priest was certainly no match for the very learned and cultivated aristocrat from Rome. In addition, De Nobili could use the success of his mission as an argument. In any case, Fernandez had failed, for he had not succeeded in converting one Hindu.[7] In contrast, the mission of the Christian *sannyāsī* had at least produced a vital community.

De Nobili's argument was intended to convince the reader that Brahmins were no different from the hereditary class of teachers of wisdom. In his view, they constituted the elite of Indian society and cut themselves off from others through their purity rules. He tried as much as possible to unlink the religious aspects from the concept of caste. In his eyes, Brahmins were certainly not

7 Apart from one or two terminal patients, as De Nobili rubbed in at the beginning of his defence without a great deal of subtlety. Cf. Dahmen 1931:62.

priests, at least not primarily, for a number of the members of the caste did not perform any sacrifices. All Brahmins were, however, scholars. Just as those in Europe who had gained their doctorate wore caps, so Brahmins wore the figures on their foreheads as badges of honour (Rajamanickam 1972b:88 [Latin]).[8]

Indeed, De Nobili gave a number of good arguments for the 'civil side' of Brahmanical characteristics. The most convincing is that, although the Brahmins who converted to Christianity were treated badly by their fellow caste members, they were never denied their right to wear the sacred thread (Rajamanickam 1972b:73 [Latin]; 95–96 [English]). Nevertheless, it is still intriguing to see that he completely denied the connection between the sacred thread of the Brahmins and the sacrificial cult. Traditionally, the thread had an intrinsic connection with the sacrificial activities of the Brahmin priests. This is perfectly clear in the ritual of consecration, in which the sacred thread was hung for the first time around the neck of a Brahmanical boy. This sacrament of the *upanayana* is still celebrated today in Brahmanical circles all over the world.[9] The original Sanskrit term for what is called 'sacred thread' in English is *yajñopavīta*, i.e., "thread of the offering." It is central to this ritual of *upanayana* in which the sacred Gāyatrī Mantra is passed on and Agni is worshipped in particular as the divinity of the sacrifice. After all, the old Vedic writings state: "The sacrifice of one who wears the thread prospers, but that of one who does not wear the thread does not prosper."[10]

9 *Conversion and* Accomodatio

De Nobili held that attempts at converting others always entailed an adaptation to local circumstances. Already in 1608, he wrote in a letter to his superior Laerzio that his example was Paul, who had seen an altar in Athens that was dedicated to the unknown god and then based his Christian proclamation on that (Acts 17) (Cronin 1959:90). De Nobili pointed out how old customs from heathen antiquity were preserved in honour in the Church. A marriage was not rejected because it previously stood under the protection of an idol. And conquerors were still at that time crowned with laurel wreaths, even though that custom was once dedicated to Mars (Rajamanickam 1972b:106 [Latin]; 142 [English]). In this way, the missionary from Madurai made a passionate plea to

8 Cf. p. 117 of the English text: "fits in with our conception of the Doctor's cap."
9 See the detailed description in De Klerk 1951:103–14.
10 Taittirīya-āraṇyaka 11,1,1; cited in Scharfe 2002:106.

adopt customs and rites from the local context and thus Christianise what was part of a heathen environment.

A concrete example of this can be found already at the beginning of his activities. At the start of each year, Hindus celebrate the *poṅkal* feast in which new rice is cooked for the first time, and the pan is placed before an idol. The Brahmanical members of De Nobili's community were very strongly attached to this ritual, and that is why De Nobili let them cook rice in front of a crucifix standing on the ground, and he blessed the new rice in a Christian way. Thus, an acceptable new form was found for an old feast (Cronin 1959:116).

Considerably more engrossing than the intense questions of exterior appearance and clothing was the question of the concepts that the new community of Christians would use. In the Christian villages on the Pearl Coast a kind of mixed speech of Tamil and Portuguese had developed. No native term could be found for 'holy Mass,' and thus, using Portuguese as a basis, they arrived at the term *mīsai*. That was not a happy choice, however, for the Tamil word that is pronounced that way means 'moustache.' Instead of this, De Nobili introduced a Tamil form of the classic Hindi word for 'sacrifice': *pūjā*.[11]

The most important consideration here was, of course, the question what term to use for God. In the catechism for the fishing population on the Pearl Coast, the word *Tampirāṉ* was used. This word, which already appears in the classic work by Māṇikka Vācakar, means 'lord with no lord above him.' In his *Apologia*, De Nobili recognised that this was a correct term. But, the word was also used by the people in the capital to address each other in a polite way as 'sir.' Initially, De Nobili preferred *Śiva* because *śaivas* had taught him that that was the name for the only supreme deity. He slowly began to see the objections to the mythological connotations and then chose the neologism *Carvēcuraṉ* (from the Sanskrit *Sarveśvara*), 'master of all.'[12]

These examples show that De Nobili had a preference for the classic Hindi terminology, usually stemming from Sanskrit. It was precisely this sacred language that led him to the most consecrated texts and rituals, where notably the Brahmins were in their element. It is hardly surprising then that this missionary in Madurai made an official request to the Vatican to use Sanskrit in the church services instead of Latin (Cronin 1959:173). At the high point of the Counter-Reformation, when the Roman pontiff was forcibly opposing the introduction of local languages in northern Europe in the Mass, this request did not stand a chance. But it does show where De Nobili stood.

11 De Nobili defends this choice in his *Apologia*; cf. Dahmen 1931:157.

12 In his *Apologia*: Dahmen 1931:156–57. Cf. Tiliander 1974:118–19, 175.

10 Affinity with Hinduism?

One looks in vain in De Nobili's writings for an appreciation of the Hindu faith. On the contrary, especially in his writings in Tamil, he argues against various views that were present in his environment, such as divine incarnations (*avatāras*), the reincarnation of human beings, and the automatism of reward and punishment through karma. In particular, his very apologetic work *Tūṣaṇat Tikkāram* is quite compelling, if only because of the title, which means: 'Refutation of Calumnies' (Rajamanickam 1972:123–26; Rocaries 1967:197–230).

It would be too quick to conclude, however, that De Nobili had no appreciation whatsoever for Hinduism and that his only intention was to combat the ancestral religion of his dialogue partners.[13] Because of his activities as a 'Christian *sannyāsī*,' Church authorities kept an extremely close eye on him. If he was caught making any positive statements about the religion of the heathens, he would be in deep trouble. The active inquisition in Goa often went into action for much less.

De Nobili took care that the regular accusations of apostasy and syncretism that his opponents made could never be proven on the basis of his own works. For the well-intentioned, however, he did make his affinity with the Hindu culture in which he worked clear. He attempted to integrate the existing customs and festivals as much as possible into the Christian framework of his community, and that is why they had to keep celebrating the *poṅkal* feast, even if the forms were adapted to the Christian faith. For the marriage celebrations of the Brahmins, De Nobili wrote various songs that could be sung in the same classic metre that people were accustomed to in India. The Church owes the way in which terms with a Hindu background could be used in a Christian framework to this missionary (Rajamanickam 1972a:55; cf. Tiliander 1974:passim). It was a Hindu culture that was 'baptised' by him.

Of course, De Nobili believed in his mission to bring Hindus to Christ. But he also demonstrated in detail that the good deeds of those who did not know the Gospel were also due to the grace of God.[14] One could expect that God would not reject those who were ignorant of the Christian faith through no fault of their own. His starting point was that each person was enabled by reason to discern some traces of God and to make right moral choices in his or her life. The religions of India apparently play a supporting role in this. The almsgiving and the asceticism of the Hindus came from a desire for ultimate redemption. Thus, the missionary could appreciate the motives of the Hindus

13 This was the conclusion drawn by Clooney 1990:26.

14 Especially in *Tūṣaṇat Tikkāram*, see Arokiasamy 1985.

and that is why he himself could recognise God's hand in the good that he saw in the other religion, however wrong its doctrinal system might be.

De Nobili was very motivated to analyse and discuss differences and similarities. Right from the beginning, when he began his work as a Brahmanical *sannyāsī*, he was able to discuss issues with his dialogue partners in the way they were accustomed to discussing things. Apparently, the Brahmanical way of thinking and arguing appealed to him. Using typical Hindu reasoning, the missionary argued, for instance, for the existence of ranks and classes, namely, that the microcosm is the same as the macrocosm: the hierarchy in society corresponds to the hierarchy in the human body. Regarding this point, he even indicated explicitly that "the people of this land" would agree with this (Rajamanickam 1972a:206–07).[15]

11 Caste as a Stumbling Block

This also, however, immediately reveals the weakness of De Nobili's accommodation approach. His fascination with the culture and religion of the Brahmins also made him blind to the position of the other castes. Whether or not he was influenced in this by his own aristocratic birth, he was completely uncritical of the strongly hierarchical Indian society. With no reservations, he complied with the purity rules of the highest caste in order to reach those he was concerned with: the Brahmins.

He also accepted the hard, cruel sides of the culture he wanted to penetrate as a matter of course. When the local prince died and his 400 wives died with him in the act of *satī*, his primary reaction was that of being impressed by what he saw as heroic proofs of marital fidelity (Cronin 1959:54–55).

Because of De Nobili's orientation to the Brahmin community, the Roman Catholic Church in South India was essentially changed. Indeed, something happened that had seemed to be unimaginable before that: a community of Brahmins was formed in Madurai who had devoted themselves completely to Christ. But the price was high. For decades, there was, consequently, no place for the lower castes in their community, even though there was a great need for pastoral care and instruction among the people in the lower castes. A new system was finally introduced in 1640: in addition to *sannyāsīs* who focused on the Brahmins, special missionaries were also appointed for the lower castes. They were distinguishable from the earlier *sannyāsīs* by strict rules of behaviour and dress and were called *paṇṭāracāmi* (*paṇḍāra-svāmī*). Here as well Hinduism

15 The example is from De Nobili's work, *Puṉar ceṉma ākṣēpam.*

provided the model: a *paṇṭāracāmi* was a non-Brahmanical *śaiva* ascetic. It was also a typical Hindu structure: each caste was separately organised in the area of religion.

The caste paradigm had assumed a legitimate place in the Church forever. There were special pastors for the highest castes who did not concern themselves with lower-caste believers in any way. The new *paṇṭāracāmis* looked after the middle castes but could not visit the lowest castes of all during the day—in public view—for then they would lose their prestige. At night—in secret—they could possibly attend to the lowest castes, the pariahs. The different groups were separated from each other during worship, if they ever did meet in the same building.

12 De Nobili as an Example?

De Nobili was highly esteemed for centuries. He was rightly admired for his phenomenal knowledge of languages and scriptures; he was "the first oriental scholar" (Rajamanickam 1972a); he was "the Christian sannyasi" (Rocaries 1967), and he could be described poetically as a pearl in Indian (church) history (Cronin 1959). His attempts to open the door in Brahmanical circles to the Gospel was more successful than people thought it would be. In the last 25 years, however, assessments have shifted considerably. The rise of the Dalit movement has made theologians in India strongly aware of the injustice that results from caste differences and thinking in terms of purity.[16] De Nobili is cited in this school of thought primarily as someone who allowed the caste differences of Hindu society and the accompanying oppression to become part of church life.[17]

In principle, the critics are right, for De Nobili did indeed have a blind spot with respect to the injustice and oppression exercised against the lower castes and untouchables. He did not understand the liberating power of the Gospel with respect to this. Nevertheless, it would be a shame if that meant that his great achievements in coming to know and understand classic Hindu culture were summarily dismissed. In a time when Christian faith was largely viewed as identical with the European way of life, he was attuned to what was unique about India. At that time, it was certainly a major undertaking to so immerse oneself in an almost unknown culture, and it led to impressive results.

16 On Dalit theology, see Schouten 2008:235–54.

17 E.g., Rajkumar 2016:27; see also Fernando and Gispert-Sauch 2004:101–02; Rajaiah 2016:120–21, 238–39.

13 Thomas Stephens in Goa

Roberto de Nobili's attempt to penetrate Brahmin culture left a deep impression on his fellow Jesuits and other contemporary theologians—and rightly so. Nevertheless, his was not the only attempt by the young Jesuit order to present the Gospel in such a way that it could find a foothold in the Hindu environment. A contemporary of De Nobili also sought ways to connect with the culture and religion of the local population in Goa. This was an English Jesuit who worked his whole life as a missionary on the Salcete Peninsula, on the south side of the Portuguese colony of Goa.[18] His name was Thomas Stephens or, in his Portuguese environment, Thomas Estevão.[19]

Stephens was born in 1549 in the county of Wiltshire in England. As a young man who wanted to remain faithful to the classic Catholic Church, he left England and joined the new order of the Jesuits in Rome. He was sent for missionary service to India and arrived in Goa in 1579, when he was thirty years old. He carried out pastoral care in the growing Christian communities in the hinterland of Goa until his death in 1619. In Salcete, the Portuguese, including the missionaries, regularly dealt harshly with the inhabitants in their zeal to root out heathenism. Temples were destroyed, sacred cows killed, and religious scriptures burned. Stephens, however, distanced himself from the cruelties of colonial policy and attempted to build connections with the local population.

It fit his attitude towards the native inhabitants that he studied the local language and culture intensely. He mastered Konkani so that he could communicate with his parishioners in that language and could hear confession. He himself was the first to write (in Portuguese!) a grammar of this language and also authored a catechism in Konkani in order to promote the transmission of the faith.

The work that made him famous, however, is of a different nature. Stephens mastered not only Konkani, the language of the common people, but also Marathi, the traditional language of the cultural elite of the area. He published a very comprehensive poem on the coming of Christ in this language, an epic in two books comprising more than 10,000 four-line stanzas. With this work, Stephens aligned himself with classical literature in Marathi to which important poets like Jñāneśvar and Eknāth had contributed.

---

18 This is not to be confused with the island of Salsette, which was 600 kilometres further north and on which Mumbai (Bombay) was built. This is a common mistake, as found in, for example, Prasad 1980:6.

19 On Thomas Stephens, see Saldanha 1907; Falcao 2003; Prasad 1980:Ch. 1; Schurhammer 1957.

Stephens' book was published in 1616, but not one single copy of this first edition has survived. The censor's permission, which has been preserved, shows that the work was referred to by a Portuguese title: *Discurso sobre a vinda do Salvador ao mundo, em alingoage bramana marastta* (Discussion of the Coming of the Saviour in the World, in the Brahmin Marathi Language). But it was not long before the book became known as "The Purāṇa." When Stephens died a few years later, he was remembered in his order as the writer of "the book that is called Purana."[20] This title is very suggestive. Stephens thus attempted to write a religious poem in which the praise of Christ is expressed, following the example of the classic Hindu sacred texts that sing the praises of a divinity.

There was also every reason to compose such a work. The Portuguese government had shown itself to be fervently opposed to singing and reciting classical Hindu literature. In particular, the new Christians had no single alternative for what had been done for centuries in life cycle rituals. The 'Christian *purāṇa*' now provided songs that could be sung at the celebration of a birth (Prasad 1980:15). And for those who remained true to the religion of their ancestors, the new work was in any case a work clearly recognisable as poetry in the Hindu tradition.

14 The *Purāṇa*

The *Kristapurāṇa*, the title under which Stephens' work ultimately came to be known, fit in completely with the genre of the Hindi poems that had been written in Sanskrit and Marathi throughout the centuries. For this extensive work, Stephens used the *ovi* metre, which was often used in Marathi for long narrative poems. It consists of stanzas of four lines, of which the first three rhyme and the fourth is shorter and does not rhyme.

The work is divided into two parts. The first part describes history prior to the coming of Christ; the second tells the story of Jesus' life as related in the gospels. In a cosmic presentation, which would be familiar to Hindus, the first part begins with a description of the heavenly reality in which the angels are the actors. The revolt by a group of angels, led by Lucifer, is narrated and then the expulsion of the rebellious angels from heaven and the consequences of that for life on earth. Then comes the biblical primal history: the creation of humankind, the fall into sin, and the expulsion from Paradise. The struggle against the seductive power of Satan continues on. Every time a new beginning

20 In the necrology from 1620; see Schurhammer 1957:82: "Purana, ita inscriptus liber."

is made with chosen people like Noah at the time of the flood, Abraham and his descendants, and ultimately the people of Israel. Then, finally, Stephens speaks of the Redeemer, who would definitively defeat Satan and establish the Kingdom of God. Christ's coming is not only announced by the prophets of Israel but also by the sybils among the peoples. In the second part, the birth of Jesus Christ is described in more detail, including the apocryphal accounts of his mother. Then follow the accounts of his public ministry and his teaching, closely following the accounts in the gospels. His suffering and death are described in detail, followed by his resurrection and ascension into heaven. In the end, the power of Satan is broken, and humankind redeemed. Stephens succeeded in giving his epic a convincing unity of action.[21]

Stephens deliberately presented his work as a *purāṇa*. In the dedication in which he offers the book to the archbishop (preserved in the archives), he describes the book as "a work in accordance with the fashion of this land and in a style that most pleases the native people."[22] Indeed, there is no doubt that the missionary, in his account of the Christian history of salvation, closely links up with the style that was familiar to people in that area because of Hindu literature.

The question remains as to how far Stephens—like his fellow Jesuit De Nobili in Madurai—also made use of typical Hindu concepts to describe Christian doctrine. It is very difficult to answer this question. The seventeenth-century prints of the *Kristapurāṇa* have not, unfortunately, been preserved, and thus we have to look at manuscripts. And these show many differences. The manuscripts that Saldanha used in 1907 for his edition of the *purāṇa* show a text that is peppered with Portuguese terms. Thus a sacrifice is called *sacrifiçiu* and baptism *bautismu*. There is a manuscript, however, allegedly early eighteenth-century, in which the terms are adapted to the Indian idiom. There 'sacrifice' is rendered by the term usually used in Hindu circles, *pūjā*, and the lovely term *jñāna-snāna* (Sanskrit for 'bath of knowledge') was chosen for 'baptism.'

This latter manuscript, the Marsden codex, is viewed by some as Stephens' original version.[23] If that is so, Stephens has made a bold attempt to describe Christian teaching in Hindu terms. He would then have distanced himself

21 Saldanha 1907:xliv: "a marvellous unity of action that is among its essential charms."

22 Saldanha 1907:xci: "uma obra composta a modo da terra, e no estilo de que os naturaes mais gostam."

23 This manuscript is in the library of the School of Oriental and African Studies in London. It was discovered by Justin E. Abbott, who saw it as Stephens' original version. A new edition by Nelson Falcao is based on this manuscript, which allows Falcao the opportunity to discuss far-reaching considerations on inculturation in Stephens' work. See also Bornet 2017 who has serious doubts as to whether this is in fact the original version.

quite far from the Portuguese-oriented church culture in Goa and taken the remarkable step of speaking to Hindus in their own language. It is, however, hard to imagine that such an unusual undertaking was possible in Goa, under the eye of the Portuguese inquisition. It seems more likely that his *purāṇa* was used to take another step in the direction of the Hindus. The experiments that Roberto De Nobili dared in his very isolated position in Madurai were far out of Stephens' reach in the Portuguese colony. Nevertheless, he did show how seriously he took the Hindu culture and how much of an effort he made to speak to the Hindus with his Christian message.

Later generations also followed the same line in Goa. The foundation was there, thanks to Stephens. When they dared to leave the clumsy Portuguese terminology that went back to Francis Xavier behind, Jesus Christ could be called *Kristu Svāmī*, who gave his life as a *pūjā* and thus destroyed the *karma* of the *saṃsāra*. And then the discussion could begin on the question if such terms did justice to the message of the Christian faith.

Bibliography

Text Editions and Translations

Dahmen, Pierre (1931). *Robert de Nobili, l'apôtre des Brahmes: Première apologie*, 1610. Paris: Spes.

Rajamanickam, S. (1972). *Roberto de Nobili on Indian Customs: Informatio de quibusdam moribus nationis Indicae*. Palayamkottai: De Nobili Research Institute.

Saldanha, Joseph L. (1907). *The Christian Puranna of Father Thomas Stephens of the Society of Jesus*. Mangalore: Simon Alvares.

Secondary Literature

Arokiasamy, Soosai (1986). *Dharma, Hindu and Christian, according to Roberto de Nobili: Analysis of its Meaning and its Use in Hinduism and Christianity*. Documenta missionalia 19. Rome: Editrice Pontificia Università Gregoriana.

Arokiasamy, Soosai (1985). "De Nobili on Non-Christians and Non-Christian Religions." *Neue Zeitschrift für Missionswissenschaft* 41: 288–93.

Bachmann, Peter R. (1972), *Roberto Nobili 1577–1656: Ein missionsgeschichtlicher Beitrag zum christlichen Dialog mit Hinduismus*. Bibliotheca Instituti Historici S.I. 32. Rome: Institutum Historicum S.I.

Bornet, Philippe (2017). "Review of N. Falcao, Father Thomas Stephens' Kristapurana I & II." *Exchange* 46: 73–77.

Caland, W. (1924). "Roberto de Nobili and the Sanskrit Language and Literature." *Acta Orientalia* III: 38–51.

Chakravarthy, Ananya (2014). "The Many Faces of Baltasar da Costa: Imitatio and Accomodatio in the Seventeenth Century Madurai Mission." *Etnográfica* 18: 135–58.

Clooney, Francis X. (1990). "Roberto de Nobili, Adaptation and the Reasonable Interpretation of Religion." *Missiology* XVIII: 25–36.

Coleridge, Henry James (1881). *The Life and Letters of St. Francis Xavier*. Volume I. London: Burns and Oates.

Cronin, Vincent (1959). *A Pearl to India: The Life of Roberto de Nobili*. London: Hart-Davis.

DeSmet, Richard (1991). "R. de Nobili as Forerunner of Hindu-Christian Dialogue." *Journal of Hindu-Christian Studies* 4: 1–9.

Dumont, Louis (1980). *Homo Hierarchicus: The Caste System and Its Implications*. Transl. Mark Sainsbury, Louis Dumont, and Basia Gulati. Chicago/London: University of Chicago Press.

Falcao, Nelson (2003). *Kristapurāṇa: A Christian-Hindu Encounter. A Study of Inculturation in the Kristapurāṇa of Thomas Stephens, S.J. (1549–1619)*. Pune/Anand: Snehasadan Studies.

Fernando, Leonard, and G. Gispert-Sauch (2004). *Christianity in India: Two Thousand Years of Faith*. New Delhi: Penguin-Viking.

Filliozat, Jean (1953). "Les premières étapes de l'indianisme." *Bulletin de l'Association Guillaume Budé* 3/3: 80–96.

Halbfass, Wilhelm (1981). *Indien und Europa: Perspektiven ihrer geistigen Begegnung*. Basel /Stuttgart: Schwabe.

Klerk, Cornelis Johannes Maria de (1951). *Cultus en ritueel van het orthodoxe Hindoeïsme in Suriname*. Amsterdam: Urbi et Orbi.

Lach, Donald F., and Edwin J. van Kley (1993). *Asia in the Making of Europe*. Vol. III. Book 1. Chicago/London: University of Chicago Press.

Plattner, Felix A. (1955). *Pfeffer und Seelen: Die Entdeckung des See- und Landweges nach Asien*. Einsiedeln: Benziger.

Prasad, Ram Chandra (1980). *Early English Travellers in India: A Study in the Travel Literature of the Elizabethan and Jacobean Periods with Particular Reference to India*. Delhi: Motilal Banarsidass.

Rajaiah, Jeyaraj (2016). *Dalit Humanization: A Quest Based on M.M. Thomas' Theology of Salvation and Humanization*. Utrecht: Utrecht University.

Rajamanickam, S. (1972). *The First Oriental Scholar*. Tirunelveli: De Nobili Research Institute.

Rajkumar, Peniel (2016). *Dalit Theology and Dalit Liberation: Problems, Paradigms and Possibilities*. London /New York: Routledge.

Rocaries, André (1967). *Robert de Nobili s.j. ou le "sannyasi" chrétien*. Toulouse: Prière.

Scharfe, Hartmut (2002). *Education in Ancient India*. Handbuch der Orientalistik Indien 16. Leiden/Boston: Brill.

Schouten, Jan Peter (2008). *Jesus as Guru: The Image of Christ among Hindus and Christians in India*. Transl. Henry and Lucy Jansen. Currents of Encounter 36. Amsterdam/New York: Rodopi.

Schurhammer, Georg (1957). "Der Marathidichter Thomas Stephens S.I. Neue Dokumente." *Archivum historicum Societatis Iesu* 26: 67–82.

Schurhammer, Georg (1955–1973), *Franz Xaver: Sein Leben und seine Zeit*. Four parts. Freiburg: Herder.

Tiliander, Bror (1974). *Christian and Hindu Terminology: A Study in Their Mutual Relations with Special Reference to the Tamil Area*. Skrifter utgivna av Religionshistoriska Institutionen i Uppsala (Hum. Fak.) 12. Uppsala: Almqvist & Wiksell.

Xavier, Ângela Barreto, and Ines G. Županov (2015). *Catholic Orientalism: Portuguese Empire, Indian Knowledge (16th–18th Centuries)*. New Delhi: Oxford University Press.

Županov, Ines G. (2001), *Disputed Mission: Jesuit Experiments and Brahmanical Knowledge in Seventeenth-Century India*. New Delhi: Oxford University Press.

CHAPTER 4

Dutch Ministers in the VOC: Rogerius and Baldaeus

1 The Oldest Manual

Various works on Hinduism had been published prior to the seventeenth century, but that century saw the publication of a survey work that would serve as the manual par excellence on Hinduism for 200 years. It was written by a Dutch minister, Abraham Rogerius, and the book was called *De Open-Deure Tot het Verborgen Heydendom* (The Open Door to Hidden Heathenism). In the second half of the nineteenth century, the well-known British orientalist Arthur C. Burnell (1840–1882) praised this old work that he called "still, perhaps, the most complete account of S. Indian Hinduism, though by far the earliest" (Burnell 1879:98).[1]

It might occasion some surprise that it was precisely a Christian theologian—and a Calvinist one at that—who wanted to publish so much information on the religion of India. The surprise was also once expressed by the Leiden Sanskrit scholar Willem Caland (1859–1932), who prepared a new edition of Rogerius' work in 1915. He wrote in his foreword that the work was captivating and objective, "in general free of that annoying and fanatical critique that characterises the work of many other clergymen" (Caland in Rogerius 1915:xxii).

2 Pastor and Missionary

Who was this minister who was able to write so objectively about a foreign religion? He grew up as Abraham Rogiers but Latinised his name during his studies, as was usual among academics.[2] Since then, he was known as Abraham Rogerius. He studied in Leiden, where he was one of the students at the Seminarium Indicum (De Lind van Wijngaarden 1891; Joosse 1992:481–500; Jongeneel 2015:46–48). This was an institute for the training of theologians who wanted to enter the service of the United East Indian Company (the VOC). The seminary was established in the home of one of the most famous professors at

1 W. Caland, who published a new edition of Rogerius' work in 1915, wrongly dates Burnell's article as in appearing in 1898 and many simply followed him here. See Rogerius 1915:xxi.

2 His original name is reported once in the Batavia church council minutes: 15 December 1642; see Mooij 1927–1931:I, 626.

 | DOI:10.1163/9789004420076_006

Leiden, Antonius Walaeus (1573–1639), who was also rector magnificus of the university for a number of years.

The students took the usual courses at the theological faculty but were given additional classes in the seminary on the history of religion (Judaism, Islam, and 'heathen religion') and in Malaysian. Practical training, such as sick visits, was also included in the program. After all, the students would later, as ministers sent in the service of the VOC, be given a double task: on the one hand, they would have to communicate the Gospel to the native population and on the other be responsible for pastoral care among the Company's employees. It was this double task that led the VOC to feel responsible for the programme and to finance the institute for 10 years, including the students' living expenses and study costs. Pastoral care would thus not only be carried out by the numerous, low-educated 'comforters of the sick' but were supervised by true, academically schooled ministers (Nagel 2006:108–09). And they were also entrusted with spreading the Christian faith among Muslims and Hindus. The VOC saw this as a debt of honour because of the economic advantage that the trade in India yielded. Profit and mission responsibility were connected. When Rogerius' main work was published shortly after his death, the foreword to the governors stated that they had no doubts about why God had made them so strong in Asia and blessed their trade: it was to make the expansion of Christ's kingdom possible (Rev. Jacobus Sceperus in: Rogerius 1915:xxxiv).

3 Rogerius' Career in the East

Rogerius graduated in 1630. And that fall he was examined by the Amsterdam classis and was taken on by the VOC to serve as minister in India. Shortly before, in Leiden, he married Maria Tijmans, a girl from Woerden who—just like him—lived on the Rapenburg.[3] He is officially described in the notice of marriage registry as "Dienaer des goddelijcken Woorts gedestineert tot den dienst des Evangeliums in Oostindien," i.e., "Servant of the Divine Word Destined for the Service of the Gospel in the East Indies." The young couple left a short time later for India and, after the usual long sea voyage, with a port of call at the Cape of Good Hope, they arrived on 5 June 1631 in Batavia (Jakarta). After their ship, the *Wesel*, arrived, the new minister reported to the church council of Batavia.[4] His first task was to provide pastoral care for a trading fleet to Surat on the northwest coast of India, where the VOC had an important trading post

3 Ondertrouw Ned.-Geref. 12 September 1630; see also Prins 2002.

4 Batavia church council, 5 June 1631; Mooij 1927–1931:I, 371.

(Van der Pol 2011:97–105). It was thus a large fleet that sailed there, with a crew of no less than 1400. There was no established living for a minister in Surat itself; a comforter for the sick did the pastoral work there. After a year, in July 1632, Rogerius returned to Batavia from this expedition and was then able to leave for his first real posting, Paliacatta, on the southeast coast of India where he would stay for ten years. Upon arrival, he was ordained as minister of the congregation by his predecessor, Nicolaus Molinaeus.[5]

Paliacatta (Pulicat), fifty kilometres north of Chennai (Madras), was the principal town of the Dutch on the east coast of India, the Coromandel Coast. This was the location of the main trading post of the VOC and the seat of the governor of all settlements on the Coromandel Coast. It was one of the few Dutch settlements with a real fort, called Geldria. This fort, constructed in accordance with the Dutch model with a moat around it and four bastions, was located within a walled city. For that matter, the population of this strong fortress was not that impressive in size: it is quite probable that not many more than 100 Europeans employed by the VOC lived in and around the fort.[6] 45 to 50 of them were members of the Reformed Church. Rev. Rogerius also, however, had to provide pastoral care to all the other baptised people who lived in the city and the fort. This number was estimated at about 1000.[7] Numerous natives could always be found at the VOC trading stations, usually of mixed ancestry (*mestizos*). Many people in this population group had been baptised already during the period of the Portuguese missionaries. The Dutch ministers continued the open church of the people policy of their Roman Catholic predecessors: they baptised the children and extended their pastoral care to this segment of the native population.

There are few details available on the activities of the minister; such details that we have are found mainly in the incidental reports in the Batavia church council minutes. Nothing whatsoever of the church archives of Paliacatta itself has been preserved. Completely missing are any details about this minister's personal family life. As stated above, Rogerius had begun the journey to India with his wife, Maria, but we have no idea of what happened to her, not even if she ever reached Paliacatta. In February 1636, the church council in Batavia received a letter from him that indicated that he was looking for a new marriage partner.[8] Apparently, he had been a widower for some time already then.

5 Molinaeus reported on the arrival of his successor to the Batavia church council, 3 February 1633; Mooij 1927–1931:I, 417.

6 The number of Europeans in all settlements on the Coromandel Coast amounted to no more than 439 in 1664; Peters 2002:13.

7 Batavia church council, 3 February 1633, Mooij 1927–1931:I, 417.

8 Batavia church council, 6 February 1636; Mooij 1927–1931:I, 474.

It turned out that the young woman in Batavia whom he had his eye on had married someone else already before the arrival of his letter. His suggestion that he marry a native woman if the church council did not provide him with a spouse did lead them to take action. The church council made him the generous offer of providing a replacement for him so that he could take a leave of absence for some months in order to travel to Batavia to find a wife. In October of that same year, however, he had made no progress. Rogerius again asked Batavia to send him a suitable marriage partner ("een eerlijk partuijr" [an honest match]).[9] It seems that he had made an official request in the meantime to marry a native woman, but the various government bodies (the governor of Coromandel, the governor-general, and the councils of India) wanted nothing to do with that. Finally, a solution was found. When Rogerius returned to the Netherlands in 1647, he had already been married to Emmerentia Pools for some time, and the couple settled in Gouda, where she probably came from. After his death, two years later, it was apparent how much his wife was involved in his work. She published his major study of Hinduism and attempted to get his other manuscripts published as well.

In total, Rogerius served for three periods of five years each in Asia. For the first ten years, he was stationed in Paliacatta, and then for another five in Batavia. In addition to his pastoral work, during his first ten years he also studied the social and religious environment in which he lived in particular. He composed a detailed and thorough study of the religion of the country, by means of very extensive interviews with a number of Brahmins and also strengthened the position of the non-Dutch people by regularly holding services in Portuguese. He also wanted to become so adept in Tamil so that he would be able to preach in that language;[10] but we do not know if he was successful. We do know that he made various translations into Portuguese to aid his work in the church, translating the New Testament and the Catechism, and a rhymed version of the Psalms. He continued this work in the five years that he was a minister in Batavia, from 1642 on. As a pastor, he was primarily oriented to the "native nation" and, in addition to church services in Portuguese, also conducted services in Malaysian. He wrote a Malaysian dictionary, made a rhymed version of the Psalms in that language, and prepared a volume of sermon outlines for other ministers who led services in Malaysian.

9 Batavia church council, 3 November 1636; Mooij 1927–1931:I, 487.

10 Batavia church council, 10 August 1637; Mooij 1927–1931:I, 505.

4 Study on Hinduism

His most famous work was also his study on Hinduism, the material for which he had collected in Paliacatta. He completed his manuscript in Batavia, where he presented it to the church council for their assessment in 1643.[11] The title was originally *Baäls Priester of een waere beschrijvinge van het leven der Brahmines* (Baal's Priest or a True Description of the Life of the Brahmins). Rev. Laurentius Persant and elder Arnoldus Vlamingh were given the task of assessing the work. The assessment was apparently favourable, for the manuscript lay on the meeting room table of the top executives of the VOC in Amsterdam, the 'Heren Zeventien' in the next year.[12] Rev. Robertus Junius, who himself had served for a period in Asia, was appointed to make any possible corrections, but the decision to publish it had already been made immediately. But the VOC did not publish it, however. That was not the fault of the corrector, who was himself greatly interested in the field of Oriental Studies that was now just emerging. The book was not published until seven years later, in 1651, and then by the printer Françoys Hackes in Leiden on the commission of Rogerius' widow. The title became *De Open-Deure tot het Verborgen Heydendom.*

The new title invokes the image of interested study. At that time, the word 'heidendom' (heathenism) did not have any negative connotations; it was the usual term for all religions that were not Jewish, Christian, or Islamic. The term used earlier, 'Baäls Priester' (Baal's Priest) did have negative connotations of course. In biblical jargon, Baal's priests were, after all, the most prominent enemies of the God of Israel (e.g., 1 Kings 18:20–46). Did the fact that the book was now published privately make it possible to drop the apologetics? In any case, the writer did his best to describe the religiosity in South India with understanding and respect. The approach in his chapter on the existence of God is typical. In this chapter he vigorously rejected the presumption that these people lived like animals, without any understanding of God: "No one should think that this people are simply like animals, with no knowledge of God or religion. On the contrary, we have to witness about them" (Rogerius 1651:103; 1915:85).

5 Sources

Rogerius' sources for his knowledge consist first of all of communications from a number of local Brahmins whom he regularly cites throughout his account.

11 Batavia church council, 7 December 1643; Mooij 1927–1931:I, 687.

12 Resolutions of the Seventeen, 16 September 1644; Mooij 1927–1931:I, 24.

His primary source was a certain Padmanābha, who had gotten into trouble in his home town after a conflict with one of his concubines, whose hair he had cut off. After this scandalous treatment, his fellow caste members turned against him, and he then fled and sought the protection of the Dutch governor of Paliacatta. Through Rogerius' intercession, he was allowed to live in safety in the fort. He and Rogerius became friends, and Padmanābha, who spoke Portuguese, was inclined to tell him a great deal about his ancestral religion and sometimes included fellow caste members from the neighbourhood. For instance, there was a certain Damersa who spoke better Portuguese and was thus consulted for a more precise explanation. In situations in which complicated items were discussed, even more experts were consulted. In the difficult question of the origin of the soul, no fewer than four Brahmins were called in to provide Rogerius with the best explanation (Rogerius 1651:146; 1915:110).

More than once, Rogerius supplemented the information he received from the Brahmins with information from others. He thus cited the 'heathen' governor of the city by name when describing the disagreements about the bride price that was given precisely among the Brahmins. If the father of the bride was offered more from someone else than the bridegroom, the father was inclined to give his daughter to the one who offered the most. Rogerius assumed that his Brahmanical informants were too ashamed to tell him this and that is why he consulted the governor (Rogerius 1651:45; 1915:37).

What is also very important in this voluminous account by this minister is his own observation. He repeatedly states that certain customs were not only prescribed but were also actually practised. And we are told in relation to some events that he not only heard about them but also saw them with his own eyes in Paliacatta. That, for example, is the case with his detailed, extraordinary description of a woman being buried alive and following her husband into death. *Satī* took on its own form in caste groups that did not practise cremation: the woman was placed in the grave with the body of her husband in her arms, the hole was then slowly filled up with earth, and at the last moment, she was administered poison and her neck broken (Rogerius 1651:99–100; 1915:81–82).

Because Rogerius was such an active observer, different voices can be detected in his writing. The description of the ritual self-flagellation with back hooks, hook-swinging, is a typical example. During a celebration in Paliacatta, Rogerius witnessed some people, including women, being raised by means of hooks in their back muscles. He relates that they convinced each other that it did not hurt at all but adds that it was striking that the bystanders burst out in such loud screams when it happened so that one could not hear if the victims also screamed in pain. He then recounts how one of the governor's slaves confided to him later how greatly deceived she felt. She had undergone the ritual because she had been convinced that it did not hurt. But she testified later that it was very painful and that she would never do it again (Rogerius 1651:186–87; 1915:143–44).

Another example concerns the various views of informants. Rogerius describes in detail the ascetic practices of some *sannyāsīs* that he witnessed in Paliacatta. He even notes time and place and does so very carefully sometimes. Thus, he describes the extreme devotion of a man whom he saw in the temple of Pārvatī on the Śiva temple square on 17 January 1640. Standing on his head, this man quoted the sacred texts in the temple and then came outside, lit a fire, and hung upside down from a scaffold, with his feet in ropes and his head swinging through the fire. The Brahmin Padmanābha, Rogerius' permanent informant, explained to him that the man was thus ensuring a better place in heaven for himself. But the other Brahmin, Damersa, doubted whether this ascetic was all that holy, for a true holy man would have withdrawn into solitude or travelled to a holy place like Varanasi (Benares). This shows how certain religious phenomena can also be assessed differently by experts in the community (Rogerius 1651:193–94; 1915:148–49).[13]

6 An Honest Report

This VOC minister made an impression with his report on religious life on the Coromandel Coast. In the ten years that he worked there, he was obviously a close observer of his environment and of the culture where he ended up. He questioned his Brahmanical conversation partners thoroughly and regularly and accurately states who his source was and if there was a difference of opinion. Perhaps the best evidence of his sincerity is that he honestly admits if he cannot place something properly or cannot investigate its background. Thus, he gives a survey of the myths of the ten incarnations of Viṣṇu, the *avatāras*, in which he also reports the fourth incarnation, where Viṣṇu appears as half-human, half-lion but admits that he does not understand the story: "I have not understood what the reasons for that are" (Rogerius 1651:121; 1915:95). It is remarkable, however, that the myth of the man-lion (*Narasiṃha*) that played a major role in modern Hinduism escaped him.

Rogerius also came to understand that not all aspects of Hinduism are so easily shared with outsiders. What is striking and not unentertaining is the fact that he had repeatedly asked his chief conversation partner, Padmanābha, about the image of the *liṅga* in the Śiva temple in Paliacatta that he had often visited. He had never received an answer to his questions. Only when Rogerius

13 This characteristic episode is also illustrated on the top left of the title page of the book.

was ready to leave for Batavia, after having stayed in Paliacatta for ten years did the Brahmin return to this question on his own. He apparently felt guilty for withholding information from Rogerius. But the latter had to promise first that he would not laugh at the explanation. And only then, after he had promised this, was this well-known myth explained.

Rogerius relates that it was with a sense of shame that the Brahmin told him the meaning because he was embarrassed about his own religion, " apparently .... that such things were found in it that so badly fit with the divinity." Then the story follows of the great wise man who goes to heaven (Kailāsa), where Śiva was found in bodily form. When he reported at the gate, he had to wait a long time, however, because Śiva was having sexual intercourse with his divine spouse Pārvatī. Becoming angry, the wise man cursed the god so that he would become what he was now doing. Since then, Śiva has been worshipped in the form of the *liṅga* in a *yoni* (Rogerius 1651:117–18; 1915:92–93).[14]

That Rogerius in the end—although with hesitation—did hear the myth of the *liṅga* shows that he enjoyed the trust of his Brahmanical friends. Another good illustration of the good contact between him and the priests is the explanation of the rituals before the sun. Rogerius describes in detail the state of affairs in the Brahmanical circles. This also included the morning ritual at sunrise. He first of all describes what he saw. Each of the Brahmins took water in their hands, said a prayer text three times, and threw the water on the earth in honour of the rising sun. Rogerius then passes on what he was given as an explanation. There is, apparently, a myth behind this ritual. There were once devils in the mountains that wanted to prevent the sun from rising. The Brahmins travelled through the passes to the sun and threw water to the sun; the devils were frightened by the sound of that and fled. What is peculiar about this story by Rogerius, however, is that he can recount how the Brahmins experienced this old custom in his time. He managed to convey that the Brahmins were aware of the fact that their ritual did not help the sun, but they kept on doing it as an expression of their good will and their affection for the divine sun. Rogerius has thus come much closer to the experience of the religion than all those who unquestioningly repeated the old texts, i.e., that the sun would not rise if the Brahmins did not make their sacrifice (Rogerius 1561:72; 1915:59).[15]

---

14 The myth is found in the *Padma Purāṇa*, VI, 255.

15 The famous text (Śatapatha Brāhmaṇa 2,3,1,5) reads: "The sun would certainly not rise, if he did not make that sacrifice."

7 The Structure of the Book

De Open-Deure Tot het Verborgen Heydendom consists of three parts. The first part, on the life and morals of the Brahmins, is a sociocultural sketch of the society in which Rogerius found himself. He limited himself not exclusively to the Brahmins, but, as the leading figures in religion, they did constitute his starting point. He described how there were four social classes (*varṇa*) among the Hindus and beneath them a fifth layer of very untouchable people, the pariahs. The caste pyramid is described with the appropriate hierarchy, mutual relations, and everyone's profession and obligations. Then he directs his attention to the Brahmins, who were divided into six different sects that are carefully described. Rogerius also makes use of a distinction between the Brahmins who lead an ordinary social existence and the various homeless Brahmins who had withdrawn from the world and lead a wandering life.

Rogerius emphasises that the Brahmins had a privileged position in society. He distinguishes five privileges of the priestly caste: they could hold a sacrificial ceremony (*yajña*), they could teach others about the sacrifice rituals, they could read the Veda, they could teach the Veda to others in their caste, and they could beg for gifts and give others alms. He also describes the system in which the Brahmins were supported by others, especially by kings, because of their ritual position.

Rogerius then provides an overview of the rites of passage that the Brahmins underwent during the course of their lives. We hear about the rituals after a birth, about teaching and training Brahmin boys, marrying off their daughters at a young age, marriage rituals and polygamy. He always gives examples from the other castes, but the Brahmanical example sets the tone.

The material on the importance that the Brahmins—and other Hindus as well—attach to omens and propitious and unpropitious days is interesting. The list of activities that are to be avoided or carried out on certain days covers more than six pages. On Wednesday, for instance, sexual intercourse leads to pregnancy, but sex on Friday is considered to be fatal. Sexual intercourse should therefore be avoided on that day. It was bad to take medicine on Wednesday for a snakebite, but on Friday it was good.

Rogerius also gives information about the daily rituals among the Brahmins. For instance, he relates, with obvious delight, the myth of Gajendramokṣa in which Viṣṇu comes to the aid of a king who has been changed into an elephant and is threatened by a crocodile. This colourful story had to be read, according to Rogerius' Brahmanical informants, every morning in order to receive forgiveness of sins. This seems to be a specific devotion rather than a fixed prescription, however.

Finally, he discusses extensively how the Brahmanical community dealt with death. He looks of course at the burning of widows, and this is one of the few occasions where he abandons his role of objective observer. That went too far for him: "O inhuman cruelty! Who is not horrified by such terrible things that are still current and practised in those places?" (Rogerius 1651:97; 1915:79).

These 21 chapters are followed by a second part of 21 chapters that deal with faith and religious practice. The starting point is the belief in the one God that Rogerius also recognised among the Hindus. But the concepts of God differed quite considerably from his, and he also gave that his full attention. The first thing that struck him was that female partners were added to the figures of the gods. That seems hardly to have surprised him, however, because these people had a anthropomorphic concept of God. With apparent approval, he relates many mythological narratives about the chief gods Viṣṇu and Śiva as well as about the lower divinities like Garuḍa and Hanumān.

Rogerius acknowledged that the Hindus believed the world to have been created. In any case, he finds that position chosen above Aristotle's idea of the eternality of the world. When he describes the four ages (*yuga*), he does feel compelled to remark that, according to the Bible, the earth is much younger: "thus, we will find that, in the view of Hinduism, the world has existed many hundreds of thousands of years more than the Holy Truth reports" (Rogerius 1651:135; 1915:105).

In this part as well, however, Rogerius looks for more similarities than differences. This is clear especially in his description of the temple cult. He explains that the Hindus did not really believe that the gods need the food that was offered. It was, however, an expression of gratitude to the gods for the food. If the believers placed the food in the temple, only to eat it afterwards themselves (*prasād*), it was to have the food hallowed by the gods.

His description of the female temple dancers (*devadāsīs*) is very striking in this connection. It seems very strange, of course, that the Brahmins placed women whom everyone knew to be prostitutes in the place that was the holiest of all. But one had to be aware of the background: "But if one hears how they feel about the prostitutes, it will not seem that strange." Then his explanation follows: the temple prostitutes had their own morality: if they were faithful to their lovers and received them properly, they would be blessed. By way of illustration, he gives the story of Indra who tested the faithfulness of his lover in the temple: the god pretended to be dead, and then saw that the *devadāsī* was prepared to be thrown on the cremation pyre with him in an act of *satī* (Rogerius 1651:165; 1915:125).[16]

16 Goethe reworked this story into his ballad "Der Gott und die Bajadere," most likely after having read it in Rogerius; cf. Rogerius 1915:125.

After these two descriptive parts in the sense of religious studies, the third part consists of a translated text. These are proverbs from the poet Bhartṛhari, from the seventh century CE. The proverbs were written in Sanskrit and were divided into three books: love (*śṛṅgāra*), the art of living (*nīti*), and renunciation of the world (*vairāgya*) (von Glasenapp 1961:220–21). The Brahmin Padmanābha had this text available and translated it into Portuguese for Rogerius. He did not want the minister to know about the amorous verses and therefore limited himself to the last two books. This text was the first to be translated into a European language from Sanskrit.

> It is an ornament for the rich man that he be generous;
> for a good soldier that he does not boast;
> for a wise man that he does not bother about injustice done to him;
> for the scholar that he treats everyone properly;
> for money that it be given to the good;
> for the promise that people not become angry about it;
> for a prominent man to be gentle;
> for him who gives alms to do it without expecting something for himself;
> for everyone it is an ornament to walk the good path.
>
> ROGERIUS 1651:248; 1915:201[17]

8 An Appealing Book

Rogerius' book, which was finally published in 1651, was appealing to the public. At that time there was great interest in the still unknown world of Eastern culture and religion, which led to a number of great publications. The book was not only one of the first but also had the advantage of being written on the basis of his own observations and thorough research. The translation of Bhartṛhari, which will remind many of the biblical book of Proverbs, made it even more interesting.

The illustrations also contributed to the attractiveness of the edition. No illustrations are included in the text, but the title page contains eight unique illustrations. What is special about these prints is that they are not standard depictions of Indian culture, like those found in such books since the Middle Ages. These illustrations, though not very artistic, are closely connected to the text. They are, without a doubt, inspired by the reality of India (Mitter 1977:60).

17 Rogerius is still honoured as the first translator of a Sanskrit text: the inaugural address by Hans Bakker begins and ends with it; cf. Bakker 1997:5, 19–20.

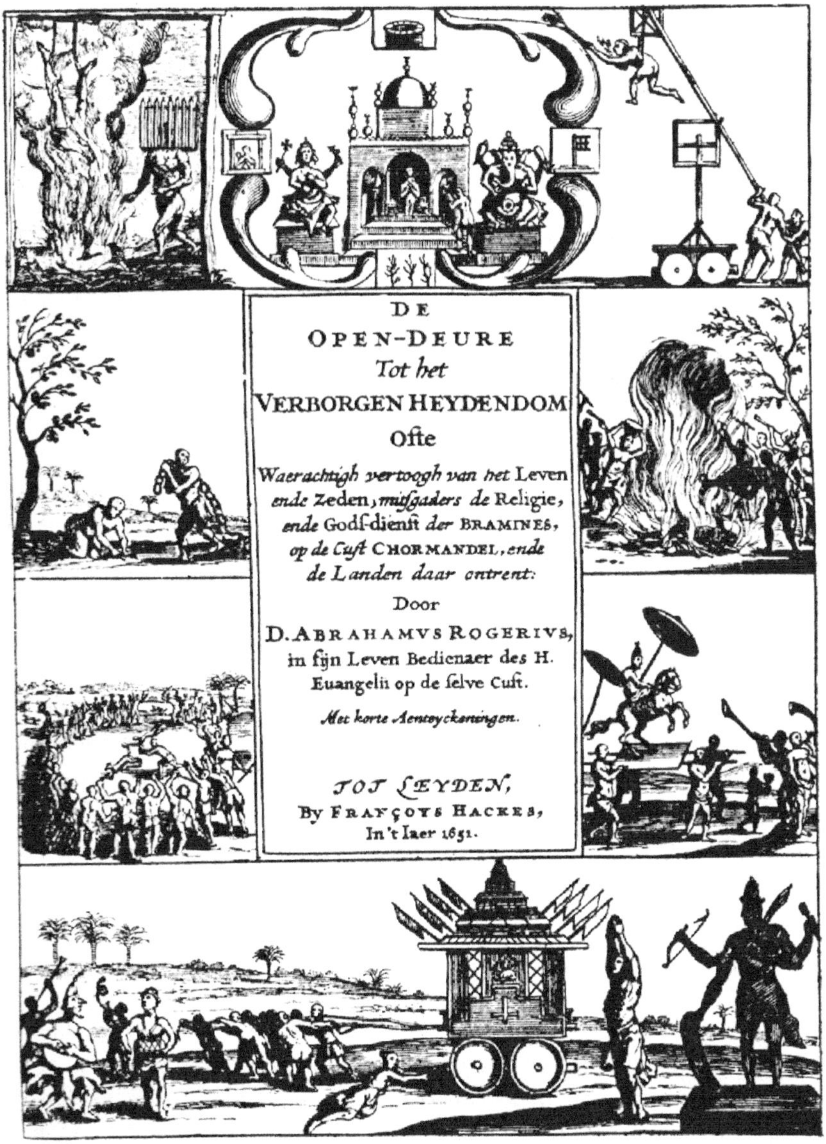

FIGURE 6 Illustrated title page of Rogerius' De Open-Deure Tot het Verborgen Heydendom, 1651

The illustrations are all scenes that are described in the book. Thus, on the upper left, we see two examples of extreme ascetic devotion that Rogerius describes. The next shows the interior of a temple with an altar for Hanumān, flanked by images of Śiva and Gaṇeśa. It is striking that the four-armed Śiva has

South Indian attributes: a gazelle and a hand drum (Von Wyss-Giacosa and Isler 2006:68). On the upper right we find an adherent who is being lifted by means of meat hooks (hook-swinging). On the next row we also see two illustrations of events described by Rogerius: the asceticism of two men dragging heavy chains and the ritual suicide of a widow (*satī*). Below that is the slaughter of goats for a local divinity (incorrectly called Gaṅgā by Rogerius) and an image of a god being carried in a procession. Finally, at the bottom, we find a depiction of a temple wagon being pulled forward while spectators show reverence.

We do not know who did the engravings, but it is obvious that the example was prepared by Rogerius himself or came from his immediate environment in Paliacatta. The link between text and illustration is too striking to allow any other origin.[18]

The Dutch edition of Rogerius' book was followed by German and French translations. In the next century, an English edition appeared based on the French translation. Obviously, this was a book Europe needed: it offered detailed and objective information on a religious culture that had been neglected until then. The work had great influence, particularly via the translations.[19]

Modern authors also praise the remarkable attitude of Rogerius, "who was prepared to study Hinduism as a living religion that had to be understood on its own terms" (Lach and Van Kley 1993:II, 1056). In recent years, the academic debate has primarily concerned the question how Western researchers presented themselves to their informants in colonial circumstances. Rogerius is striking in this as well, given that he was one of the few who based themselves on local knowledge and treated the native sources with respect (Noak 2012:355).

9 Baldaeus and Mythology

Rogerius was not the only minister in the service of the VOC to make an intense study of his surroundings. A younger contemporary was Philippus Baldaeus (1632–1671), who arrived in Batavia in 1655. After a short stay in Malacca, he was given a permanent post on Sri Lanka (Ceylon), where he worked from 1656 to 1666.[20] He was ordained as a minister in Jaffna, on the north side of the island.

18 Von Wyss-Giacosa and Isler (2006:67) write about "wohl selbst angefertigtes Bildmaterial" (pictures most probably produced by himself).

19 See, e.g., Sweetman 2003:90; Dharampal 1982:209 (on Diderot, among others).

20 Batavia church council, 16 October 1656, Mooij 1927–1931:II, 501; Batavia church council, 25 January 1666, Mooij 1927–1931:III, 3.

After returning to the Netherlands, he was a minister in Geervliet. During this time, he edited his large collection of data into a standard work on South India and Sri Lanka. It is a solid work in three parts, called *Naauwkeurige Beschryvinge van Malabar en Choromandel, Der zelver aangrenzende Ryken En het machtige Eyland Ceylon* (A True and Exact Description of the Most Celebrated East-India Coasts of Malabar and Coromandel; as also of the Isle of Ceylon).

The first two parts offer a very extensive geographical report on, respectively, India and Sri Lanka. A number of peculiarities in the area of history, opportunities for trade, and the culture are also discussed here. In addition, it includes a concise grammar of Tamil, complete with the Lord's Prayer and the Apostle's Creed in that language. The third part is called *Nauwkeurige en waarachtige ontdekking en wederlegginge Van de Afgoderye der Oost-Indische Heydenen* (The Idolatry of the East-India Pagans, Giving a Full and True Account of the Religious Worship of the Indosthans, the Inhabitants of Coromandel, the Malabars, and the Ceylonese).

One would expect that this work by Baldaeus on religion would yield a similar description to that of Rogerius. That is not the case, however. Baldaeus is primarily interested in mythology and thus relates in great detail the stories about gods and saints in Hinduism. In that sense, it is a supplement to the earlier *Open-Deure*. We saw that there were gaps in Rogerius' work, among others with respect to the incarnations of Viṣṇu. Rogerius had honestly admitted that he had not understood the myth of the fourth *avatāra*, the form of a man-lion. Baldaeus does present this story of *Narasiṃha* but does so in detail and even adds an engraving of the man-lion. The theme is the effectiveness of an appeal to the intervention of Viṣṇu. Because of his asceticism, the conceited giant Hiraṇyakaśipu had received the assurance from Brahmā that he would not be killed by man or animal, by means of any weapon, day or night, inside or outside. His son Prahlāda, however, was a true worshiper of Viṣṇu and sustained his faith in the face of his tyrannical father's oppression. When the boy called on the name of Viṣṇu, the deity appeared from out of a pillar in the palace, as a man-lion. In this form (neither man nor animal), he killed the giant with his claws (thus with no weapon). The judgement occurred at twilight (neither by day or night), on the threshold of the palace (neither inside nor outside) (Baldaeus 1672:III, 56–59; 1917:58–62; myth from Bhāgavata-Purāṇa and Padma-Purāṇa).

Baldaeus records a great number of mythological stories in that same detailed way. The first eight chapters of his *Afgoderij* contain myths from Śaivism. The well-known stories about Śiva and Pārvatī were included of course. There is also a great deal of attention paid to Gaṇeśa and Subrahmaṇya while Bhadrakālī is also given ample space. The *liṅga* is of course not skipped either. Baldaeus then turns to the *vaiṣṇavas*. First was what was for Baldaeus obviously the principal part of Hindu mythology: the ten incarnations of Viṣṇu, which are described in striking detail. This section is comprised of eleven chapters. Finally, in seven chapters, he discusses a number of separate doctrinal topics and rituals of the Hindus. He treats them using Christian terminology: creation, angels and demons, the human soul. The rituals he describes include the temple building, the sacred ashes, feasts and fasts, marriage, and funerals.

10 Sources

A new edition of Baldaeus' *Naauwkeurige Beschryvinge* was published in 1917, edited by the Roman Catholic Sanskrit scholar, A.J. de Jong. He expresses great appreciation for Baldaeus because the latter was one of those ministers "who stood out both through his science and his character and devotion to duty" (De Jong in Baldaeus 1917:xliii). With appreciation, De Jong reports the great admiration this Calvinist minister showed for the missionary work of his Catholic predecessors, particularly the Jesuits. De Jong was struck by the fact that the text of Baldaeus' work sometimes shows remarkable similarities to those of other authors, contemporaries or later writers, and he concluded that many books relied on the same source.

What were Baldaeus' sources? In the first place, he made ample use of Rogerius' book, which he often cites, mentioning the author. Just like Rogerius, Baldaeus asserts that he also had conversations with local Brahmins. That is rather a vague claim, however, and it is not clear what he derived from those conversations. Baldaeus did say that he borrowed a great deal from Catholic sources, including, among other things, manuscripts by "Portuguese papists" (De Jong in Baldaeus 1917:lxix). Allegedly, the Dutchmen had appropriated various documents and other property as plunder during their conquests of Portuguese forts; the VOC was probably able to seize a great deal, particularly during the occupation of Cochin (Kochi).

In the 1920s, the Swedish Sanskrit scholar Jarl Charpentier was able to reconstruct some of Baldaeus' sources (Charpentier 1923, 1924). The result was revealing. It appeared that Baldaeus made extensive use of earlier sources, particularly from the Jesuits. Thus, there was a very comprehensive manuscript, called *Livro da Seita dos Indios Orientas*, dating from the first years of the seventeenth century, written by the Jesuit Jacobo Fenicio (ca. 1558–ca. 1632). A hundred pages from Baldaeus' famous book turns out to be nothing more than a translation of this Portuguese manuscript. Baldaeus also seems to have been inspired in the same way by an anonymous manuscript on the ten *avatāras* of Viṣṇu.

The discovery of these sources caused a great deal of commotion. A caustic article was published in the Roman Catholic journal *Studiën* on this Calvinist minister who had become famous by plagiarising Jesuit missionaries (Wessels 1935). The criticism extended to De Jong who had wanted to issue a new edition of this work. Nevertheless, this critique can be mitigated somewhat: in previous centuries, people were less strict with respect to taking over someone else's work. Moreover, De Jong had already relativised Baldaeus' work considerably. He denied that its value lay in Baldaeus' own research on Hinduism—in contrast to Rogerius' book. The book was valuable, however, because "Baldaeus recognised the value of the Indian stories ... he took the trouble to collect as many as possible and to share with the public his knowledge of Hinduism, gathered by the Jesuits" (De Jong in Baldaeus 1917:lxxxv).

11 Refutation

The complete title (in the Dutch original) of the third part of Baldaeus' major work, which discusses the Hindu religion, is *Nauwkeurige en waarachtige ontdekking en wederlegginge Van de Afgoderye Der Oost-Indische Heydenen* (An Accurate and True Exploration and Refutation of the Idolatry of the East Indian Pagans). Thus, the author intended not only to explain the religion of this people but also to refute it. In the new edition of the book in 1917, this double purpose has disappeared. De Jong held that all arguments against Hinduism had to be omitted as "polemical passages that had no importance for us" (De Jong in Baldaeus 1917:lix). That is indeed a shame because that leaves us with no understanding of what Baldaeus thought of these strange religious phenomena. Whoever consults the original from 1672, however, finds the minister's judgment alongside the myths he narrates.

It is striking of course that the religion of the Hindus is frankly called "Idolatry" in the title. That is certainly different from Rogerius' approach, who refrained in general from judgment and was primarily interested in similarities. Baldaeus does look for similarities sometimes but gives his assessment many times, as well as his indignation and condescension about so much that appears to him to be made up, foolish, or despicable.

The story cited above of the man-lion who judges the tyrannical giant gives Baldaeus the occasion for a long digression. Here he is looking primarily for similarities, particularly in the area of morals. He does that in the way that was usual in his time: examples from classical antiquity and from the world of the Bible alternate. Baldaeus cites four parallels to this myth (Baldaeus 1672:III, 59–60). The pride of the strong Hiraṇyakaśipu, who exalted himself to divine

FIGURE 7 Philippus Baldaeus with servant in Sri Lanka
Painting by Jean de la Rocquette

status, has many parallels in antiquity, including the figure of Icarus. The theme of the divine judgement of tyrants also appears in the Bible—for example, in the account of the Judean king Rehoboam. We know from the Bible that it ends badly for those who blaspheme God (Leviticus 24:14) as well as from the history of antiquity. Finally, Baldaeus remarks appreciatively about Prahlāda's attitude: "We see with surprise that this child feared God more than he did his father," and he illustrates this attitude with a quote from the Church Father Jerome. The myth is thus placed in the larger framework of divine judgement and admirable human piety.

This is certainly not the case all the time. Baldaeus can also be extremely critical of and denigrating towards Hindu ideas that he finds objectionable. This happens, for example, in connection with the worship of the *liṅga* that depicted the presence of Śiva in the temples (Baldaeus 1672:III, 8–9). He bursts out in great indignation and sketches in detail the different forms of the phallic cult that he knew from antiquity, from Priapus to Osiris. People have thus "scandalously displayed their animal lecherousness." And the conclusion about the East Indian pagans should also be "that the teacher of this people is the unclean devil and the evil spirit."

12 Other Ministers

Other ministers who were in the service of the VOC also saw their task as one of recording in print the wondrous culture of Asia for their compatriots. The most productive writer was undoubtedly François Valentijn (1666–1727), who wrote a monumental encyclopaedic work in five parts on the Asian possessions of the Netherlands. His interest was primarily, however, in the history of the colonial powers, whose martial activities, trade, and missionary activities he described down to the smallest detail.

Valentijn was a minister for many years on Ambon. The greatest part of his work thus dealt with the Moluccans. But Hinduism does come up a few times. When he describes the island of Bali, which was always Hindu, he also mentions *satī*: "the burning of their wives with them" (Valentijn 1724–1726:III, 256). In his description of Java, he reports that, in addition to Islamic, Chinese, and the Christian religion there were still traces of the previous religious civilisations. He states that this religion came from South India, but he is wrong when he calls the main gods Brahmā and Śiva. He also refers to the books by Rogerius and Baldaeus, where the interested reader can find all kinds of information (Valentijn 1724–1726:IV, 1). Much more detailed are the facts Valentijn gives in his fifth part, in which he describes the Coromandel Coast. Here as well he refers primarily to his predecessors, Rogerius and Baldaeus, whose work he presents in detail. He also has something to say, however, about the content of the Veda, and he argues vigorously that future ministers should learn Sanskrit and study these sacred texts (Valentijn 1724–1726:V, 72–73).

More fascinating, though rather brief, is the work of Jacobus Canter Visscher (1692–1735), who was a minister in Kochi (Cochin) for a few years. From this Keralese post, he wrote dozens of letters to family members and acquaintances in the Netherlands, which were published after his death. With respect to religion, Canter Visscher did not share Rogerius' appreciation for Hinduism. He writes about "the most repugnant of all heathens who worship the most horrible monsters of all as their gods" (Canter Visscher 1743:78; 2008:112). He realised, however, that much of this religion remained strange to him because he did not speak the languages, and he argued for sending candidates with a wide knowledge of languages, given that "Malabaars" (Malayalam and Tamil) were needed as the language of oral communication whereas the Brahmins described the mysteries of their religion in *zwamkerdamsch* (Sanskrit) (Canter Visscher 1743:136; 2008:135).

The value of Canter Visscher's letters lies primarily in his description of the caste system. He provides many details about the division of the various population groups, their professions, and their religious culture. It already begins with him providing a good definition of 'caste': "a certain group of people who, by virtue of their birth are obligated to observe certain services and obligations, by virtue of which they also enjoy certain privileges" (Canter Visscher 1743:147; 2008:140). In his letters he describes not only the Brahmins, about which interested readers had already learned a great deal from other publications. He also describes a number of lower castes, with the peculiarities of their position and culture. He pays attention precisely to the specific Keralese castes, such as the *nāyars* with their polyandry. In modern Kerala, Canter Visscher is an important historical source, and his letters have also been translated into Malayalam.

Bibliography

Archival Records

Regional Archives Leiden (Erfgoed Leiden en omstreken): Kerkelijke huwelijksproclamaties der gereformeerden deel 1626–1633, inv. no. 1004/10.

Text Editions and Translations

Baldaeus, Philip (2000). *A Description of the East India Coasts of Malabar and Coromandel and also of the Isle of Ceylon with Their Adjacent Kingdoms and Provinces*. New Delhi/Madras: Asian Educational Services. https://archive.org/details/trueexactdescripoobald.

Baldaeus, Philip (1917). *Afgoderye der Oost-Indische Heydenen*. Ed. A.J. de Jong. 's-Gravenhage: Martinus Nijhoff.

Baldaeus, Philip (1672). *Naauwkeurige Beschryvinge van Malabar en Choromandel, Der zelver aangrenzende Ryken, En het machtige Eyland Ceylon, Nevens een omstandige en grondigh doorzochte ontdekking en wederlegginge van de Afgoderye der Oost-Indische Heydenen*. Amsterdam: Janssonius van Waasberge en Van Someren.

Canter Visscher, Jacobus (2008). *Mallabaarse Brieven: De brieven van de Friese predikant Jacobus Canter Visscher (1717–1723)*. Ed. Bauke van der Pol. Zutphen: Walburg Pers.

Canter Visscher, Jacobus (1743). *Mallabaarse Brieven: Behelzende eene Naukeurige Beschryving van de Kust van Mallabaar, Den Aardt des Landts, de Zeden en Gewoontens der Inwoneren, en al het voornaamste dat in dit Gewest van Indië valt aan te merken.* Leeuwarden: Abraham Ferwerda.

Rogerius, Abraham (1915). *De Open-Deure tot het Verborgen Heydendom.* Ed. W. Caland. 's-Gravenhage: Martinus Nijhoff.

Rogerius, Abraham (1651). *De Open-Deure Tot het Verborgen Heydendom Ofte Waerachtigh vertoog van het Leven ende Zeden, mitsgaders de Religie, ende Gods-dienst der Bramines, op de Cust Chormandel ende de Landen daar ontrent.* Leyden: Françoys Hackes.

Valentijn, François (1724–1726). *Oud en Nieuw Oost-Indiën: Vervattende Een Naaukeurige en Uitvoerige Verhandelinge van Nederlands Mogentheyd In die Gewesten.* Five volumes. Dordrecht/Amsterdam: Joannes van Braam/Gerard onder de Linden.

Secondary Literature

Arasaratnam, S. (1960). "Reverend Philippus Baldaeus: His Pastoral Work in Ceylon, 1656–1665." *Nederlands Theologisch Tijdschrift* 14: 350–60.

Bakker, Hans T. (1997). *De Schaamteloosheid tot het Uiterste Gedreven.* Amsterdam: Koninklijke Nederlandse Akademie van Wetenschappen.

Beumer, Mieke (1999). "Philippus Baldaeus en Gerrit Mosopatam: een buitengewoon portret." *Bulletin van het Rijksmuseum* 47: 144–73.

Bodewitz, H.W. (2002). *De late 'ontdekking' van het Sanskrit en de Oudindische cultuur in Europa.* Farewell Lecture. Leiden: Leiden University.

Burnell, A.C. (1879). "On Some Early References to the Vedas by European Writers." *The Indian Antiquary* VIII: 98–100.

Charpentier, Jarl (1924). "The Brit. Mus. Ms. Sloane 3290, the Common Source of Baldaeus and Dapper." *Bulletin of the School of Oriental Studies* 3: 413–20.

Charpentier, Jarl (1923). "Preliminary Report on the 'Livro da Seita dos Indios Orientais' (Brit. Mus. Sloane, 1820)." *Bulletin of the School of Oriental Studies* 2: 731–54.

Dharampal, Gita (1982), *La religion des malabars: Tessier de Quéralay et la contribution des missionaires européens à la naissance de l'indianisme.* Supplementa Nouvelle Revue de science missionnaire XXIX. Immensee: Nouvelle Revue de science missionnaire.

Glasenapp, Helmuth von (1961). *Die Literaturen Indiens von ihren Anfängen bis zur Gegenwart.* Stuttgart: Alfred Kröner Verlag.

Havart, Daniël (1693). *Op- en ondergang van Cormandel, In zijn binnenste geheel open, en ten toon gesteld.* Three volumes. Amsterdam: Jan ten Hoorn.

Jongeneel, J. (2015). *Nederlandse zendingsgeschiedenis: Ontmoeting van protestantse christenen met andere godsdiensten en geloven (1601–1917).* Zoetermeer: Boekencentrum Academic.

Joosse, L.J. (2001a). "Baldaeus, Philippus." In: C. Houtman et al. (eds.). *Biografisch Lexicon voor de geschiedenis van het Nederlandse Protestantisme* 5. Kampen: Kok. Pp. 35–36.

Joosse, L.J. (2001b). "Rogerius, Abraham." In: C. Houtman et al. (eds.). *Biografisch Lexicon voor de geschiedenis van het Nederlandse Protestantisme* 5. Kampen: Kok. Pp. 433–34.

Joosse, L.J. (1992). *'Scoone dingen sijn swaere dingen': Een onderzoek naar de motieven en activiteiten in de Nederlanden tot verbreiding van de gereformeerde religie gedurende de eerste helft van de zeventiende eeuw*. Leiden: Groen.

Lach, Donald F., and Edwin J. van Kley (1993). *Asia in the Making of Europe*. Volume III. Books 1 and 2. Chicago/London: University of Chicago Press.

Lind van Wijngaarden, Jan Daniël de (1891). *Antonius Walaeus*. Leiden: Los.

Mitter, Partha (1977). *Much Maligned Monsters: History of European Reactions to Indian Art*. Oxford: Clarendon Press.

Mooij, J. (1927–1931). *Bouwstoffen voor de geschiedenis der Protestantsche Kerk in Nederlandsch-Indië*. Three volumes. Weltevreden: Landsdrukkerij.

Nagel, Jürgen C. (2006). "Predikanten und Ziekentrooster: Der Protestantismus in der Welt der Verenigden Oostindischen Compagnie." In: Michael Mann (ed.). *Europäische Aufklärung und protestantische Mission in Indien*. Heidelberg: Draupadi Verlag. Pp. 101–21.

Noak, Bettina (2012). "Kennistransfer en culturele differentie. Abraham Rogerius en zijn *Open deure tot het verborgen heydendom* (1651)." *Tijdschrift voor Nederlandse Taal- en Letterkunde* 128: 350–64.

Peters, Marion (2002). *In steen geschreven: Leven en sterven van VOC-dienaren op de Kust van Coromandel in India*. Amsterdam: Stichting Historisch Onderzoek in Woord en Beeld/Bas Lubberhuizen.

Pol, Bauke van der (2011). *De VOC in India: Een reis langs Nederlands erfgoed in Gujarat, Malabar, Coromandel en Bengalen*. Zutphen: Walburg Pers.

Prins, Yvonne (2002). "Leidse vrouwen naar de Oost." *Jaarboek van het Centraal Bureau voor Genealogie* 56. The Hague: Centraal Bureau voor Genealogie. Pp. 179–216.

Sweetman, Will (2003). *Mapping Hinduism: 'Hinduism' and the Study of Indian Religions, 1600–1776*. Neue Hallesche Berichte 4. Halle: Verlag der Franckeschen Stiftungen.

Terpstra, H. (1946). "Tropische levenskunst in de XVIIe eeuw." *Cultureel Indië* 8: 199–210.

Troostenburg de Bruijn, C.A.L. van (1893). *Biographisch Woordenboek van Oost-Indische Predikanten*. Nijmegen: Milborn.

Troostenburg de Bruijn, C.A.L. van (1884). *De Hervormde Kerk in Nederlandsch Oost-Indië onder de Oost-Indische Compagnie (1602–1795)*. Arnhem: Tjeenk Willink.

Veth, P.J. (1884). *Ontdekkers en onderzoekers: Zevental levensschetsen*. 2nd ed. Leiden: Brill.

Wessels, C. (1935). "De verzwegen bronnen van Philippus Baldaeus' 'Afgoderije der Oost-Indische Heydenen'." *Studiën* 67: 482–85.

Wyss-Giacosa, Paola von, and Andreas Isler (2006). "Die 'Offne Thür zu dem Verborgenen Heydenthum': Frühe Titelkupfer zu Indien." *Librarium* 49: 58–68.

Zubkova, Luba (2004). "Pioneers of Orientalism at the VOC." *IIAS Newsletter* 35: 14.

CHAPTER 5

A Pietistic Preacher in Danish Territory: Bartholomäus Ziegenbalg

1 A Danish Undertaking

Many European countries opened trade offices in India in the seventeenth century, mostly on the southern coast, the Coromandel. The Portuguese, the English, the French, and the Dutch all had settlements there. One of the smaller settlements here was the Danish one, which was an initiative by the Danish East Indian Company (see Nørgaard 1988; Schmidt 2006) and consisted of a fort in the city of Tharangambadi (Tranquebar), 270 kilometres southeast of Chennai (Madras).

Although Tharangambadi was not a great success as a centre of trade, this Danish settlement played an important role in the history of mission. Two Lutheran missionaries arrived here on 9 July 1706: Bartholomäus Ziegenbalg (1682–1719) and Heinrich Plütschau († 1752). Their arrival in India is generally viewed as the beginning of the history of Protestant India, although that claim does not do any justice at all to the labour performed by the Dutch preachers of the Gospel in the seventeenth century.[1] In contrast to the Dutch preachers, Ziegenbalg and Plütschau were not, however, involved in pastoral care for the employees of the trading company; their only task was to spread the Gospel.

Whether the limitation of their task to purely missionary work was a good thing is open to doubt. The early history of mission in Tharangambadi was a succession of conflicts and opposition. It began already with setting up the mission undertaking. This was a personal initiative of the Danish King, Frederick IV,[2] and the board of the Danish East Indian Company had not even been informed that clergy would be sent. Nor did the colonial government in Tharangambadi have any idea what was going on, and it was also strongly opposed to the missionaries from the beginning. There was no interest in these preachers because the company had already hired two Danish ministers for pastoral work among the employees (Nørgaard 1988:14–16).

1 Jeyaraj, who describes the account of Ziegenbalg as "the father of modern Protestant missions" also admits this (2006:2, n. 3).

2 Nørgaard 1988:55: "ein königliches Privatunternehmen."

 | DOI:10.1163/9789004420076_007

2 Pietistic Germans

The greatest problem, however, was that the two missionaries had an entirely different background than the Danish ministers. When the king formed the plan to commence missionary work in the colony, there did not appear to be any suitable Danish theologians available. The plan had also been conceived in the king's consultation with his court preacher, Franz Julius Lütkens (1650–1712), who was of German descent and belonged to the pietistic wing that was strongly present in many German countries. The king gave him the task of finding potential missionaries in Germany, and, from the circles he was acquainted with there, he managed to interest Ziegenbalg and Plütschau for the plan.

Both German theologians had studied at the University of Halle, the centre of the pietistic wing, where they had been taught by August Hermann Francke (1663–1727) (Deppermann 1992:91–107). The latter was not only famous as a professor but also and primarily as the founder of many educational and charitable foundations. Thousands of children and young people were able to make something of their lives thanks to the orphanages and schools in Halle. The institutions taught the deep spirituality of pietism: personal conversion, obtained through struggle and the experience of God's grace, was central. It is obvious that mission among the 'heathens' was highly regarded.

Denmark was also Lutheran, but in an entirely different ecclesiastical climate. Both pietistic Germans were greeted with suspicion, and their ideas about conversion and being born again were critically questioned. No one in the hierarchy of the Church was looking forward to preachers like them. Moreover, the whole plan of missionary work abroad was very sensitive. The conservative Danish church only had ministers who were called by a local congregation, and there was no place for ministers working outside the boundaries of the church. Under pressure from the king, the bishop did finally ordain Ziegenbalg and Plütschau, but that was of course anything but a strong beginning.

It only became worse when they arrived in India. The Danish governor of Tharangambadi had received secret instructions from the headquarters of the Danish East India Company to make it as difficult as he could for the missionaries, and that is what he did (Jeyaraj 2006a:43). The governor intervened to show his power with every new initiative, and there were constant financial problems because salaries were not paid or donations from the king disappeared. Ziegenbalg even went back to Denmark once to complain to the king. In 1708, he was also imprisoned by the governor in a cell in the Danish fort. In the end, all the opposition broke him psychologically. He died at the age of 36, disillusioned by all the injustice and oppression he encountered in his idealistic work.

Ziegenbalg did not, however, always take the right approach himself. His intentions were certainly good when he took the initiative to preach in his mother tongue, German, for the many German members of the garrison, but that of course got him in trouble with the Danish colony ministers. Moreover, the relation between both missionaries was tense as well, which certainly came to light later. When two new members were added to the team, it became clear that Ziegenbalg and Plütschau were not always in agreement on this entirely new enterprise.

3 Preaching in Tamil

When the two missionaries arrived in Tharangambadi, they quickly discovered that their first task was to learn languages. The language of general everyday life in the colony was Portuguese, so of course they had to master that language. In addition, it appeared that they could not really build up contact with the local population without learning Tamil. They began to learn Portuguese with the help of books and hired a former schoolteacher to get them started in Tamil. The latter, however, did not understand any European languages and could only teach them some elementary principles of writing and grammar. In the end, they came into contact with a certain Aleppa, an interpreter who had previously worked for the East Indian Company and could speak several languages (Liebau 2008:116, 253). Through this intensive instruction in language, the missionaries succeeded in acquiring a solid knowledge of Tamil within a year, in addition to Portuguese. Ziegenbalg himself reported that he "could read, write, and speak this difficult language after eight months." He added: "I could even understand what was said to me when I met people" (cited in Jeyaraj 2006a:65).

Some specialisation was inevitable, however, for it was impractical for both of them to master two strange languages. And thus they made the decision in a way often used in pietistic circles: they cast lots so that they would not have to choose themselves but could leave it to God. The result was that Ziegenbalg would continue to study Tamil, whereas Plütschau would limit himself to Portuguese (Jeyaraj 2006a:66). In hindsight, that was a good move, for Ziegenbalg proved to be a genius in learning an extremely difficult language like Tamil. Plütschau was less capable in languages, but when he left in 1711, he had been able to make a solid contribution to congregational work because of his knowledge of Portuguese.

The mission community grew slowly. The first catechists were baptised in May 1707: five people employed by Danish functionaries, some slaves, others freemen. Baptism more or less meant becoming Danish, and the five Tamils were renamed Friedrich or Hedwiga (Jeyaraj 2006a:66–67). This baptism occurred in the Danish church, the Zion Church. Normally, however, Indians were not welcome in this church, and they held their services in the missionaries' homes. That is why a new church of their own was built in a short period of time, the Jerusalem Church. Here the missionaries held church services and catechism classes for the indigenous members of their congregation and other people who were interested. Two services were held on Sunday in which both Portuguese and Tamil was used.

According to the division of tasks agreed upon, Ziegenbalg took care of the Tamil part. He had the Danish liturgy translated into Tamil and also quickly completed translations of the New Testament and Luther's *Small Catechism*. His greatest achievement, however, was the fact that he was also able to preach in Tamil. Initially, he wrote his sermons in that language and memorised them. There are still a few dozen sermons in Tamil in the archives of the Franckesche Stiftungen in Halle, written—following Indian custom—with an engraving pen on a palm leaf. In the spring of 1707, however, his grasp of the language had advanced to such an extent that he could preach without the help of a written text (Jeyaraj 2006a:70).

He was famous among those who knew him for his gift for languages. Friend and foe praised him for this. One missionary who worked for a short time in Tharangambadi and could not get along with the two missionaries at all for the rest wrote: "Mr. Ziegenbalg, a man of about 28 years old, has—because God gave him a fine intellect—come very far in Tamil, for he speaks Tamil fluently and, conversely, understands the native Tamils, which is exceptionally difficult."[3]

4 Sources of Language and Religion

Ziegenbalg not only devoted himself to translating Christian texts in Tamil but also studied what the Tamil culture had to offer. He collected manuscripts in Tamil, and his "Bibliotheca malabarica"—as he called his collection—already numbered 119 books in 1708. The collection grew steadily in the years following, and he supplemented his book knowledge with information he acquired orally.

3 Johann Georg Bövingh, cited by Caland in Ziegenbalg 1926:5: "Herr Ziegenbalgh, ein Mann von etwan 28 Jahre, hat, nachdem Gott ihm ein herrliches Ingenium gegeben, es in der Malabahrischen Sprache sehr weit gebracht, denn er redet Malabarisch fertig, und verstehet hinwiederumb die gebohrenen Malabahren, so doch überaus schwer ist."

Many informants he spoke with deepened his knowledge of their culture and religion.

A very special project here was the correspondence of the missionaries, in which Ziegenbalg again played a prominent role. Whenever they came into contact somewhere with someone who was able to provide written information about the country, the culture, and the religion, they wrote him a letter with questions. This resulted in a collection of 99 letters from Tamils who put their insights and opinions down on paper for Ziegenbalg and Plütschau. This collection of letters is known as the "Malabar Correspondence." In addition, Ziegenbalg translated in particular various religious and other writings from Tamil and collected his constantly expanding knowledge of the religion of the Tamils in important studies.

Everything that Ziegenbalg and the other missionaries wrote—and that was quite a lot—was shipped to Halle for publishing. The mission enterprise was, namely, supported by a publicity campaign that was constructed along modern lines. The reports of the "Royal Danish missionaries" were published at regular intervals, as a journal, usually called the *Hallesche Berichte*, which was sent to contributors but sold in bookshops in many countries as well. Commercially, this was a successful approach. Distribution was enormous, both in print and in reach. There were even translations into Dutch and English. Towards the middle of the eighteenth century, the mission in Tharangambadi enjoyed wide name recognition.

This recognition is also apparent from a number of publications about the mission in Tharangambadi that were not from Halle. In 1732, for instance, two curious books were published in which Ziegenbalg is the central figure in a discussion that takes place in the realm of the dead.[4] The anonymous author has Ziegenbalg give an enthusiastic description of his mission work from the hereafter. His conversation partners are a fictional Dutch ship's minister called Johannes Coccejus (!)[5] and the historical person who taught the missionaries Tamil, Aleppa Kuru. The texts that are put in Ziegenbalg's mouth are all derived from the reports that the missionary had published in the *Hallesche Berichte*. Aleppa's dialogue consists of texts that were also published previously in Halle: they are fragments from the letters by Hindus in the "Malabar Correspondence."

4 *Ost-Indisches Gespräch, In dem Reiche der Todten* and *Continuatio oder Rotsetzung des Ost-Indianischen Gesprächs in dem Reiche der Todten*. Cf. Schouten 2010.

5 This is obviously an allusion to the seventeenth-century Dutch Reformed minister, Johannes Cocceius. Cf. Schouten 2010:148: "A famous Calvinist is used in the dialogue to show Lutheranism's superiority."

FIGURE 8 Ziegenbalg in conversation with Aleppa Kuru
Frontispiece of Ost-Indisches Gespräch: In dem Reiche der Todten

Thus, outsiders could also go all out with the material from Halle. And although the anonymous author's intentions were probably completely commercial, Ziegenbalg's mission movement became even more famous. The publication of the mission reports in Halle, however, also entailed a great disadvantage.

The missionaries were dependent on what the leaders in Halle wanted to publish. It was August Hermann Francke himself in particular who, as the uncrowned king of the pietistic institutions, decided what could and could not be published. The texts of the missionaries were subjected to a radical censorship. Offensive texts were modified, and the pious sauce of pietism was liberally served in the notes and introductions.

Worse for Ziegenbalg and his associates was the fact that whole manuscripts were laid aside if they did not sufficiently serve to edify and build up believers. None of the major studies on Hinduism that Ziegenbalg wrote and the writings that he translated from Tamil were published in his lifetime. His Tamil grammar is the only book that was published in Halle, since it could help future missionaries prepare for their work. But the other books on 'Malabar heathenism' all disappeared into the archives. Francke's response—which has become proverbial—to Ziegenbalg's manuscript *Genealogie der malabarischen Götter* was typical: "The idea of publication cannot be entertained at all, for the missionaries were sent out to uproot heathenism, not to spread that heathen nonsense in Europe."[6]

It was, however, not possible either just to include pious reports of the growth of the mission church in the *Hallesche Berichte*. There was a great deal of interest in distant countries and strange cultures in the first half of the eighteenth century. The readers of *Berichte* also wanted to know something about that exotic country where the missionaries worked. That is why the questions the missionaries asked their native correspondents and their answers were allowed to be published. The entire "Malabar Correspondence" was published in the *Berichte*, and the missionaries were even subsequently asked by Halle to send more letters (Liebau in Gründler and Ziegenbalg 1998:30). This entirely new approach was apparently appreciated by the readers.

5 The "Malabar Correspondence"

The first part of this collection of letters is found in the seventh *Continuation* (issue) of the *Hallesche Berichte*, that was published in 1714. The second group of the letters were published a few years later, in 1720, in the eleventh

6 "An einen Druck könne gar nicht gedacht werden, die Missionare seien ausgesandt das Heidenthum in Indien auszurotten, nicht aber den heidnischen Unsinn in Europa zu verbreiten," A.H. Francke, cited by Germann in Ziegenbalg 1867:vii. Cf. Dharampal-Frick 2006.

Continuation. In total, there were 99 letters published in the Halle journal.[7] What is immediately striking is the great variety, both in subject and in style, in the correspondence. That is completely in line with the missionaries' intent: they selected their correspondents according to knowledge and ability. And they asked questions in such a way that the readers in Europe could receive a comprehensive picture of the culture and religion in the land of the Tamils.

Some correspondents were scholars and provided a fundamental knowledge of the classical writings in their works. The missionaries had thus asked them questions in which theoretical knowledge played a greater role. Thus, the first three letters are entire explanations, in response to at least 9, 18, and 14 questions respectively. Alongside these experts, allegedly Brahmins, there were also representatives from other backgrounds who contributed. There is a correspondent, for instance, who described the cultus of the village gods among the lower castes (letter I/8). A teacher was asked to explain the instruction in arithmetic, and he did this in a detailed way and with evident interest (letter I/10). A short letter on the taboo against eating beef did not present many arguments but instead narrated a quaint legend-like story (letter I/32).

The letter writers also demonstrate very different positions regarding their own religion and that of the missionaries. Some were true believers in the ancestral religion who wanted to have nothing to do with the message of the Europeans. There are also writers who were quite positive about the message but had a negative view of the Christians' lifestyle in the Danish colony. There are also correspondents who were almost ready to join the church. And finally, there are people who were able to accept others as they were and to make the meaning of all individual religions the primary issue.

The subjects of the questions and the answers given fall into four categories. Together they give a reasonably complete picture of life and faith in seventeenth-century Tamil Nadu.

In the first place, there are letters about the country itself and its political history. The governments of the successive rulers, the relationship with the Mogul emperors, and the coming of the Europeans are explained in broad strokes (particularly letters II/5, II/18 and II/6). A special subject here is the allowance of the slave trade in the colony (letter II/21). The criticism of Danish policy that is vented in this letter would have been welcomed by the missionaries, for the slave trade for reasons of economic gain was an abomination to them.

7 A nice new edition of 44 letters was published in 1998 by Kurt Liebau: cf. Gründler and Ziegenbalg 1998.

A wide range of topics are then examined that gave the reader in Europe a better picture of the environment in which the missionaries worked. There is a letter about agriculture (letter I/25), one on the activities of women (I/23) and one on inheritance law (I/21). Another letter answers the question of the position of the kings in relation to Brahmins (letter II/19). The letter mentioned earlier from the instructor on arithmetic also belongs in this category of course.

Many of the questions paid extra attention to the religious culture, and several letter writers take up those questions all too readily. Thus, we find interesting and detailed treatments on the preparation of the sacred ashes (letter I/24) and on eating habits (I/14). Polygamy is of course discussed (letter I/24), as is the position of widows (letters I/2 and I/23). But questions about evil spirits and ghosts, as well as ones concerning various ascetic practices and marvels, are also willingly answered (letters I/17 and I/7).

The main issue for the missionaries is of course the content of the religion and its differences from the Christian faith. In the letters that talk about this we find a great deal that has also been taken up systematically in Ziegenbalg's books. But it should be remembered that those books were not allowed to be published in his lifetime—not until the nineteenth and twentieth centuries did they appear in print. The readers of the *Hallesche Berichte* had to make do with what was reported in the letters of the "Malabar Correspondence."

These included of course the expected overviews of the gods, particularly in Śaivism. The various persuasions among the Brahmins and the accompanying writings were also nicely sorted out. What would truly be new for the European readers, however, is the look at the religious practice that the letters every now and then offer.

Letter I/22, for instance, contains an interesting sketch of the temple dancers. These *devadāsīs* were trained to sing and dance as young girls. They were ultimately in service to the temple so that they would be present during rituals, and they also performed at weddings and parties. They were free to have relations with men, which was not viewed as improper in society. The pietistic missionaries had other ideas about this, however. In the published version of letter I/22, the commentary they added was more extensive than their commentary on other letters. The letter itself, however, was written by an Indian who attempted to bring out the artistry and impressiveness of these women in a sympathetic way. He describes in detail the rich clothing of the *devadāsīs* and their extensive cultural training: in addition to practising their art, they were also very well read and played string and wind instruments. The missionaries' footnotes, however, candidly talk about the "prostitutes' trade" and report with indignation that even Christian Europeans ("sadly!") hired these women for musical performances.

6 On the Path to Salvation?

The core question for the missionaries from this pietistic background was obviously how a human being could attain salvation. Their starting point was certainly that Christ had opened the way to heaven. But how were the other religions to be viewed? Ziegenbalg and his associates also had to ask this question of many correspondents as well, even though one can well ask whether the missionaries and their correspondents defined words like "salvation" and "heavenly bliss" in the same way.

The most pregnant question was probably the one raised in 11/7: "Whether people could find salvation in the Tamil religion or the Islamic religion?"[8] It does appear that the letter writer has difficulty with the question right from the start. Placing religious systems over against each other did not fit well into his way of thinking. He was, after all, a Hindu.

In answering the question, he first emphasises how old his own religion is—it goes back to the beginning of creation. And in all that time, since its beginning, it has preached pluriformity. He sums up ten forms of religious activity, all of which lead to salvation:

1. If one sacrifices to the eternal Supreme Being, believes in it in with one's heart, confesses it with one's mouth, and loves this Being.
2. If one brings a "sacrifice of the heart" with no conception or idea of God in his heart. And the letter writer (who obviously includes himself in this group) adds that such a person makes no distinctions between religions and does not disparage adherents of other religions.
3. Making a *liṅga* out of mud and sacrificing to it (and then letting it be washed away).
4. Withdrawing to the desert and practising ascetism.
5. Living a quiet life without wife or children and doing penitence daily.
6. Living one's life directed at sacrificial practices in an ordinary daily life and breaking with lies, deceit, and passion.
7. Whoever has no understanding of divine things and of good and evil turning to priests and other wise people and following their example.
8. Receiving salvation as the result of a virtuous life: "agreement between heart and mouth," good deeds like giving rice and clothing to the poor, paying for the wedding of another, building houses for Brahmins, building

8 'Ob man in der Malabarischen oder Mahometanischen Religion die Seeligkeit erlangen könne?' *Hallesche Berichte*, Eleventh *Continuation*, 904–07. This letter is not included in Liebau's miscellany.

gardens, renovating or building temples, building dykes, places for people to stay, and water stalls.

9. Whoever has no money for such good deeds obeying the commandments and practising faith, love, and hope.
10. Sacrificing and praying to Viṣṇu and singing to him.

The conclusion is that, in essence, all comes down to the same thing; they differ only in name. And Muslims? They hold that their faith system ('law') is better; "but we think ours is better." But there are many wise people among the Muslims as well, and many miracles occur. Their religion also includes a great deal of understanding and piety. If Muslims follow their commandments, they will also attain salvation. Thus the Hindu writer; the missionaries, however, had other ideas about this.

But the letters also yield something else. The question that is posed a number of times to the Hindus is: What actually prevents them from becoming Christians? Also: how do they view Christians? The answers vary, but one theme regularly returns: Christian teaching may be indeed be exalted and true, but the practice of its adherents falls far short (letters 1/1, 1/13 and 1/26).

The Indian writers are troubled by the lifestyle of the Europeans in their world: they drank strong drink, did not follow the purity rules, did not let the poor share in their joy at weddings and in their grief at funerals. They did not take the difference between high and low castes and the difference between men and women seriously. Worst of all was that they slaughtered cattle and ate beef. The criticism actually served the missionaries' purposes well. When one of the correspondents wrote that "The Christians have a holy law but no works," the missionaries wrote in a note: "This is the absolute worst that the heathens can reproach the Christians for, namely, that their law was indeed good, but their lives had no good works." Pietism, after all, focused on two fronts: the sanctification of church members and the conversion of those outside the church. There was enough to do on both fronts in Tharangambadi, and the readers in Europe could use some exhortation as well.

7 Systematic Work

In addition to the "Malabar Correspondence" and the missionary reports in the *Hallesche Berichte*, Ziegenbalg sent several manuscripts to Halle. These include, first of all, three translations of short ethical tractates that he wrote already in 1708, two years after his arrival in India.[9] He also prepared two

9 The last of the three was published during his life in Denmark; the others not. The three were finally published together in 1930 for the first time: Ziegenbalg 1930.

systematically arranged treatments of the religion of the inhabitants of the country. In 1711 he wrote his main work *Ausführliche Beschreibung des Malabarischen Heidenthums* and two years later a shorter study, *Genealogie der malabarischen Götter*. Although both works were not published during his life because of strong opposition in Halle, these works should nevertheless give us an idea of how much knowledge of the strange religion Ziegenbalg had acquired in a few short years.

Ziegenbalg himself viewed the three ethical tractates as a kind of first acquaintance with the religion of the Tamils. In any case, they did show that the Tamils were not a barbaric people who had no moral knowledge. In his long introduction to the first tractate, *Nītiveṇpā*, Ziegenbalg states the following: "How far a heathen, without Holy Scripture, can still come to knowledge of the moral law on the basis of the natural light of reason."[10] The difficult text[11] contains 94 proverbs with moral instruction, clearly intended to be learned by heart. For example:

> In this world the venom of the fly is only in its head,
> In the scorpion, the venom does not go any further than its tail,
> In the snake the venom is only in its teeth,
> but in bad people, the venom is present all throughout their body and in all their pores.
>
> *Nītiveṇpā* 17 in ZIEGENBALG 1930:32

The other two tractates, *Koṉṟaivēntaṉ* and *Ulakanīti*, are less sensational. They are collections of short proverbs that are used at school to teach children morals and decency. The following is one example:

> You should not think about what you cannot obtain.
>
> *Koṉṟaivēntaṉ* 16 in ZIEGENBALG 1930:57

Why should Europeans learn about these things? The writer gives a typical pietistic argument: "that they be aroused to living a virtuous life, so that in due course, on the day of Judgment, the heathens will not shame them."[12]

The themes that Ziegenbalg had already offered in the "Malabar Correspondence" and in the translation of the ethical tractates were broadly worked

---

10 Ziegenbalg 1930:25: "[W]ie weit doch gleichwohl ein heyde, ohne der heyligen schrifft vermöge des natürlichen lichts im erkentnis des Moralgesetzes kommen kan."

11 Caland: "äusserst schwierig" in Ziegenbalg 1930:5.

12 Ziegenbalg 1930:53: "[Z]um tugendwandel dadurch aufgemuntert werden, aufdasz dermaleins an jenem gerichtstage die heyden sie nicht beschämen möchten."

out in the manuscript that became his major work, *Ausführliche Beschreibung des Malabarischen Heidenthums*. Here as well we find the remarkable tension that Ziegenbalg had indicated between the right ideas that the Indians had because of "the natural light [of reason]" and the terrible idolatry to which the devil had led them. Ziegenbalg placed the largest part by far of their religion in the latter category: "the heathens are all under the dominion of the devil, who carries out his rule in a very broad way among them so that he himself is worshiped as a god by them and has seduced them into the most repulsive idolatries and pure superstitious idol worship."[13]

Was that sufficient reason for Christians in Europe to acquaint themselves with these tractates? The writer gives four explanations for publishing his book. First, with a view to his successors, he argues that they could—more easily than he did at the time—learn the principles of these heathens. The second was so that the Christians in Europe could feel pity for these heathens and pray for their conversion. And the third reason was so that the Protestant theologians in Europe could start a discussion on how to address these heathens and thus be able to advise the missionaries on this question. Finally, he wanted it published so that preachers could refute the atheists in Europe with the views of these Indians, none of whom, though they were heathen, denied the existence of God.

This last reason indicates immediately what Ziegenbalg saw as the most positive aspect of the religion of the Tamil people. Behind the numerous gods of their mythology and the cultus there was ultimately one God, called *Parāparavastu* ('Barábarawastu'). He describes this supreme deity in a very Christian way as "a divine being by whom everything was created and on whom everything in heaven and earth depends" (Ziegenbalg 1926:39). The being of this God is, however, unknown, and he plays no role in the cultus. It was particularly the wise men, *jñānī*, who accepted his existence. This presents a point of contact for the Christian preacher, however. The way in which Ziegenbalg put this principial monotheism in the foreground and gave it central significance is correctly called "exemplary and impressive" (Halbfass 1981:63).

Another element of the Hindu religion that Ziegenbalg describes with appreciation concerns the seriousness with which it deals with the sinfulness of human beings. With approval, the pietistic preacher cites a bhakti text in which the understanding of sin is all-comprehensive: "I am a sinner, my body

13 Ziegenbalg 1926:10: "Die heiden ... stehen alle unter der Herrschaft des Teufels, als welcher sein Regiment gantz auff grobe weise unter ihnen hat, also, dasz er selbst als ein Gott von ihnen angebeten wird, und sie zu den abscheulichsten Abgöttereyen, und zu lauter abergläubischen Götzendienste verführet hat."

is corrupt through and through; in my heart is pure uncleanness. God, be my trust!" (Ziegenbalg 1926:67). This comprehensive sense of sin led to a strongly ethical understanding among the Hindus: by performing many good works they attempted to do something to balance the guilt incurred. Although, looking at it from his point of view, Ziegenbalg saw little that was redemptive in such good works as a means to reach heaven, he does appear to be very much impressed by how these Indians went to great lengths in giving alms, demonstrations of aid, and penance. They could be examples for Christians.

For the rest, the writer gives a very detailed overview of Hindu teachings, mythology, and religious praxis that he observed in his environment. The detail of some descriptions is striking. He thus illustrates his description of the temples with well-drawn maps that show the various rooms and placing of altars and images (Ziegenbalg 1926:126, 130). If the whole cultic area of this religion was to be viewed, from his background, as the work of the devil, one could ask how he himself experienced his intriguing study of this religion. Surely his meticulousness and detail reflect something of a certain fascination with the religion of the 'heathens.'

Maybe what Dharampal writes does not, after all, go deep enough: "Although the voice of the pietistic preacher can still be heard, the descriptions of the Tamil religion and society witness to an independent, questing mind and a sincere attempt to understand a strange culture" (Dharampal-Frick 2006:146). That is certainly true, but there is more going on. Ziegenbalg seems to be so struck by the culture around him that he rejects the 'heathen' in it only provisionally. This is clear from his second systematic work, *Genealogie der malabarischen Götter*. In almost 300 pages, he describes what he should find the most objectionable: the gods and their cultus. But he nevertheless saw a future for everything that he encountered and was impressed by. In the discussion of the Hindu feasts, he writes:

> The Christian mission in India must study precisely how the folklore elements of the existing feasts could be connected with the celebration of the Christian feasts and can be ennobled in order to turn them into people's feasts, just as the proclaimers of the faith who brought the gospel to our fatherland were able to do.
>
> ZIEGENBALG 1867:269

The rich Tamil culture could look forward to a good future, though that future entailed that the culture be Christianised.

Bartholomäus Ziegenbalg himself did not witness that future. When he died on 23 February 1719, the Tamil culture was not Christianised in any way: the

FIGURE 9 Monument to Ziegenbalg in Tharangambadi

fruit of all the mission labour was no more than a small Lutheran community in the Danish colony. Ziegenbalg did not live past the age of 36 and was married for only three years. His beloved wife Maria Dorothea survived him by 57 years.[14]

Bibliography

Text Editions and Translations

Ziegenbalg, Bartholomaeus (2006). *A German Exploration of Indian Society: Ziegenbalg's "Malabarian Heathenism." An Annotated English Translation with an Introduction and a Glossary.* Transl. Daniel Jeyaraj. Chennai/New Delhi: Mylapore Institute for Indigenous Studies/Indian Society for Promoting Christian Knowledge.

Ziegenbalg, Bartholomaeus (2005). *Genealogy of the South Indian Deities: An English Translation of Bartholomäus Ziegenbalg's Original German Manuscript with a Textual Analysis and Glossary.* Transl. Daniel Jeyaraj. RoutledgeCurzon Studies in Asian Religions. London/New York: RoutledgeCurzon.

14 She died on 6 November 1776 in Flensburg (Source: Stadtarchiv Flensburg).

Ziegenbalg, Bartholomaeus (1930). *Kleinere Schriften: Nītiveṇpā, Koṉraivēntaṉ, Ulakanīti*. Ed. W. Caland. Verhandelingen der Koninklijke Akademie van Wetenschappen te Amsterdam, Afd. Letterkunde, Nieuwe reeks XXIX/2. Amsterdam: Koninklijke Akademie van Wetenschappen.

Ziegenbalg, Bartholomaeus (1926). *Ziegenbalg's Malabarisches Heidenthums*. Ed. W. Caland. Verhandelingen der Koninklijke Akademie van Wetenschappen te Amsterdam, Afd. Letterkunde, Nieuwe reeks XXV/3. Amsterdam: Koninklijke Akademie van Wetenschappen.

Ziegenbalg, Bartholomaeus (1867). *Genealogie der malabarishen* [sic] *Götter*. Ed. Wilhelm Germann. Madras: Christian Knowledge Society's Presse.

Gründler, Johann, and Bartholomäus Ziegenbalg (1998). *Die Malabarische Korrespondenz: Tamilische Briefe an deutsche Missionare*. Ed. Kurt Liebau. Fremde Kulturen in alten Berichten 5. Sigmaringen: Jan Thorbecke Verlag.

Ost-Indisches Gespräch (1732a). *Ost-Indisches Gespräch, In dem Reiche der Todten, Zwischen Bartholomäo Ziegenbalg, Königl. Dänischen Missionario, und Evangelisch-Lutherischen Prediger, zu Tranquebar auf der Küste Coromandel in Ost-Indien, und Johann Cocceo, Einen Holländischen Schiff-Prediger.* Franckfurt.

Ost-Indisches Gespräch (1732b). *Continuatio oder Fortsetzung Des Ost-Indianischen Gesprächs in dem Reiche der Todten, Zwischen Bartholomäo Ziegenbalg, Königl. Dänischen Mißionarien zu Tranquebar auf der Küste Coromandel, Und Einem Heydnisch-Malabarischen Priester, Aleppa Kuru.* Franckfurt.

Secondary Literature

Caland, W. (1924). "Over Ziegenbalg's Malabarisches Heidenthum." *Mededeelingen der Koninklijke Akademie van Wetenschappen Amsterdam*, Afd. Letterkunde, Deel 57, Serie A, No. 4: 73–89.

Deppermann, Klaus (1992). *Protestantische Profile von Luther bis Francke: Sozialgeschichtliche Aspekte*. Göttingen: Vandenhoeck & Ruprecht.

Dharampal-Frick, Gita (2006). "'…ausgesandt, das Heidenthum in Indien auszurotten, nicht aber den heidnischen Unsinn in Europa zu verbreiten': Bartholomäus Ziegenbalg und die Hallesche Tranquebar-Mission zwischen pietistischem Sendungsbewusstsein und ethnologischer Aufklärung." In: Michael Mann (ed.). *Europäische Aufklärung und protestantische Mission in Indien*. Heidelberg: Draupadi Verlag. Pp. 143–63.

Fenger, J. Ferd. (1845). *Geschichte der Trankebarschen Mission nach den Quellen bearbeitet*. Grimma: J.M. Gebhardt.

Georgi, Lotte (1958). *Maria Dorothea Ziegenbalg: Tatsachenberichte aus dem Leben der ersten deutschen evangelischen Missionarsfrau in Süd-Indien*. Berlin: Evangelische Verlagsanstalt.

Gross, Andreas, Y. Vincent Kumaradoss, and Heike Liebau (2006). *Halle and the Beginning of Protestant Christianity in India*. Three volumes. Halle: Verlag der Franckeschen Stiftungen.

Halbfass, Wilhelm (1981). *Indien und Europa: Perspektiven ihrer geistigen Begegnung*. Basel/Stuttgart: Schwabe.

Irschick, Eugene F. (2003). "Conversations in Tarangambadi: Caring for the Self in Early Eighteenth Century South India." *Comparative Studies of South Asia, Africa and the Middle East* 23: 254–70.

Jeyaraj, Daniel (2006). *Bartholomäus Ziegenbalg: The Father of Modern Protestant Mission. An Indian Assessment.* New Delhi/Chennai: Indian Society for Promoting Christian Knowledge/Gurukul Lutheran Theological College and Research Institute.

Jürgens, Hanco (2014). *Roeping India: Religie, Verlichting en koloniale expansie. Duitse zendingsberichten 1750–1810*. Nijmegen: Radboud University.

Liebau, Heike (2008). *Die indischen Mitarbeiter der Tranquebarmission (1706–1845). Katecheten, Schulmeister, Übersetzer*. Hallesche Forschungen 26. Tübingen: Verlag der Franckeschen Stiftungen Halle im Max Niemeyer Verlag.

Nørgaard, Anders (1988). *Mission und Obrigkeit: Die Dänisch-hallische Mission in Tranquebar 1706–1845*. Transl. Eberhard Harbsmeier. Missionswissenschaftliche Forschungen 22. Gütersloh: Gerd Mohn.

Schouten, Jan Peter (2010). "Piëtistische propaganda in een heidens jasje: Een onbekend geschrift over het zendingswerk van Ziegenbalg." *Kerk en Theologie* 61: 143–55.

Schmidt, Yvonne (2006). "Tranquebar unter dem Danebrog: Die Rolle der Dänen im multikulturellen Handelsnetz an der Koromandel-Küste." In: Michael Mann (ed.). *Europäische Aufklärung und protestantische Mission in Indien*. Heidelberg: Draupadi Verlag. Pp. 81–99.

Sweetman, Will (2004). "The Prehistory of Orientalism: Colonialism and the Textual Basis for Bartholomäus Ziegenbalg's Account of Hinduism." *New Zealand Journal of Asian Studies* 6: 12–38.

Online Resources

Der Königl. Dänischen Missionarien aus Ost-Indien eingesandter Ausführlichen Berichten, Von dem Werck ihres Amts unter den Heyden, angerichteten Schulen und Gemeinen, ereigneten Hindernissen und schweren Umständen; Beschaffenheit des Malabarischen Heydenthums, gepflogenen brieflichen Correspondentz und mündlichen Unterredungen mit selbigen Heyden ... Teil 1–9 (Continuation 1–108) (Halle 1710–1772) [the 'Hallesche Berichte']. Accessed 6 July 2017. http://192.124.243.55/digbib/hb.htm.

CHAPTER 6

A Disappointed Missionary: Abbé Dubois

1 Reading for the Curious

The pietistic Germans were certainly not the only ones who provided their supporters back home with interesting reading and thus involved them in their missionary work. A counterpart of their *Hallesche Berichte* can be found in the *Lettres édifiantes et curieuses* that the Jesuits began issuing in 1702 (Sweetman 2003:127–53).[1] Just as with the Halle journal, the *Lettres édifiantes* were concerned with satisfying curiosity about strange cultures that flourished among the intelligentsia in eighteenth-century Europe. Although the letters were indeed sometimes pious in tone and the excellence of the Christian religion was pointed out, the writers were nonetheless able to report many things of interest to their readers. The term *édifiant* reflects the purpose behind the letters, but it was the *curieux* that attracted the readers.

Thus, writers came forward who had many interesting things to say. Among the missionaries of the Jesuit order were scholars who sometimes stayed up to half a century in India and knew the country and the languages thoroughly. One of them was Jean Venant Bouchet (1655–1732) who lived like a *sannyāsī*, following Roberto de Nobili's example. He knew the culture of his environment so well after some time that he no longer ran the risk of being taken for *paraṅgi*. His primary aim in studying the Hindu writings was to be able to use debates to convince the Indians of the foolishness of their religion. A side effect, however, was that he could also explain the religion of this far country to many people among his European public. He was convinced that much in Hinduism derived from Judaism, but the arguments he cited for support here, such as the similarities in names like Abraham and Brahmā, Sarasvatī and Sarah, were unusual, to say the least. Although this was, in retrospect, completely off the mark of course, it did help people in Europe to see the religion of India as something serious, as something other than the barbaric primitiveness that had determined their view of Hinduism until that time.

Another writer in the *Lettres édifiantes* was Gaston-Laurent Cœurdoux (1691–1779). He was much more critical of the idea that the Hindus had learned their religion from the Jews. His knowledge of the background of Indian culture

1 Gita Dharampal (Dharampal-Frick 2006:145) described the *Hallesche Berichte* as a "Protestant counterpart to the well-known *Lettres édifiantes.*"

 | DOI:10.1163/9789004420076_008

was greater than many others in his order. In the 47 years that he stayed in India, he studied the languages and literature of his surroundings closely. He was one of the first to see the similarities between Sanskrit and Latin and speculated about a common source. He is primarily known, however, as a collector of ethnological material: he contributed immensely to the understanding of Brahmanical morals and customs (see Murr 1987). The material this Jesuit provided, however, did not become known in the first place via the *Lettres édifiantes* but in an entirely different way, as is apparent from the following story.

2 A Costly Manuscript

In 1806, a French missionary, Jean-Antoine Dubois (1766–1848), went to the British resident in Mysore, Mark Wilks (1759–1831), and showed him a hefty manuscript that contained his notes on the customs and beliefs of the Hindus. This highly-placed civil servant, who was renowned as an expert in the religion of South India, studied the French manuscript intensively and became convinced of its importance. He therefore sent the manuscript to the British governor-general with the advice to buy it and publish it at the expense of the East India Company. It would be important particularly for civil servants in the colonial government and the staff of the Company to gain insight into the mores of the local population. The governor, Lord William Bentinck (1774–1839), recognised the importance of his request. He wrote, among other things, that he believed that the British were "in fact strangers in the land" and that from "a political point of view the information might be of the greatest benefit in aiding the servants of the Government " (cited in Dubois 1985:xv). The manuscript was bought for the substantial amount of 2,000 *star pagoda*s and was published in 1817 after being translated into English.[2]

In the meantime, Abbé Dubois, as the writer was generally called, continued with his work, constantly sending supplements and improvements to the British colonial government, based on his encounters with the local population and his reading of Hindu writings. Reprints of his work thus became more and more comprehensive until 1906 when, half a century after his death, a definitive edition was published that became a compendium of all knowledge about Hindu life. The great Indologist Max Müller (1823–1900) wrote a foreword in which he praised the author as a man who was strikingly free of prejudices and, as a scholar, had sufficient knowledge of Tamil to understand the work of the native population: "As a trustworthy authority on the state of India from

2 A *star pagoda* was a gold coin, equal in value to about 8 euros.

1792 to 1823 the Abbé Dubois' work will always retain its value" (Müller in Dubois 1985:vii).

In 1977, however, a massive attack on the reputation and work of Abbé Dubois began. In a notorious article, Sylvia Murr (1947–2002) claimed that the manuscript that Dubois had sold to the British East India Company had not been written by him at all (Murr 1977). Instead, she claimed, he copied it from another document that, like Dubois' manuscript, was in the library of the Indian Office in London. This document had been written by a French officer, Nicolas-Jacques Desvaulx (1745–1817), and demonstrably compiled before Dubois had arrived in India. About 10 years later, however, the history of the manuscript had expanded: Desvaulx was no longer considered to be the original author but had in turn copied his manuscript from a lost manuscript by no one less than the above-mentioned Jesuit Gaston-Laurent Cœurdoux (Cœurdoux 1987; Murr 1987).

Murr's publications used harsh words: she was aiming at nothing less than unmasking Abbé Dubois.[3] This accusation of plagiarism is not as convincing as it seems at first glance, however. It is entirely conceivable that he saw a work by a previous writer during the first phase of his stay in India, when he was stationed in Pondicherry. It is also completely logical to argue that he adopted the structure and chapter division of the overview of the caste system he found there. But, as later authors have already shown, it is highly unlikely that an expert like Dubois simply copied the manuscript and sold it as his own work to the British who were quite familiar with such literature (Mohan 2004:244; cf. DeSmet 1990). In any case, all the later additions that substantially expanded the book and made it what it is today were certainly Dubois' work. Moreover, taking over someone else's work was not viewed nearly as negatively two centuries ago as it is today. Baldaeus did this as well to a considerable extent.[4]

3 Missionaries in Turbulent Times

Jean-Antoine Dubois came from Vivarais, a former province in France, that more or less coincided with the area of the current department of Ardèche. He was born on 10 January 1766.[5] He studied at the seminary of the Society of Foreign Missions of Paris and was ordained as a priest when he was 24. Not long

3 The title of the first part (64 pages) of Murr 1987: "L'abbé Dubois démasqué."
4 See Chapter 4.
5 It is recorded in the baptismal register of the village St. Remèze that he was baptised there on the day of his birth, 10 January 1766. See Mazon 1899:50.

afterwards, he left as a missionary for the French colony in India, Pondicherry. The rumour went round later that he had fled the massacres that accompanied the French Revolution, but he himself always put this in perspective: the persecution of the religious and the accompanying bloodbaths did not begin until two years after he left.[6]

The situation in Pondicherry was tense when Dubois arrived in 1792. Dubois was not regular clergy but secular clergy under the authority of the bishop (thus his title of *abbé*).[7] This bishop was, at a certain point, expelled from the colony because he did not want take part in the ceremony of planting a liberty tree. Even worse in the eyes of the revolutionaries was the fact that the bishop and all his subordinates refused to take the oath of loyalty to the revolutionary constitution. Under immense pressure, the clergy had to flee to Tharangambadi, which was under Danish rule.

The missionary work was resumed with the Danish colony as the base. After the Jesuit order was disbanded in 1773, much of the pastoral work in India was taken over by the Society of Foreign Missions. An important area of work for the French Catholics was the principality of Mysore, also because France had been an ally of the ruler of that kingdom for a long time. The current ruler, Tipu Sultan, however, was strongly opposed to outsiders and launched a reign of terror against everything that was Christian. Abbé Dubois had originally been sent to work in Mysore, but for the time being could only reach those areas that the sultan had been forced to cede to the English. Dubois was given his first post in Salem, now Tamil Nadu, where he had to deal primarily with Indian Catholics who had personally experienced Tipu Sultan's persecution.

This pastoral care of those who had been persecuted became even more important in 1799. Then the English defeated Tipu Sultan and occupied his whole kingdom. Dubois settled in the capital city, Srirangapatna, where he attempted to gather the Catholic Christians together and to rebuild parochial life. The persecution had been severe there. Most of the Christian women had been given to Muslim men as sex slaves, whereas the Christian men were faced with the choice of either death or circumcision. Given his own experience in Paris, Dubois realised that the Church was dependent on people who remained faithful in the face of persecution, which is why he also found it difficult to accept the fact that all Indian Catholics, without exception, had denied their faith and let themselves be absorbed into the Islamic community. Even years later, in 1815, the outrage was clearly detectable when he wrote:

---

6 Dubois in the foreword of the French edition of 1825. See Mazon 1899:55.

7 Thus, he was not a Jesuit, as is often claimed.

> Oh shame!—oh scandal!—will it be believed in the Christian world?—no one, not a single individual among so many thousands, had courage enough to confess his faith under this trying circumstance, and become a martyr to his religion.
>
> DUBOIS 1823:74

4 A Hindu among the Hindus

One would, perhaps, not expect it from this strict cleric, but Dubois—like the Jesuits of Roberto de Nobili—adapted completely to the environment in which he had to work. From the moment of his arrival, he realised that he could only win the trust of the native people if he lived as they did. In one of his letters he writes: "I adopted their style of clothing, and I studied their customs and methods of life in order to be exactly like them. I even went so far as to avoid any display of repugnance to the majority of their prejudices" (Dubois 1985:ix). He thus wore a long white garment with a turban flaring into a long wrap, carried a pilgrim's staff in his hand, and walked on the classic wooden sandals. He was a strict vegetarian and also adapted to the local customs in his behaviour and manners.

The Indians responded to Dubois' adaptation to the local culture. He was looked upon very soon as a 'holy man' who should be treated with acknowledgement and respect. The resident of Mysore related that, when Dubois travelled through the principality, he was received everywhere as an important guest: "when travelling, on his approach to a village, the house of a Brahmin is uniformly cleared for his reception, without interference, and generally without communication to the officers of Government, as a spontaneous mark of deference and respect" (Mark Wilks in Dubois 1985:x).

The respect that the people had for Dubois is also apparent from the nickname he was given over the course of time: he was called *Doḍḍa svāmiyavaru*, which could be translated as 'Great Lord.' The missionary clearly owed such respect not only to his dress and behaviour as a 'holy man' but also to the fact that he committed himself to the local population in a variety of ways, and certainly not only to the Brahmanical upper crust. It is typical for him to develop plans for founding agrarian colonies in which the collaboration between the various population groups could better be achieved. He sought the support of the British colonial government for this—he was, after all, on a very friendly footing with them. Given such practical initiatives, he showed how much the people—Christian and non-Christian—mattered to him. The mission

FIGURE 10 Abbé Dubois in Indian clothing
Portrait: Thomas Hickey, 1820

work he did for the Church went hand-in-hand with care for people in their everyday life.

His most remarkable undertaking in this area was certainly the introduction of the smallpox vaccination. Mysore was repeatedly plagued by smallpox epidemics that killed a great many people. Dubois organised a vaccination campaign by sending a number of volunteers into the country to vaccinate people here and there. Dubois kept track of the progress himself: since 1 January 1803 as many as 25,432 people were vaccinated in a year and a half (Mazon 1899:107). This was a major achievement. The vaccination with cowpox was, after all, a completely new method: the British doctor, Edward Jenner (1749–1823), had developed and described this method in 1798. It says something about Dubois' character that he applied this brand-new method so energetically five years later. In addition, it was precisely in India that there was such great opposition to new Western medical practices. Dubois needed all his persuasive power to get the vaccination programme going.

5 Mission Impossible?

Dubois was able to persuade people in Mysore with respect to smallpox vaccination, but he was less successful in persuading them in the area that ultimately concerned him: the spread of Christianity. When Dubois returned to Europe, after 31 years of missionary work in South India, he published a book that attracted a great deal of attention: *Letters on the State of Christianity in India* (Dubois 1823). The subtitle already gives an evaluation of his overseas career: *in which the Conversion of the Hindoos is Considered as Impracticable.* Indeed, the book presents an extremely bleak picture of the possibilities of reaching Hindus with the Gospel.

Dubois had become convinced that the Hindus would not change in a thousand years with respect to their rejection of the religion and culture of the Europeans (Dubois 1823:49). They would continue to allow themselves to be led by their prejudices, which prevented them from being open to the Christian faith. He looks nostalgically back on the seventeenth century when missionaries from the Jesuit order managed to reach many tens of thousands of Indians by adapting to the Hindu *sannyāsīs*' way of life without compromise (Dubois 1823:7).[8] When the European powers grew stronger in India and the population became more acquainted with European culture, Christianity fell into serious decline among the indigenous population. Dubois expected that there would be no trace of it left in 50 years (Dubois 1823:13).

The book has indeed been described as "a voice of disillusionment amounting almost to despair" (Neill 1985:277). It is telling that Dubois did not write his book as a look at his time in India from a later perspective; rather, it contains reflections of his experiences during his stay in South India. After all, the book contains letters written earlier, mostly during the years 1815–1816. Thus, during all these years in India, despite his exemplary and highly praised adaptation to the local culture, Abbé Dubois felt miserable, feeling that he did not have any chance of success, even with all the effort he put into it.

---

8 For the Jesuits, see Chapter 3 of this book.

This volume of letters shows how extremely negative and threatening Dubois felt Hinduism—particularly the Brahmanical culture—to be. What is sometimes stated obliquely in his major study on Hindu morals and customs is stated clearly in these letters: Hinduism is no good and must be defeated. On his more positive days, Dubois is upbeat: "Let us take care that we do not despair; there will come a day when the standard of the cross will shine on the temples of India, just as it shines on the Capitol" (cited in Mazon 1899:57). This resembles Ziegenbalg's dream that the colourful folklore of India would have a future with Christianity.[9] Dubois is more negative, however: Hinduism cannot be incorporated into Christianity but was a despicable superstition that had to be rooted out (Mazon 1899:57; cf. Dubois 1823:140).

In *Letters on the State of Christianity in India*, Dubois attacked Hinduism with an unprecedented ferocity. The Brahmins especially were taken to task: "The Hindoos may be divided into two classes—the imposters, and the dupes. The latter include the bulk of the population of India; and the former is composed of the whole tribe of Brahmins" (Dubois 1923:87). In Dubois' view, the Brahmins represented all evil: pride, self-deception, lying, the lust for power. He was convinced that nowhere else in the world had the Gospel encountered such terrible opponents. The Hindu—and in particular the Brahmin—could be characterised as "a kind of moral monster" (Dubois 1923:100). It was thus no wonder that nothing came of conversion to Christianity.

It is clear that Dubois is exasperated and rattling on. Nevertheless, we can say something positive. Through his special knowledge of the life circumstances in India, he—much more than his contemporaries—had an eye for the major social inequalities that Hinduism caused and for the oppression of the people on the lowest rung of the caste hierarchy. Not until the end of the twentieth century would the oppressed begin to cause a stir as *Dalits* and challenge the obvious Brahmanical supremacy. Dubois had recognised their powerlessness more than a century and a half earlier.

The book by the retired Dubois did not remain undisputed—Anglicans and other Protestants especially protested (see especially Hough 1824). While Catholic colleagues of the disappointed missionary were not edified by his negative attitude to their common undertaking, Protestants, however, had a reason to express their disagreement, for Dubois had written the book to frustrate them (Launay 1898:I, 317). Dubois was annoyed by their indulgence of Hindus and, moreover, had serious objections to the new Protestant missionary tactic: the

9 See Chapter 5.

distribution of translated sections of the Bible. This was a modern development: the British and Foreign Bible Society had been founded in 1804 and since then distribution of the Bible was seen as the missionary task par excellence. As a convinced Roman Catholic, Dubois did not think that people should read the Bible themselves at all—that was reserved for priests. But he thought that Hindus should read it even less, and he did have a point here. In his *Letters* volume, he demonstrated—and not without a sense of humour—that Hindus would get the wrong idea if they started reading the Bible. What would Hindus think if they read that Abraham slaughtered a calf when three angels came to visit him and offered it to his heavenly guests? They would view the patriarch with the three angels as the lowest of the pariahs because of this murder of the holy cow (Dubois 1823:28). Dubois' book also included constant critique and disparagement of the Protestants—ecumenism was still an unknown concept at the beginning of the nineteenth century.

Dubois had got along well, for the rest, with the British in India, most of whom were non-Catholic. He was very highly esteemed for his wide knowledge of Hinduism and South Indian languages (he spoke Tamil, Kannada, and Telugu). Because of his great services, the British even gave him retirement pay. This allowed him to set himself up in France after he repatriated in 1823. There Dubois served for a few years as the vice chancellor of the seminary of the Society of Foreign Missions in Paris. He was criticised for his acceptance of this position because of his extremely negative attitude to the conversion of the Hindus. The Methodist missionary Elijah Hoole (1798–1872) characterised this as "a singular conclusion to the history of the strange inconsistencies of the Abbé Dubois" (Hoole 1844:157).

It is not at all surprising that Dubois occupied himself with his study of the culture and languages of India. This resulted in, among other things, a translation from the South Indian languages of classic literary stories, the *Pañcatantra*. Jean-Antoine Dubois died at his seminary on 17 February 1848 at the age of 82.

6 A Manual

The book that made Abbé Dubois famous, *Hindu Manners, Customs and Ceremonies*, has 741 pages in its final, definitive edition of 1906. It clearly feels like a manual: offering a comprehensive overview of the rites, doctrines, social structure and customs and etiquette of Indian society. There the main accent is on the Brahmanical section, which is of course also the one that is most carefully detailed in the classic writings. Other castes are also discussed, however, right down to those lowest in rank. The book's merit lies in the fact that it is clearly written by someone who knows the culture inside out. Dubois uses his personal memories to illustrate moral practice and customs many times.

The book is divided into three parts. The first contains 14 chapters and consists of a socio-cultural overview. Here it concerns primarily the various castes, the different traditions, and the priestly functions: "General View of Society in India, and General Remarks on the Caste System." In the second part, containing no less than 36 chapters, the life of the Brahmins is examined: "The Four States of Brahminical Life." It not only deals here with the four phases of life but also provides information about purity and morality, rules for conduct, and literature. In the third part, "Religion," nine chapters provide an overview of the different gods, temples, and feasts. These three parts are followed by six appendices on specific topics. We will now describe one characteristic chapter from each part.

7 Inclusion of the Lower Castes

The fifth chapter of the first part deals with the lower castes. In the previous chapters Dubois describes the four classes in the classic writings: Brahmins, *Kṣatriyas*, *Vaiśyas*, and *Śūdras*. Now he turns his attention to the countless castes that can be included in the category of the *Śūdras*, the lowest groups in the caste hierarchy.

Dubois felt strictly bound to the schema of the four classes in classic Indian literature. That entailed that all lower castes had to be categorised among the Śūdras. A distinction was later made between the actual Śūdra castes, which still enjoy some status, and all the 'untouchables' who exist outside of the whole system of the four varṇas (*avarṇa*). For Dubois, however, they were all Śūdras, but he seems to have known about the phenomenon of exclusion when he writes about certain groups "who, owing to the depth of degradation into which they have fallen, are looked upon as almost another race of beings, altogether outside the pale of society" (Dubois 1985:49).

Dubois underscores how important these groups were in terms of numbers: the pariahs (*Paṟaiyar*) and shoemakers (*Sakkili*) made up at least one quarter of the population. The lot of the pariahs was especially to be lamented. Dubois describes them as the slaves of India and adds that he himself would rather be a slave in one of the European colonies than a pariah. The pariahs were, after all, he said, completely subject to the caprice of their masters. They had so internalised their subordinate position that it did not even occur to them to think that they could change their lot in life.

In addition, they lived in hopeless poverty. Dubois also related a few things from his pastoral work. In his various parishes, half the believers were people from the pariah caste. He tells how he often crawled into the low pariah huts on his hands and knees to attend to the dying. Afterwards, a hot bath and change of underclothes was necessary because of the immense quantity of insects and vermin. He did have some understanding for the revulsion people from the higher castes felt for the pariahs. After all, these people lived, he writes, in very unhygienic conditions, and they ate what everyone else saw as the nastiest food of all, such as rotting meat.

Nor did Dubois have a high opinion of the morality that the pariahs followed. He typified them as people who lived hand-to-mouth and knew nothing of planning and saving. They were completely unfit for the army as well because of their complete lack of a sense of honour. The editor of the definitive edition of the book, Henry Beauchamp, intervened at that point: he reports in the footnotes that much had changed for the better since Abbé Dubois' time and that the colonial army in Madras trained them to become disciplined soldiers.

A favourable circumstance for the pariahs in the cities was, according to Dubois, that they often found work in housekeeping for European families. The reason for this was, however, "for lack of better people": people from castes with some sense of class would not accept work in which they had to prepare beef, polish leather shoes, and empty chamber pots. According to him, this confirmed all the prejudices about the low status of the pariahs and did not help the attitude towards Europeans in any way.

There were other castes as well that he viewed in a very negative way, even though they had a somewhat higher status than the pariahs. In the first place, there were two service professions found in every village: barbers and laundrymen. Although everyone made use of their services, they were very low-caste because of all the impurity they encountered in their work. The same obtained for other professional groups who were per definition contaminated by their work, such as tanners who, after all, had to handle the hides of dead animals.

Finally, Dubois describes the wandering groups. These included both nomadic castes and forest-dwellers that people would now call 'tribes' (*ādivāsīs*). Most striking is the description of the *Lambāḍi* caste, which had a very bad reputation. The presumed unreliability and licentiousness is described in extensive detail. Dubois even managed to report that members of this caste were guilty of human sacrifice.

However much such sketches were sometimes based on rumour and prejudice, Dubois nevertheless deserves respect for having studied the many lower-caste groups and did not limit himself to the Brahmanical culture. His book is thus also one of the first in the line of manuals on 'castes and tribes' that became popular in the nineteenth century.

8 Contamination

In the second part of Dubois' book, three chapters describe the contamination that threatened Brahmanical life. Chapter 5 here, called "Defilements of the Soul, and the Means of Purification" is especially striking.

Dubois states that this has to do with a central theme: "Defilements and purifications form together one of the most important articles in Brahmanical doctrine and the Hindu creed" (Dubois 1985:33). It concerns here primarily sin, which had left its traces on the soul, and Dubois gives an overview of the many possibilities of liberating oneself from that stain. One could go on a pilgrimage and bathe in sacred rivers, in the sea, or under waterfalls. One could also drink the urine of a cow or recite mantras. Or one could visit a temple or see a *guru*.

The power of contamination, however, is seen from the five sins that a person cannot purify his soul of in this life: the murder of a Brahmin, abortion, drinking alcohol, stealing gold, and sleeping with the wife of one's guru. It is not until after death these missteps the Brahmin has committed will be visited on the Brahmin—by punishment in hell or a very unfavourable reincarnation.

The origin of the innumerable purity regulations is very old—there is no dispute about that. And many were already struck in Dubois' time by the fact that there were remarkable similarities between the Hindu and the Jewish regulations. Nevertheless, Dubois did not assume that the Hindus had borrowed their rules from the Jewish laws. In a very dated, historicising approach to the book of Genesis, he does suggest that this understanding of purity goes back to traditions from the time before the Deluge. The Hindus then ultimately developed their own system in India with their own criteria of purity and their own rules for behaviour. And he is certainly right about the latter, in contrast to the eighteenth-century Jesuits who saw nothing more in the morality of Hinduism than something derived from Judaism.

Dubois illustrates how strongly the sense of contamination is rooted in the Brahmanical culture by memories from his own travels. He relates that he was usually well received on his travels around Mysore. This occurred also because his servants told everyone that, as a priest of Sarveśvara, he followed all Brahmanical rules strictly and abstained from meat and alcohol.[10] Although the latter was not completely true, it did open all doors for him.

10 The divine name Sarveśvara (Master of all) had been introduced by Roberto de Nobili, see Chapter 3.

Sometimes it went wrong, however. He relates how he was reluctantly received by a Brahmanical village chief and closely watched by the latter's family. At a certain moment, the son of the family claimed he had seen one of Dubois' servants leave the house for a bowel movement and had re-entered the house without washing. A great commotion immediately ensued in which the whole village became involved. The head of the house was furious that his house had been contaminated, demanded that the servant in question be severely punished, and expected financial compensation for the costs of the ritual purification. Though the servant swore that it was not a bowel movement and that he had only urinated (for which washing was not necessary), he was not heeded. Dubois had to move with his entire company to a cow barn, and the dispute was to be resumed the following morning. Dubois was wise enough not to wait for that and fled the village in the middle of the night.

9 Reincarnation

The third part of Dubois' book concerns religious doctrines and institutions. The second chapter deals with *metempsychosis*, or reincarnation.

Dubois begins his treatment with a summary of the Indian teaching on this issue as articulated in the *Bhāgavata Purāṇa*. The emphasis lies on the automatic character of the destiny of the human being: it is purely on the basis of his merit during his life that the soul migrates to a human body or the body of an animal. The soul can end up in an insect, a reptile, a bird, a mammal, or a human being. In case one has accumulated a great deal of merit, the soul can first be rewarded with a stay in heaven (*svarga*). Serious misdeeds should first be atoned for in hell (*nāraka*).

The doctrine of reincarnation could already be found in classical antiquity, in Pythagoras and Plato. Dubois suggests that they could have been taken over from the Indians. Unlike the Greeks, however, the Indians were never tempted to connect certain lengths of time to the journey the soul had to take to achieve the highest perfection. In the sacred texts of the Hindus, the impression was given that, in any case, the soul had to undergo a very long penitence and contemplation in order to attain the final goal.

The terrors of hell are described in detail in the writings. Dubois quotes the *Padma Purāṇa* extensively, in which the punishments for the damned are described in an almost sadistic way for everyone according to the worst sin he has committed. Thus, some have to swim in pools full of dog urine; others have a string through their nostrils by which they are pulled over razor-sharp knives; still others stand between two flat rocks that slam together, crushing them without killing them.

Dubois puts the emphasis in his book on the fact that precisely in these teachings of the future after death, something is preserved of the truth that is inscribed in the human heart. Thus, the Hindus also recognised the immortality of the soul and the other existence in which good is rewarded and evil punished. Although he continually engaged in critical commentary on the idolatry that corrupted all truth, traces of the reality of the Almighty could, apparently, be detected in Hindu circles.

Bibliography

Text Editions and Translations

Cœurdoux, G.-L. (1987). *Mœurs et coutumes des Indiens: Un inédit du Père G.-L. Cœurdoux s.j. dans la version de N.-J. Desvaulx*. Ed. Sylvia Murr. L'inde philosophique entre Bossuet et Voltaire 1. Paris: École française d'Extrême-Orient.

Dubois, J.A. (1985). *Hindu Manners, Customs and Ceremonies*. Ed. Henry K. Beauchamp. 3rd ed. 5th impression. Delhi: Oxford University Press.

Dubois, J.A. (1826). *Le Pantcha-Tantra ou les cinq ruses: Fables du Brahme Vichnou-Sarme, aventures de Paramarta, et autres contes*. Paris: J.-S. Merlin.

Dubois, J.A. (1823). *Letters on the State of Christianity in India: In which the Conversion of the Hindoos is Considered as Impracticable*. London: Longman, Hurst, Rees, Orme, Brown, and Green.

Secondary Literature

Cornille, Catherine (2008). "Missionary Views of Hinduism." *Journal of Hindu-Christian Studies* 21: 28–32.

DeSmet, R. (1990). "Review of Sylvie Murr, Moeurs et Coutumes des Indiens/L'Indologie du Père Coeurdoux." *Indian Theological Studies* 27: 371–73.

Dharampal-Frick, Gita (2006). "'… ausgesandt, das Heidenthum in Indien auszurotten, nicht aber den heidnischen Unsinn in Europa zu verbreiten': Bartholomäus Ziegenbalg und die Hallesche Tranquebar-Mission zwischen pietistischem Sendungsbewusstsein und ethnologischer Aufklärung." In: Michael Mann (ed.). *Europäische Aufklärung und protestantische Mission in Indien*. Heidelberg: Draupadi Verlag. Pp. 143–63.

Hoole, Elijah (1844). *Madras, Mysore, and the South of India: Or, A Personal Narrative*. 2nd ed. London: Longman, Brown, Green, and Longmans.

Hough, James (1824). *A Reply to the Letters of the Abbé Dubois on the State of Christianity in India*. London: L.B. Seeley & Son.

Launay, Adrien (1898). *Histoire des Missions de l'Inde. Pondichéry, Maïssour, Coïmbatour. Five Volumes*. Paris: Ancienne maison Charles Douniol.

Mazon, A. (1899). "L'abbé Dubois, de St-Remèze." *Revue Historique, Archéologique, Littéraire et Pittoresque du Vivarais Illustrée* 7: 49–57, 97–109, 145–62, 193–210, 241–59.

Mohan, Jyoti (2004). "British and French Ethnographies of India: Dubois and his English Commentators." *French Colonial History* 5: 229–46.

Murr, Sylvia (1987). *L'indologie du Père Cœurdoux: Stratégies, apologétique et scientificité*. L'inde philosophique entre Bossuet et Voltaire 2. Paris: École française d'Extrême-Orient.

Murr, Sylvia (1977). "Nicolas Jacques Desvaulx (1745–1823), véritable auteur des 'Mœurs, institutions et cérémonies des peuples de l'Inde', de l'Abbé Dubois." *Puruṣārtha* III: 245–58.

Neill, Stephen (1985). *A History of Christianity in India 1707–1858*. Cambridge: Cambridge University Press.

Sweetman, Will (2003). *Mapping Hinduism: 'Hinduism' and the Study of Indian Religions, 1600–1776*. Neue Hallesche Berichte 4. Halle: Verlag der Franckeschen Stiftungen.

CHAPTER 7

British Government Officials: John Muir and Nascent Indology

1 The East Indian Company

The interest of the British East Indian Company in Abbé Dubois' ethnological treatises was not an isolated incident. The trading company had already shown a great curiosity earlier in the culture and religion of the areas in the Indian subcontinent that were under their control. That was not so much because of commitment to Christian missionary work, for the East India Company had long disapproved of missionary work. The Company was dedicated exclusively to trade, and the activities of missionaries could lead to unrest and have a detrimental effect on trade interests. It was therefore standard policy to bar all forms of missionary activity from British territory. The missionaries who sought to make contact with the Indians thus worked out of the forts that served the Danes or the French as colonial support centres: Tharangambadi and Serampore, as well as Pondicherry.

At the end of the eighteenth century, the Company broke through the monopoly held by the Christian missionaries until then on the knowledge of the native languages. The Company stimulated their employees to learn the languages of the inhabitants and to study their literature. And it began to make greater use itself of the knowledge that missionaries had acquired, as is apparent from their purchase of Abbé Dubois' work.

2 An Influential Translation

The first example of the new course that the Company was taking was the publication of a translation of one of the most important sacred texts of Hinduism. In 1785, the directors published an English version of the Bhagavad Gītā, announced in the foreword to be "a very curious specimen of the Literature, the Mythology, and Morality of the ancient Hindoos" (Wilkins 1785:5). That foreword was written by no one less than the governor-general, Warren Hastings (1732–1818). Not only was he the one who presented the final result, he had also played a significant role at the beginning of the whole translation project. One of the staff members, Charles Wilkins (1749–1836), was given the task of

 | DOI:10.1163/9789004420076_009

translating this work by the governor-general. On the title page Wilkins was very expressly referred to as a "Senior Merchant" of the East India Company.

Wilkins was a linguistic genius: not only had he mastered the language used for diplomacy, Persian, but the everyday language of the people as well, Bengali. A printer by training, he made himself useful by designing fonts for the latter language. He was chosen by the governor to also learn the holy language of the Brahmins, Sanskrit. When he needed a leave of absence for health reasons, he was transferred for some time to Varanasi (Benares), where he had the opportunity to be instructed in Sanskrit by a Brahmanical scholar. Wilkins was not afraid to dream big: he was determined to use his newly acquired linguistic knowledge to translate the whole of the *Mahābhārata*, which consisted of at least 100,000 couplets. He never completed a full translation of this old epic, but he did translate some parts of it, including the Bhagavad Gītā, into English within a few years.[1]

For his translation, Wilkins had to design a system of diacritical marks to be able to reproduce Sanskrit names and terms in Latin script. It is already apparent from the title of his book how carefully he went about this transcription, making a meticulous distinction between short and long vowels: *The Bhăgvăt-Gēētā, or Dialogues of Krĕēshnă and Ărjŏŏn*. His reverence for the text that emerges here was also instrumental in gaining him access to this sacred work. About this work he wrote that "[t]he *Brahmans* esteem this work to contain all the grand mysteries of their religion; and so careful are they to conceal it from the knowledge of those of a different persuasion …." (Wilkins 1785:19). Wilkins, however, believed that it was because of the wise administration of the British government that the Brahmins worked with him. It is certainly doubtful as to whether the Brahmins were happy with his conclusions. Wilkins saw the Gītā as a work that countered the polytheism of the Vedas. In line with the fashion of the time, he viewed the modern Brahmins as "Unitarians: but, at the same time that they believe but in one God, an universal spirit, they so far comply with the prejudices of the vulgar, as outwardly to perform all the ceremonies" (Wilkins 1785:20).

Hastings, the governor-general, also used the translation of the Bhagavad Gītā as proof that there were modern aspects to be found in Hinduism. Europeans might have viewed the Hindus as half-savage, but, according to him, whoever studied their literature would have come to a different conclusion. Hastings appeared to be especially impressed by the call in the Gītā to spiritual

1 An episode from other parts of the *Mahābhārata*, namely, the myth of the churning of the oceans (Mbh. 1:15–17), is added to this translation of the Bhagavad Gītā. See Wilkins 1785:106–11.

discipline. Spiritual exercises that included concentrating on the divine reminded him of what was practised in some Roman Catholic churches. With great approval, he cited the verse that he saw to be the conclusion to the Bhagavad Gītā:

> Hath what I have been speaking, O *Arjoon*, been heard with thy mind fixed to one point?
> Is the distraction of thought, which arose from thy ignorance, removed?
>
> WILKINS 1785:96 [Bhagavad Gītā 18:72]; cited in Hastings in WILKINS 1785:8

3 A Learned Society

The British in India who were interested in the languages and culture of India found each other in these years. In 1784, they founded an academic society to promote the study of India in all its aspects, and the Asiatic Society of Bengal was formed by thirty European men. Governor-General Hastings had stimulated the founding of such a society, but the actual founder was another prominent British administrator who would play a decisive role in the development of the nascent Indology, William Jones (1746–1794).

Jones already knew several languages before he arrived in India in 1783, including Persian and Arabic, but Sanskrit was not taught in Europe at that time. When he was appointed judge in the supreme court of Kolkata (Calcutta), he did, however, have the opportunity to master the ancient language of the Hindus. He also had a good reason for doing so. Arguments were regularly made in court based on the classic Hindu legal tradition, and the British, in principle, wanted to take these arguments into consideration in court. Native scholars were therefore employed to supply and translate Sanskrit texts. Jones did not want to be dependent on the contribution of these 'court pundits' without being able to check their work in any way.

After failing to appropriate Wilkins' Sanskrit teacher for himself, Jones managed—with difficulty—to find his own teacher in Krishnanagar, Nadia, almost a hundred kilometres north of Kolkata. This *paṇḍit*, Ramalocana Kanthavarna, taught him the first principles of Sanskrit (Rosane Rocher in Cannon and Brine 1995:56–58). Jones, however, also experienced how difficult it was to be admitted, as a non-Hindu, into the circle of those who knew the sacred language. Although Ramalocana himself was not a Brahmin, he did have great objections to bringing an unclean, non-vegetarian foreigner into the sacred domain of Sanskrit. Purification rituals had to be carried out, and, according to tradition, Jones had have his lessons in the morning, without breakfast. He could only—by way of exception—have a cup of tea once every so often (Franklin 2011:35).

His instruction was quite fruitful, for after a year he was already able to read, on his own, the old lawbooks that were the reason why he started this process. An even greater achievement was that he was also able, after some time, to comprehend the literary Sanskrit of classical poets like Kālidāsa (fifth century C.E.). The first text that Jones published in English was thus *Śakuntalā*, Kālidāsa's famous play, taken from a legend in the *Mahābhārata*. The play caused a sensation when it appeared in English in 1789: for the first time, people in Europe realised that there was a literary tradition in India that was the equal of that on their own continent (Bakker 1988:101).

The study of old lawbooks did lead to an important publication in the area of law. The *Institutes of Hindu Law or, the Ordinances of Menu, according to the Gloss of Cullúca* was published in 1796. This was the translation of the traditional 'lawbook of Manu,' the *Mānavadharmaśāstra*, a very comprehensive body of legal and moral provisions and the result of hundreds of years of ethical reflection. This publication was of great importance for Jones' own work and that of his colleagues on the supreme court, and it also proved to be a goldmine for many others who were involved in law and ethics.

Jones became most famous, however, for a lecture delivered to the Asiatic Society, which was also published in the society's journal, *Asiatick Researches*. At that time, Jones had been studying Sanskrit for no more than half a year. Nonetheless, he had acquired such insight into the grammar and vocabulary of that language that he dared to present the thesis that Sanskrit was related to Latin and Greek and all the languages that developed from them. He argued:

> The *Sanscrit* language, whatever be its antiquity, is of a wonderful structure; more perfect than the *Greek*, more copious than the *Latin*, and more exquisitely refined than either, yet bearing to both of them a stronger affinity, both in the roots of verbs and in the forms of grammar, than could possibly have been produced by accident.
>
> Cited in FRANKLIN 2011:36

It was Jones who discovered that Indo-European was the common source of European and Indian languages. The activities of the Asiatic Society of Bengal also strongly stimulated the study of the languages and cultures of India at European universities. In particular, it was German linguists who continued the research into the common source of the Indo-European languages. Thus, Friedrich von Schlegel (1772–1829) and Wilhelm Freiherr von Humboldt

(1767–1835) taught Sanskrit and even started studying the philosophy of ancient India that went along with the language (Bakker 1995:101–07). Germany, which had no colonial connection with Asia, became the teacher in this area: "Germania docet." It was also a German who would ultimately make the biggest contribution to opening up early Hindu literature: Friedrich Max Müller from Dessau (1823–1900) became a professor at Oxford and saw to it that the Upaniṣads and the Ṛg-Veda became accessible to the European public.

4 The Serampore Trio

More and more was discovered about the Hindu heritage during the nineteenth century in India, an activity that both missionaries and government officials were involved in. There was remarkable collaboration between the two groups sometimes, even though they were often adversaries of each other. Thus, in the Danish colony of Serampore, close to Kolkata, were three Baptist missionaries: William Carey (1761–1834), Joshua Marshman (1768–1837), and William Ward (1769–1823). Together, they are known as the Serampore Trio. These missionaries chose to stay in a city that was under Danish authority because they were not welcome in the area administered by the British East India Company. The Company was, after all—as stated above—opposed to the activities of missionaries, and, moreover, these missionaries were not even members of the state church but were Dissenters.

One would expect that the British officials would not want to have anything to do with the three missionaries, but practical interests dictated otherwise. After some time, William Carey became especially proficient in Bengali, and the British were regularly confronted with translation problems. They therefore hired Carey to translate the laws and regulations of the government. And when a college was founded in Fort William in Kolkata in 1800, Carey was appointed professor in Bengali and Sanskrit. There was no other choice—no European was better at Bengali than he (Smith 1913:158).

One of the projects Carey took up at the college in Fort William was the editing and translation of classic Sanskrit literature. This was a joint undertaking of the college and the Asiatic Society of Bengal. Carey prepared the text editions that would be printed at the printing department of his mission in Serampore, and it was hoped that, via the Society, the published works would also reach university circles in Europe. Carey suggested that they publish the *Rāmāyaṇa* first. It was not, perhaps, the most sacred text of the Hindus, but the dry Vedic literature would not keep the attention of the Europeans for very long. In contrast, he viewed the *Rāmāyaṇa* as a book that gave the best understanding of

Hindu mythology and, moreover, would be sensational enough to interest readers (Smith 1913:171).[2]

The first part of the *Rāmāyaṇa* rolled off the presses of the Mission Press in Serampore in 1806. It was a great achievement with respect to printing techniques. The Sanskrit text of the epic was printed in *devanāgari* letters, with an English translation underneath—in European script of course—and finally, at the bottom of the page, there were notes in English that helped explain the text. William Carey and Joshua Marshman took care of the text and translation, while the third missionary, William Ward, looked after the printing. With this publication, the Serampore Trio proved they were up to the challenge of academic work. And the British government officials would have had no regrets about their decision to work with these missionaries. A second and third part published respectively in 1808 and 1810 completed the publication.

5 'Little Britain' in a Foreign Society

The government official who would attract the most attention because of his knowledge of Indian languages was certainly John Muir (1810–1882). Not only did he speak Bengali and Persian and read Sanskrit, he was also able to write treatises in the latter language. That made him stand head and shoulders above his colleagues who had certainly acquired some knowledge of the languages during their education but did not improve much after arriving in India. In general, it was so that life in the circles of the British government officials was largely directed at reproducing the atmosphere of the mother country. They were more British than the British and attempted to keep a great distance between themselves and the surrounding culture. A popular picture book, *Curry and Rice*, published in the middle of the nineteenth century was typical. It gave a humorous picture of life in a colonial setting that was a faithful reproduction of English village life, complete with horse races and dance parties.[3]

There were, of course, exceptions—men who were sincerely interested in the world in which they found themselves and attempted to study what was foreign to them. Frederick Shore (1799–1837), who was stationed for several years in the remote Dehra Dun at the foot of the Himalayas, became the foremost expert of Indian nature, particularly in the area of ornithology. He was thus someone to whom the small, closed culture of the officials meant nothing,

2 Smith quotes Carey here, who wrote: "the best account of Hindoo mythology that any one book will, and has extravagancy enough to excite a wish to read it through."

3 This work was first published in 1859 and was reprinted several times.

"faith turned in on itself of their own superiority and a banishment outside of the English horizon of what almost unchangeably is called the 'black fellows'" (Kolff 1993:638). But not many would go as far as Shore: he would go to annual fairs disguised as a native doctor so that he could hear what the people were talking about.

6 The Christian Faith Disseminated

John Muir was a less striking figure, an ordinary civil servant who was set for a nice career in the department of the interior.[4] He did have, however, an enthusiasm that went beyond the ordinary, and he was also exceptionally talented. Originally from Scotland, he had studied literature as a young man at the University of Glasgow and then attended the college of the East India Company in Haileybury, north of London, for two years. At that time, the programme at the college was very much focused on languages and also offered Sanskrit. After arriving in British India, he took a short follow-up course at the Fort William College in Kolkata. In 1829, Muir could begin his duties at his first post, Nadia (West Bengal).

Muir was Presbyterian and belonged to the Church of Scotland. His family felt a strong affinity with the Evangelical movement that had started at the end of the eighteenth century, and Muir was also inspired by this movement throughout his life, with its heavy emphasis on personal experience and missionary ideals. It was primarily Anglicans he met in India, for the Company was traditionally connected with the Church of England. But there as well, he sought and found contact with those who shared the same affinity for Evangelicalism.

That faith and theology were supremely important to him was generally well known. When he began corresponding at an advanced age with the professor of theology Abraham Kuenen in Leiden, the latter even addressed him by a clerical title. Muir protested politely:

> I may also mention that I have no title to the honourable appellation of "Rev^{d}" which you give me on the address of your letter, as I am a layman. I was long in the Civil Service of our late East India Company in Bengal. The interest which I take in theological matters is not therefore a professional one, though not the less legitimate on that account.
>
> Letter from JOHN MUIR to ABRAHAM KUENEN, 8 May 1869

4 For a more extensive treatment of John Muir and his brother William, also a colonial civil servant and well-known Islamologist, see Powell 2010.

The Evangelicals among the government officials found each other easily, and they also maintained contact with those who had come to India to serve as missionaries. Missionary projects, particularly in the area of education, could certainly count on the support of Muir and his circle. Many a missionary school in his successive posts profited from his commitment to the faith and the Church. After his start in the area around Kolkata, he spent most of his career in what were called the 'North-Western Provinces,' the area of the Ganges delta, which gave him ample opportunity to converse with Brahmanical scholars. It was this aspect of his appointment that drew him the most. He even served as principal of the well-known Sanskrit College in Varanasi (Benares). He could thus increase his own knowledge of Sanskrit and work on what mattered most to him: presenting the Christian faith in the world of classical, scholarly Hinduism.

Not every government official was inclined to let so much of his own faith and missionary zeal show through in his administrative work. The company was, after all, a commercial enterprise, and, for that reason, some felt very strongly about maintaining neutrality with respect to religion. Muir, however, assumed that there could be no objection to an objective presentation of Hinduism and Christianity, also if the differences between both traditions were clearly indicated in such a presentation (Powell 2010:86). This led to one of the most interesting projects in the area of mission in India carried out by a government official.

7 Writing in Sanskrit

John Muir was very much at home in Sanskrit. He knew the religious literature of India well, and he was also familiar with the new Christian use of the language. In Kolkata, shortly after his arrival, he came into contact with William Carey, who had translated the Bible into Sanskrit. Following Carey, Muir was convinced that the top layer of Hindu society could be reached with the Christian message if Sanskrit was used. After all, Brahmins took presentations of religion and morality seriously only if they were done in their own sacred language.

This was supplemented by an argument from experience. Missionaries usually proclaimed the message of the Christian faith in India by speaking in the markets. This 'bazaar preaching' was often characterised by a blunt condemnation of the faith of those listening and an ungracious pronouncement of eternal damnation for those who did not convert. Muir had often been irritated by this approach, which he found to be unworthy and did not see as effective. If the street preachers did not appear to have any knowledge of what was sacred to their audience, they would be ignored. Muir repeatedly referred to the example of Paul, who addressed his audience in Athens in a way that connected with the Athenians' own culture and religion.

Muir was one of the few who was able to do it in a different way, for he had mastered Sanskrit so well that he could also write treatises in that language that the learned reader could understand and appreciate. Thus, in 1839 he published for the first time a treatise on religion in an 'Indian' form. The book was written in Sanskrit, in the form of a dialogue between a student and his teacher, in a total of 379 verses in a certain metre (*anuṣṭubh*). It is called *Mataparīkṣā*, An Examination of Religions. What those religions were and what the writer's purpose was is immediately clear from the English subtitle: *A Sketch of the Argument for Christianity and against Hinduism*.[5]

Muir continued to work on this after its first publication in 1839. A second edition was published In the following year that was three times as large. And in the period from 1852 to 1854, he published a definitive *Mataparīkṣā* in two parts. The first analysed the Hindu writings, and the second presented the Christian faith. This edition also includes an English translation so that Westerners who were interested could follow the argument.

8 Divine Properties

In the first edition, however, Muir shows clearly what his purpose was and how he saw such a work as being beneficial for Hindu readers. He used a short quote, neatly printed in Greek, from Paul's letters as a motto for the book. Even though the intended readers would not have understood it, it probably showed them that Christians had their own esteemed holy language. The quote was from 1 Corinthians 9:19–22, in which Paul argued that he had adapted to others in his preaching of the message of salvation: he had "become all things to all men."

Muir has very appreciative things to say about Hinduism, the ancientness of their nation, the reverence for their priestly caste, the holiness of their writings. It was very important to him to express himself in such a way that *paṇḍit*s would want to listen to the message. The message that Muir wanted to bring linked up closely with the theological fashion of the time. The starting point was that reason and revelation complemented each other: knowledge of God could be acquired through reason. The Anglican theologian William Paley (1743–1805) argued for this position, and it was this evidential theology that the

5 Muir's project and the reactions it evoked are extensively described in Young 1981.

Mataparīkṣā linked up with. Muir had also been taught that theology while attending the college of the East Indian Company in Haileybury, where Paley's books were required reading (Powell 2010:56; cf. Young 1981:70–71).

The structure of the *Mataparīkṣā* is thus remarkably rational. The first chapter starts off firmly with describing the properties of God, which true religion has to reflect. The earth displays the glory of the all-present God. The knowledge of good and evil, which is innate to everyone, goes back to Him, and God will reward the good and punish sin. This is followed by a short chapter on the necessity of revelation. Religions are always different in the various countries. There are traditions that blaspheme God and worship other spirits, which is why people turn to their scriptures.

But what is then the criterium for true scriptures? In the third chapter, the teacher presents different answers. First of all, the founder of a true teaching has the power to perform miracles. Then comes the argument about holiness:

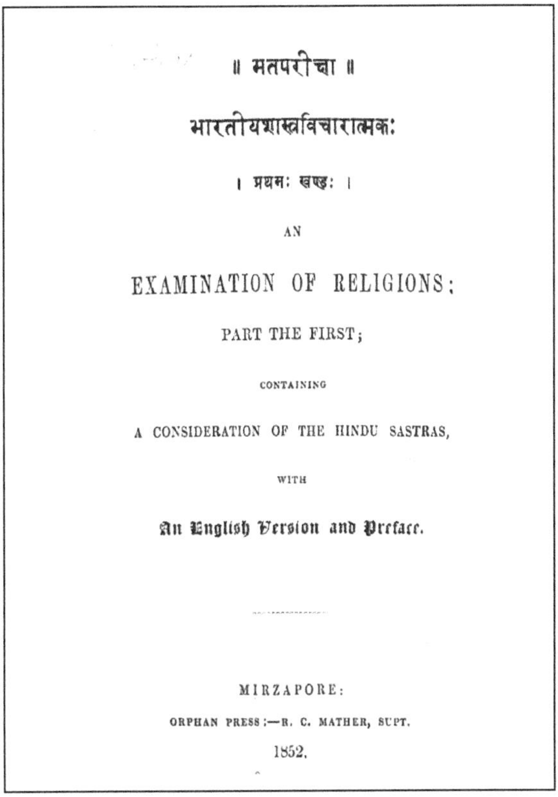
॥ मतपरीक्षा ॥

भारतीयशास्त्रविचारात्मकः

। प्रथमः खण्डः ।

AN

EXAMINATION OF RELIGIONS;

PART THE FIRST;

CONTAINING

A CONSIDERATION OF THE HINDU SASTRAS,

WITH

An English Version and Preface.

MIRZAPORE:

ORPHAN PRESS:—R. C. MATHER, SUPT.

1852.

FIGURE 11 Title page of the final edition of Muir's Mataparīkṣā (1852)

God is holy and scriptures that include embarrassing stories are thus not divine. The final answer has to do with universality: there is only one God and thus only one true religion. A teaching that is not for everyone does not come from God.

"Which scriptures then have all three characteristics of truth?" the student asks at the beginning of chapter 4. And then the teacher gives the expected answer: "Only the Christian teaching has all three." He continues with a presentation of the life of Jesus Christ, paying a great deal of attention to the miracles he performed and to the perseverance of the first disciples who are not even deterred from their faith by oppression. The moral elevation of the commandments of Christianity is also praised. Then the argument ends in the idea that is central to the book: "Now, I say, third, that Christian dogmatics teaches correctly about the doctrine of truth that it is universal."[6] The Christian faith is not intended for one caste. To the contrary, all had sinned, and all, Westerners and Indians, can be saved by God's grace.

This is followed by a long chapter that closely examines Hinduism. But here Muir does not reach the same level as the earlier chapters. Many of the traditional objections of Christian preachers to the religion of India are simply repeated here, albeit in beautiful Sanskrit versification. Muir does not find the miracle stories in the Hindu myths convincing and calls the stories about demonic and divine figures childish and deceptive. But it is unclear as to what criterion he is using to claim this. If it is a matter of the holiness of God, which the scriptures have to reflect, Hinduism does not score very high: Brahmā, Viṣṇu, and Śiva are criticised severely. And Muir brings out the contradictions especially in the Hindu writings, although one could point to contradictions in the Bible as well. Finally, Hinduism fails, according to Muir, also with respect to the third characteristic of true scriptures: universality. The way in which the Brahmins exalt themselves above other castes cannot be harmonised with the true teaching that had to be equal for all people. And the rules for living in the ethical scriptures, the *dharmaśāstras*, did not apply at all to foreigners.

It is apparent from his work that Muir was well informed about what was known in his time about the development of religion in India. He gives a flawless picture of the development of the religion from Vedic times to belief in God in the *Purāṇas*. He was also quite familiar with the various philosophical systems but found it difficult to deal with different positions that, according to Hindus, certainly could exist alongside each other. And he could not understand that mythological narratives belong to another genre than historical reports.

6 *Mataparīkṣā* 21 (IV:63): "idānīṃ satyaśāstrasya tṛtīyaṃ vacmi lakṣaṇaṃ sāmānyamiti khṛṣṭīye dharme samyak pradarśitaṃ."

9 Hindus Respond to the Challenge

The *Mataparīkṣā* was intended to tempt the Brahmanical scholars into a debate with Christians. Muir was successful in this, for a number of Brahmins responded in public to his presentation of Hinduism and Christian faith. That means, however, that they were not at all convinced by Muir's arguments. In divergent ways and with varying intensity, they all sprung to the defence of their ancestral religion.[7]

The first apologist for Hinduism was Somanath Vyas (1807–1885).[8] As a Brahmanical scholar, he was primarily interested in the natural sciences, astronomy in particular. His acquaintance with Western ideas such as the Copernican worldview also brought him to a certain reorientation in his religious tradition. Fascinated as he was by the technical developments of the discoveries of the Europeans—steamboats and hot air balloons—he was open to a comparison of cultures. The much used argument of Europeans that it was also because of the influence of Christianity that their continent had brought about this progress roused him to respond.

As a response to the *Mataparīkṣā* (An Examination of Religions), he wrote the *Mataparīkṣāśikṣā* (A Study in the Examination of Religions) in the same year, i.e., 1839. His starting point was that all religion was ultimately one and that the various religions did not contradict each other. He argued that God created the different human races on earth in their diversity and that He had given each their own revelation with their own scriptures. That took away the need Christians felt to convert others. And the only task for Hindus was to examine their own tradition for elements that could give direction in new circumstances.

Much different was the approach of the second Brahmin to respond to the *Mataparīkṣā*. Harachandra Tarkapanchanana represented the most strongly conceivable antithetical approach to Christianity.[9] His *Mataparīkṣottara* (A Response to the Writer of An Examination of Religions) was published in 1840. It is a vicious attack on the missionaries and their faith. He also ridiculed those Hindus whom the missionaries had managed to convert: they were only after the missionaries' pretty daughters or were hankering for alcohol or meat. But it was the faith itself that was wrong. In connection with the birth of Jesus, Harachandra reported that his mother Mary had stayed in a

7 Three of the responses are very well explained in Young 1981.

8 For him, see Young 1981:80–92, 143–49, and also Young 2008.

9 Young 1981:93–101, 149–53.

temple where she had had sex with many priests. The virgin birth had been invented to conceal the abuse.

In contrast to that, Harachandra was completely convinced of the superiority of Hinduism and saw Christianity as a newcomer in the world of religions. As a new book, the Bible was not even worthy of standing in the shadow the ancient Vedas that had existed for centuries. There was therefore no reason for Hindus to pay any attention to it—given the Hindus' venerable tradition, such a preposterous religion like Christianity could only be met with ridicule. Understandably, Harachandra's work was characterised by Christian readers as "Extra Vedos nulla salus."[10]

Finally, a Brahmin responded to the *Mataparīkṣā* who was just as opposed to the Christian faith as Harachandra was but he converted years later and was baptised. Nilakantha Goreh (1825–1885) was nowhere near that point when he wrote the *Śāstratattvavinirṇaya* (The Proof of the Truth of the Scriptures) in 1844.[11] The scriptures whose truth he wanted to defend were the Hindu ones. That was why he was so opposed to the work of the Christian street preachers, certainly when that occurred in the holy city of Vanarasi (Benares). He resisted by engaging in conversations with missionaries and by also responding to Muir's book.

Nilakantha's work was a very specific rejection of Christianity, which made dialogue almost impossible. He assumed that Christianity was a heresy (*mohadharma*), which, according to the Hindu religion, was a teaching that was created by a divinity with the express purpose of misleading people. In previous lives, Christians had apparently built up such bad karma that they, by way of punishment, were caught up in a delusion they could not free themselves from. It was their own fault that they could not even see how wrong their religion was.

That it was precisely this well-armed opponent of the Christian faith who was later baptised and ultimately became the first native systematic theologian of India can be called an irony of history. In any case, it proves the strength of Muir's work. Nilakantha, who was later called Nehemiah, always said that it was precisely because of the *Mataparīkṣā* that he came to the Christian faith.

---

10 This is a play on the saying by the church father, Cyprian (3rd century): "Extra ecclesiam nulla salus" (There is no salvation outside the Church); it was Paul Deussen (1845–1919) who first coined the phrase in relation to Harachandra's work. See Young 1981:152.

11 Young 1981:101–08, 153–61. For Nilakantha Goreh, see also Schouten 2008: 35–53.

10 Other Research into Hinduism

After this remarkable publication, Muir continued to study the history of Hinduism. The results of that can be found in the later edition of the *Mataparīkṣā*, which appeared in 1852–1854. Now the book had expanded into two parts: Hinduism was first described in detail and evaluated in the first part, and the Christian faith was discussed in just as extensive a way in the second. Interested Hindus were now even confronted with the stories and writings of numerous church fathers from Clement of Rome to Eusebius of Caesarea. It is striking how Muir worked many new discoveries of British and German Indologists into the first part of his work (Powell 2010:91).

Nonetheless, Muir could make his greatest contribution in the area of research into Hinduism only after he retired in 1853 and had gone back to Scotland. As a lifelong bachelor, retirement allowed him to devote all his time and energy into studying and writing about Indology.

The five-volume *Original Texts*, in which he published what could be seen as prooftexts for the religious and mythological ideas, as well as the social and ethical rules of the Hindus, was very impressive. Thus, the first part includes a staggering amount of texts in Sanskrit and translations of all passages from the sacred texts on which the caste system is based. Other parts describe the origins of the Aryans and the development of the religion from the Vedic period into the later forms of Hinduism. It is this publication on sources that increased Muir's status as Indologist. The many accolades he received, including honorary doctorates from three universities, probably led to forgetting that he began his career as a lowly official with the East Indian Company.

Nevertheless, what drove him was not pure science for the sake of science. Until his death in 1882, he was always concerned what could help the people in India make progress. He dedicated himself to the expansion of the Christian faith as an alternative to Hinduism. In later life, however, he thought less in terms of contradiction and contrasts and was more inclined to search in Hinduism for what could be connected with Christian morality in the area of ethics and could also help guide India's development (Powell 2010:283; see also Van der Veer 2001:24).

In a little book that was published in 1874, he presented a number of short texts from Indian sources in which he himself was struck by the similarities with the Christian faith. In the foreword, he emphasised that he had not tried at all in his translations to make the similarities greater than they were in the original. Apparently, the religions that he once saw as complete opposites were more aligned with each other than he previously thought.

Death comes, and makes a man his prey,
A man whose powers are yet unspent,
Like one on gathering flowers intent,
Whose thoughts are turned another way.

Begin betimes to practise good,
Lest fate surprise thee unawares
Amid thy round of schemes and cares;
To-morrow's task to-day conclude.

For who can tell how things may chance,
And who may all this day survive?
While yet a stripling, therefore, strive,–
On virtue's arduous path advance.

MUIR 1874:2–3, 22[12]

Bibliography

Archival Records

Leiden University, Special Collections.
Correspondence of John Muir with Abraham Kuenen 1869–1881 (BPL 3028).

Text Editions and Translations

Carey, William, and Joshua Marshman (1806–1810). *The Ramayuna of Valmeeki, in the Original Sungskrit, with a Prose Translation.* Three Volumes. Serampore: s.n.

Jones, William (1796). *Institutes of Hindu Law; or, the Ordinances of Menu, according to the Gloss of Cullúca.* Calcutta/London: Government/J. Sewell and J. Debrett.

Muir, J. (1874). *Religious and Moral Sentiments Freely Translated from Indian Writers.* Edinburgh.

Muir, J. (1860–1872). *Original Sanskrit Texts on the Origin and History of the People of India, their Religion and Institutions.* Five volumes. London: Trübner & Co.

Muir, J. (1852–1854). *Mataparīkṣā: An Examination of Religions.* Two volumes. Mirzapore/Calcutta: Orphan Press/Bishop's College Press.

Muir, J. (1839). *Mataparīkṣā: A Sketch of the Argument for Christianity and against Hinduism, In Sanskrit Verse.* Calcutta: Bishop's College Press.

12 In the notes he indicates Mahābhārata XII:6534ff. as a source and refers here to Ecclesiastes 9:10 and 12:1.

Wilkins, Charles (1785). *The Bhăgvăt-Gēētā, or Dialogues of Krēēshnă and Ărjŏŏn.* London: C. Nourse.

Secondary Literature

Atkinson, George F. (1859). *Curry & Rice (on Forty Plates) or the Ingredients of Social Life at 'Our' Station in India.* London: Day & Son.

Bakker, Hans (1988). "De culturele ontdekking van India: Romantische Geestdrift en de Opkomst der Oriëntalistiek." In: Hans Bakker and Martin Gosman (eds.). *De Oriënt: droom of dreiging?* Kampen: Kok Agora. Pp. 94–112.

Cannon, Garland and Kevin R. Brine (eds.) (1995). *Objects of Enquiry: The Life, Contributions, and Influences of Sir William Jones (1746–1794).* New York/London: New York University Press.

Franklin, Michael J. (2011). *'Orientalist Jones': Sir William Jones, Poet, Lawyer, and Linguist (1746–1794).* Oxford/New York: Oxford University Press.

Frasch, Tilman (2008). "'Deliver their land from error's chain': Mission und Kolonialherrschaft in Indien, 1793–1857." In: Michael Mann (ed.). *Aufgeklärter Geist und evangelische Missionen in Indien.* Heidelberg: Draupadi Verlag. Pp. 103–16.

Halbfass, Wilhelm (1981). *Indien und Europa: Perspektiven ihrer geistigen Begegnung.* Basel/Stuttgart: Schwabe.

Kolff, D.H.A. (1993). "Een Brits-Indische omwandeling." *De Gids* 156: 635–45.

Powell, A.A. (2010). *Scottish Orientalists and India: The Muir Brothers, Religion, Education and Empire.* Worlds of the East India Company 4. Woodbridge: Boydell Press.

Schouten, Jan Peter (2008). *Jesus as Guru: The Image of Christ among Hindus and Christians in India.* Transl. Henry and Lucy Jansen. Currents of Encounter 36. Amsterdam/New York: Rodopi.

Smith, George (1913). *The Life of William Carey: Shoemaker and Missionary.* 2nd ed. London/New York: J.M. Dent/Dutton.

Veer, P. van der (2001). *Imperial Encounters: Religion and Modernity in India and Britain.* Princeton/Oxford: Princeton University Press.

Young, Richard Fox (2008). "Can Christians Be Bhaktas?" *Journal of Hindu-Christian Studies* 21: 56–62.

Young, Richard Fox (1981). *Resistant Hinduism: Sanskrit Sources on Anti-Christian Apologetics in Early Nineteenth-Century India.* Publications of the De Nobili Research Library VIII. Vienna: Indological Institute University of Vienna.

CHAPTER 8

The Image of the East in the West: Nineteenth-century British India in Fiction and Travel Reports

The new field of Orientalistics continued to develop during the course of the nineteenth century. The sacred language of the Brahmins, Sanskrit, was gradually completely deciphered and the basic texts of Hinduism slowly appeared in translation. The first English translation of the Bhagavad Gītā had already been published at the end of the eighteenth century, in 1785. It was, however, in the nineteenth century that the majority of the sacred texts were translated and published. Major series like Original Sanskrit Texts and Sacred Books of the East made these ancient texts accessible to interested Europeans.

Moreover, at the instigation of the colonial administrators, extensive social-geographical descriptions of many regions of India were produced. The so-called "Gazetteers" not only described the geographical position and natural conditions but also provided detailed information about the population composition, culture, and religions of the regions in question. An enormous quantity of cultural-historical information was collected in series on the castes (Castes and Tribes). The great empire was slowly being mapped.

1 Romantic Orientalism

Nevertheless, this storehouse of information, which was very advantageous especially for academics and civil servants, had only a limited influence on the image that the greater public had of the Indian subcontinent. This image was determined primarily by other kinds of publications, such as literary fiction and well-written travel reports. These helped people form an image of what life in these distant parts of the world was like. After all, the culture and religion of the various parts of India appealed to the imagination precisely at the beginning of the nineteenth century, when Romanticism was at its peak.

It was in this period that a book was published that influenced the picture the reading public had of India more than any other work. This was the extremely successful poem by the Irish writer, Thomas Moore (1779–1852), that bore the mysterious title of *Lalla Rookh* (Moore 1817:1–152).[1] Expectations were

1 For an extensive discussion on *Lalla Rookh*, see Sharafuddin 1994:135–213.

 | DOI:10.1163/9789004420076_010

high already before it was published: the publisher had invested the vast amount of three thousand pounds in its publication. Moore's poem remained extremely popular during the whole of the nineteenth century: numerous reprints appeared, and it was translated into various languages. The work was also the basis for various operas and other musical works.

Lalla Rookh is a textbook example of the movement that would later be called Romantic orientalism. Using stereotypical images of a different, Eastern culture, this tradition created a world in which love, bravery, and beauty dominated life. In any event, it was a world that was radically different from the Western culture of the writer and his readers. Edward Said (1935–2003) was certainly right in this respect in his well-known work, *Orientalism*, when he reproached the "orientalists" for their self-interest in creating a completely different world in their descriptions of the East (Said 1978:passim; see also Rietbergen 2007:55–62). In Moore's case, however, there is nothing that indicates that the invented Eastern world is inferior to the powerful Western one. To the contrary, in Moore's poem, life in the East still offers hope for oppressed people, whereas people in Europe had no future. The struggle of the people in *Lalla Rookh* has rightly been seen as a metaphor for the struggle of the Irish to escape the yoke of the English (Vail 2005).

This very comprehensive work consists of a prose frame surrounding four large poems. The frame describes the journey of Lalla Rookh ('tulip-cheeked'), the daughter of Emperor Aurangzeb (1618–1707), from the court in Delhi to Kashmir, where she is to marry the prince of Bukhara. The bridegroom has sent several servants to Delhi to escort the bride to her new home, among whom is the minstrel Feramorz whose task is to make her journey more pleasant by singing to her. The princess is gradually drawn to the minstrel more and more and falls in love with him. The royal wedding takes place after they arrive in Kashmir, and there it turns out that the bridegroom is none other than Feramorz who escorted his bride disguised as a minstrel.

As can be expected, love is the theme of the songs the minstrel sings for the princess, but these songs are not about uncomplicated relationships in which love can flourish unhindered. Impossible love is the central theme of two very long poems. In "The Veiled Prophet of Khorassan," the protagonist is a soldier in the army of the usurper Mokanna. This cunning villain has managed to add the woman the soldier is in love with to his own harem by announcing that the soldier was dead. In the end, the warlord commits suicide, and the woman is killed by the soldier himself as the result of a misunderstanding. The other large poem, "The Fire-Worshippers," is also about ill-fated love. Here, it is a Zoroastrian warrior who falls in love with the daughter of one of the Arab invaders who oppress his people. Both the warrior and the woman ultimately perish.

Between the two long dramatic poems are two shorter poems with a lighter tone. In "Paradise and the Peri" we meet an angel who has been driven from Paradise and can only return if she brings a precious gift back with her, a gift that turns out to be nothing less than the tear of a remorseful sinner. The essence of this story certainly has nothing to do with Eastern religion but reflects an explicit Christian theme. Finally, the last poem is called "The Light of the Haram." This was the pet name of the favourite wife of Emperor Jahangir (1569–1627), and the verse is thus an ode to this famous empress.

Hinduism plays a subordinate role in the overwhelming pomp and the intense emotions that Moore portrays in his poem. The main characters are, after all, Islamic or Zoroastrian, whereby Islam is painted in a very negative light as the religion of the oppressors. Hinduism does have a function, however, in the poem as the exotic background against which the whole scene takes place. Thus, already immediately at the beginning it says that the princess could be "amused by those graceful dancing-girls of Delhi, who had been permitted by the Bramins of the Great Pagoda to attend her" (Moore 1817:5).[2] And the contrast with Islam is immediately emphasised: the chamberlain who protects good morals and true religion found the presence of the temple dancers abominable. The same contrast is brought out with the introduction of the minstrel. He may be Muslim, but he is viewed as "graceful as that idol of women, Crishna" (Moore 1817:5). The chamberlain will criticise and undercut the minstrel throughout the whole poem.

At one point, the princess, seated in her litter during her journey, sees a Hindu ritual being performed. This scene is particularly touching (Moore 1817: 38–39). A girl is sitting on the bank of a river; she has lit an oil lamp and places it carefully on an earthenware dish with a wreath around it. Then she lets the dish drift away and stares after it anxiously, wondering if it will stay afloat. The princess' attendants tell her that this is a way of offering up a vow for someone who has gone on a journey. If the dish stays afloat, the person who is travelling is assured a safe journey. The princess is touched by the ritual and by what that could mean for her own undertaking.

Moore makes good use of various Eastern motifs in his poem, presenting Hinduism as the religion that represents harmony and beauty. His work was highly esteemed in English-speaking areas, which is apparent from the numerous references to *Lalla Rookh* found in English literature.[3]

2 The chamberlain also refers to the dancing girls later as "worshippers of cows"; cf. Moore 1817:74.

3 The English travel accounts that are discussed in this chapter are no exception. See Eden 1978:223; Urwick 1885:178.

For that matter, the name Lalla Rookh has a special meaning for the Hindus in the Netherlands. There was, namely, a large sailing ship christened after the princess. The first British Indian contract labourers travelled to the Dutch colony of Suriname on the *Lalla Rookh* in 1873 (Schouten 2008a:254).

2 The First Detective Novel

A work of an entirely different nature in English fiction is the novel *The Moonstone* by Wilkie Collins (1824–1889), a writer from a group associated with Charles Dickens (1812–1870). The book appeared in 1868 and ranks as the first detective novel, standing at the head of a long tradition of English detective novels. Collins' book already displays the structure that later became classic: there is a mysterious crime immediately at the beginning—the robbery of a rare costly diamond in this case. A number of intrigues and insinuations ensue from this until a clever police inspector manages to finally unravel the case.

Although the story of the crime and its aftermath takes place in an English country estate, British India is always close. Thus, the lives of the main characters turn out to be linked to the colonial world. Various characters have spent time in India and are able to join in the conversation about the strange Eastern culture. Three mysterious Indians also appear, having made the long journey to England to get ahold of the diamond around which the whole story turns.

The diamond that is stolen is, in essence, the connection with India and with the Hindu religion. Collins has framed his story in an ingenious way in the history of British India and the culture of Hinduism. He writes immediately at the beginning of his book about the conquests of the Muslims and the theft of Hindu treasures that went along with that. The conquest and plundering of Somnath on the west coast by Mahmud of Ghazni in the eleventh century is historical fact (Basham 1975:73). It is certainly not improbable that the Brahmins kept one of the temple images safe by taking it to Varanasi (Benares). This would have been the image of the moon god Candra or Soma, which stood in a central spot in one of the oldest temples of the city. In Collins' story, a third eye has been added to the image in the form of a large diamond.

Although this comes across as fiction, it is certainly not inconceivable. There are, after all, temple images in India that have jewels worked into them. The seventeenth-century explorer Jean-Baptiste Tavernier (1605–1689) described in detail the Kṛṣṇa image in the temple of Jagannātha in Puri, which "had two diamonds as eyes, the smallest of which was about forty carats" (Tavernier 1696:394, 402; cf. Kurin 2017:19–37). And, given that he was a jeweller who specialised in gemstones, he would have known what he was talking about.

When Collins wrote his detective novel, the theme of diamonds in the temple was of great contemporary interest. Shortly before, Emily Eden had published her old travel memoirs in which she wrote about, among other things, the death of the Sikh ruler Ranjit Singh (1780–1839) (Eden 1978:308ff.).[4] Shortly before Singh died, he had bequeathed his jewels to various temples. His most precious possession, the large diamond called Koh-i-Nur (Mountain of Light), was to have gone to the temple of Jagannātha in Puri, but the court dignitaries refused to carry out this last wish, while the British also used their influence to gain possession of the stone. The diamond did ultimately come into the possession of the British, and in 1859 it was brought to England where it has since then been included among the crown jewels. It is not improbable that the Sikh prince intended that the diamond be used as an eye for the image of the god in Puri, but it was thought that he wanted it to be placed in the treasury of the temple.

Be that as it may, the "moonstone" in Collins' book is constantly being pursued. After the fanatical Muslim emperor Aurangzeb ascended the Mogul throne, the temples in Varanasi were no longer safe for Hindus and their temple treasures. An officer of the emperor stole the stone from the image, but three Brahmins had lingered close by so that they could follow the diamond. In the end, Tipu Sultan of Mysore (1750–1799) added the stone to his collection of jewels, which had in the meantime been set in the hilt of his sword. And—again a matter of historical fact—when the British forces occupied Tipu Sultan's capital, Srirangapatna, they plundered the palace treasuries. And so the stone ended up in England, with the three Brahmins who had sworn never to give up the stone still on its trail. And the stone was of course also a dangerous possession: whoever stole the diamond called down doom and misery upon himself.

With this theme, which fits neatly and precisely into the atmosphere of Romantic orientalism, Collins wrote his story about the stone's movements in England, with the three Indians constantly in pursuit. The curse that rested on the diamond becomes visible in the story, which is full of deception and violence: suicide and murder, opium use and magic are the ingredients of an exciting narrative in which the actual theme is the effect of the savage Indian culture on ordered English society.

At the end of the book, we return to India. The last scene takes place in the remote kingdom of Kathiawar, in what is now Gujarat. There, in Somnath, we again meet the three Indian priests who secured the moonstone and returned

4 See below.

it to its destined spot. A strong Hindu element in the story, however, is that they paid a high price for their victory. For a Brahmin, a trip overseas meant he would lose his caste. Even if the trip was in service to the deity, Brahmins who travelled overseas were nevertheless now condemned to a lifelong existence of wandering as pilgrims to Hindu shrines. The moonstone had been returned to its proper place. The narrator concludes somewhat melodramatically: "And there, in the forehead of the deity, gleamed the yellow Diamond, whose splendour had last shone on me in England, from the bosom of a woman's dress!" (Collins 1955:464).

Everything is back in its proper place. The dangerous Eastern forces have been returned to their own world, and the peaceful English countryside has been restored to peace. That seems, in the end, to be the message of Collins' masterful work.

3 Emily Eden: A Lady Travelling in a Strange Land

Among the travel accounts from the nineteenth century, it is the diary of Emily Eden (1797–1869)—which we have referred to above—that first attracts one's attention. Eden was the sister of the British governor-general, George Eden, Earl of Auckland (1784–1849), and thus moved in the highest circles of the British-Indian establishment. She stayed in India for some years, along with her sister Fanny. At that time, the governor made a long business trip through the "Upper Provinces," now Uttar Pradesh, and both sisters accompanied him. They were not alone: the whole travelling company, including household staff and army units, numbered 12,000 people, transported with the help of 140 elephants and camels. The journey lasted from October 1837 to March 1840, and most of the time the group camped in enormous, luxurious tents.

Although the trip sometimes took them through areas that had been struck by famine, the ladies and gentlemen lacked for nothing. There was even a French cook along, from the court of the House of Orange in The Hague. Nevertheless, Emily was not able to enjoy the trip. Her whole diary breathes an air of great aversion to the country in which she felt herself a stranger. At the end of the travel report she still complains: "and then India is such a horrid place" (Eden 1978:385). She usually had no idea where she was because all places looked the same: "I never can make out why they have any names; there is nothing to give a name to" (Eden 1978:34).

Emily showed talent at drawing and was thus regularly making sketches in her sketchbook. A few times the ladies went off by themselves to picturesque ruins or a tomb, while the men went hunting. She was much more intrigued,

FIGURE 12 A Hindu ascetic, Drawing by Emily Eden

however, by the social life of the small European group during their trip: their dance parties and fancy fairs received most of her attention.

The world outside her own circle was eccentric, and she viewed it with distrust. Moreover, the writer felt even more unsafe because she was a woman. Her contribution to the conversation with native guests was never encouraged, and so she concluded: "The poor ignorant creatures are perfectly unconscious what a very superior article an Englishwoman is" (Eden 1978:133). These words do of course have an irony that is intended to be somewhat humorous, but the impression of condescension cannot be completely ignored, however.

The religious life of her surroundings remained completely foreign to her. When one of the native princesses showed her the house altar, she was unable to describe it in any other way than as "quantities of horrid-looking idols—Vishnu, and so on" (Eden 1978:29). And a visit to a Sikh shrine resulted in a description that showed little understanding of their faith: "The priest read us a little bit of their Bible (not the Koran), and they brought out a sword in a red scabbard, which they worship" (Eden 1978:14).

Even in the centres of the Hindu religion, she had no idea at all what those in her environment, including her own staff, were actually experiencing. The group visited Kurukshetra where, according to tradition, Kṛṣṇa unfolded the teaching of the Bhagavad Gītā. Emily observed that the native soldiers bathed here en masse in the holy temple pond. And she was also witness to a conflict that broke out with the Muslim camel drivers who attempted to chop down holy pīpal trees. When the Brahmins were desperate and began to complain, the camel drivers were punished with a fine. Emily came to the conclusion that "[t]he Hindu religion has two merits—this constant ablution, and the sacredness of their trees" (Eden 1978:272–74). But she remained impervious to what was special about this place.

4 Mary Carpenter: A Visitor in Search of Renewal

Two years after Emily Eden's travel report was published, another travel report by a British woman was published, that of Mary Carpenter (1807–1877). It should be observed that the state journey that Eden participated in had already taken place a quarter of a century before her diary was published. Carpenter's report, in contrast, concerned a trip she had just recently undertaken.

The difference between both travel experiences is extraordinary. For Carpenter, it was not an official state visit by elephant but a fast journey via the new means of transport, the train. The extremely luxurious life with dances and dinners that Emily Eden knew so well was not part of Mary Carpenter's world and would not, for that matter, have appealed to her.

The daughter of a Unitarian minister, Carpenter had already distinguished herself in England by her great social involvement and her work for social change. She had founded a school for the poor as well as various reform institutions for juvenile offenders. She was also active in the anti-slavery movements. Her great example here was the Indian reformer Raja Rammohan Roy (1772–1833), who visited Bristol, where she lived, shortly before he died.[5]

In 1866–1867 this enthusiastic advocate for social progress made a study trip for half a year through India. Her travel account, which was published in 1868,

5 On Rammohan Roy see Schouten 2008b:5–34.

was dedicated to Rammohan Roy: his portrait appears before the title page, and she pays explicit tribute to his memory. He was the one, it states in the dedication, "who first excited in the author's mind a desire to benefit his country" (Carpenter 1868:I, xiii).

Carpenter's focus on this trip was education for women and girls. She visited countless schools and penitentiaries in which her primary interest lay in women and girls. She writes that the purpose of her visit to the country was "friendly sympathy" (Carpenter 1868:I, 23). With this attitude, she hoped that she could do something for social progress, particularly with respect to women's education. During her numerous working visits to schools and institutions, she certainly fulfilled her promise. Her report reflects a sincere interest in what the staff accomplished. And she very quickly became involved in actions in which the government was urged to make improvements, such as establishing training schools for female teachers (Carpenter 1868:I, 69–70, etc.).

Each initiative—particularly in the area of education—to help the country move forward could count on Carpenter's warm interest. Nevertheless, Indian culture remained foreign to her. She was quite at home in the British-oriented higher circles of the native population, but she vacillated between annoyance and compassion—the one emotion no less condescending than the other—when coming into contact and dealing with ordinary people. For example, Carpenter could be extraordinarily bothered by how indecently people she met were dressed. She had already been shocked at the beginning of her trip when she saw women bathing half-naked in the river in the morning ("wholly devoid of any feeling akin to delicacy") (Carpenter 1868:I, 85). And during her whole trip she was constantly irritated by the labourers and sailors who did their work stripped to the waist. It was a typical example of Victorian sensitivity.

Carpenter connected this immorality directly with Hinduism. She gave full vent to her feelings primarily in connection with visits to temples and Brahmanical neighbourhoods. After a walk in Mumbai (Bombay) through the narrow streets where Brahmins who were so-called 'holy' lived, she wrote: "A more degraded-looking set of men I have rarely beheld, and all the human beings we saw in that village appeared to be sunk in squalor and filth. A sacred cow was the least repulsive creature we beheld" (Carpenter 1868:II, 21–22). Her own Christian faith made it impossible for her to discover something more positive in the world of Hinduism. Even the nicest temple ultimately reflected "an idolatrous and degraded worship, containing nothing to elevate or refine the mind" (Carpenter 1868:I, 118).

There was an exception, however. Did Raja Rammohan Roy after all not offer his compatriots a new orientation with respect to faith in his monotheistic reform movement in which Jesus Christ had also received an important place? Carpenter was disappointed when she became acquainted with the Brāhma Samāj in Kolkata (Calcutta), for the movement had in the meantime become strongly anti-Christian. Rammohan Roy's book on Jesus' ethics was no longer even known. She did find the Raja's old ideas in a movement, the Veda Samāj, that had split off from the Brāhma Samāj under the leadership of Keshab Chandra Sen (1838–1884).[6] Her meeting with the leader and his community convinced her that the future of Hinduism lay in this monotheistic faith that excluded any worship of images (Carpenter 1868:I, 155–98).

5 D.C. Steyn Parvé: Fear of Rebellion in the Colonies

One of the most remarkable books on British India to be published in the Netherlands was the extensive study by Parvé on the Rebellion of 1857–1858 called "the Mutiny" in India. This was a very widespread insurgency against British authority, which began with a mutiny by native soldiers, the *sepoys*, and was caused by the introduction of a new type of rifle whose bullets were greased with fat from slaughtered cows and pigs, which was unclean in the eyes of Hindus and Muslims. The Mutiny spread over a large part of the subcontinent, and, while the English did manage to put it down, it cost them a great deal of effort and difficulty.

Daniël Steyn Parvé was a lawyer who had filled some important positions in the government of Indonesia. At the time of the Mutiny, however, he was living as a private citizen in London. Parvé had previously published some things on the colonial system of the Netherlands, in which he was an expert because of his own experience. He also knew a great deal about the situation in British India, where he had travelled a few years previously. His book was published in the Netherlands under the supervision of P.J. Veth (1814–1895), professor in Eastern languages in Amsterdam (later Leiden), who also wrote the foreword.

Parvé's book consists of two parts. The first gives a general introduction on the setup of the state, the culture, and the religion of British India. The second part then describes the events during the years of the Mutiny. The subtitle makes it clear what Parvé sees as the connection between both parts. The *Tafereel van Britsch-Indië en van de opstand des inlandschen legers aldaar* (A Tableau of British India and of the Mutiny of the Native Army There) was,

6 On K.C. Sen see Boyd 1975:26–39.

in his view, obviously intrinsically intertwined with the religious differences between the native population groups and the occupying forces—hence, the main title: *De Bijbel, de Koran en de Veda's* (The Bible, the Qur'an, and the Vedas). The first reviews on the book that appeared relativised this connection, by the way.[7]

Parvé does his best in the first part to give a sketch of the nature of the people who, under the influence of religion, make such a rebellion possible. For Dutch readers, it was important to know those factors, for a similar insurgency could, of course, also have broken out in the related colony of Indonesia. Parvé considered the insurgency in British India to be "a struggle between barbarism and civilisation," with Islam and Hinduism on the side of barbarism and Christianity on the side of civilisation. He expresses the opposition in a less than subtle way: "between the exalted and purest doctrine and the most horrible and inhuman superstition" (Parvé 1858–1859:I, 2).

The threat of Hinduism is obviously visible in a number of cultural customs that are extensively described: the burning of widows (which, for that matter, hardly happened any more in those years) and the murder of newborn girls are the first to be discussed. But he also wrote about the continuing threat posed by the professional thieves and murderers, the stranglers also known as *ṭhag* (Thugs). In addition, he also detailed the complete capriciousness that characterised the policy of the native princes. The dangerous sides of the Islamic population also became clear when he described the conquests by Muslim rulers.

6 Willam Urwick: A Reflective Tour

Twenty-five years later, the situation in British India looked very different. The confusing and threatening years of the Mutiny were over, and a major political shift had occurred. The East Indian Company was dissolved, and India was ruled from that point on directly by the Crown as an empire: The Raj was born.

Various accounts of the expanded British Empire in British India appeared at this time. A good example is the fine work by William Urwick (1826–1905) that was published in 1885. It was a typical picture book, generously illustrated with copper engravings. This book contains the description of a major tour that began in Sri Lanka (Ceylon) and continued from the south of the mainland to northern mountain regions and then via Rajasthan to the area around

7 See *Vaderlandsche Letteroefeningen* 1859, 418–27, anonymous review.

Mumbai (Bombay). The author, a congregationalist minister, had made the largest part of the journey himself, but he sometimes bases his story on the travel experiences of others. After a century, a new edition of the book was published as a striking picture of the "the infinite variety and exotic splendours of the British Raj at its zenith" (Urwick 1985).[8]

The book is indeed oriented to the beauty of the landscape and culture. Hinduism comes into view primarily in connection with the description of very many beautiful temples. In general, Urwick is very positive about the beauty he sees around him. But the confrontation with this other religion also had a flipside. The buildings might be beautiful, but the cultus it was all about in the end repelled Urwick. He writes about the temple of Srirangam at Tiruchirappalli:

> The contrast between the vastness, majesty and grandeur of the temple precincts, embodying the skill and toil of thousands of labourers and lapidaries for years, and the hideous, dirty, greasy, little idol before the dimly burning lamp in the centre, is most strange and striking.
>
> URWICK 1885:60–61

And the author then continues to talk about the "degraded idolatry." Nevertheless, the book does show pictures of people who had roles in that strange religion: a Brahmin during his preparations for a *pūjā* and various ascetics with their religious attributes.

Sometimes, however, it went too far, and Urwick found it impossible to experience the Hindu religion in its entirety. This was the case when he visited a temple where erotic depictions could apparently be seen on the *gopuram*. He found that shocking and wrote: "It is, in fact, a mass of obscenity cut in stone, such as one could hardly imagine depravity itself capable of inventing" (Urwick 1885:88).

This book clearly foregrounds the exotic aspect of India that can be rejected, but it was precisely that exotic aspect that accounted for much that was beautiful. Moreover, Urwick did indeed see how Hindu society was developing. What was new in his time was that the whole subcontinent could now be traversed by train. And that brought about a great deal of change: Brahmins and pariahs sat next to each other on the train. He concluded, not unjustifiably: "The railway is the great antagonist to caste in India" (Urwick 1885:66).

8 Text on dust jacket.

FIGURE 13 A Brahmin preparing for his pūjā; illustration in Urwick's Indian Pictures, 1885

7 A Princely Picture of India: Prince Bojidar

In the final years of the nineteenth century, a book on India caught on that, more than many other travel reports, gave a persuasive picture of what the subcontinent had become around the turn of the century. The writer was Bojidar Karageorgévitch (Božidar Karađorđević, 1862–1908), a member of the royal family of Serbia—he was a second cousin of King Peter I, who ascended the throne in 1903.[9] Prince Bojidar, however, had lived his whole life in France, where he was known as a writer, painter, and interior decorator. In 1896, he undertook a journey of several months through British India.

Unlike the previous travel accounts that have been discussed above, this author had no particular sympathy for the colonial policy of the British, and he was not very impressed by the progress that the British had brought about in India. Already in his foreword he sharply criticised the business-like way in which the English described their colony and the insensitivity they showed in their behaviour towards the native people (Karageorgévitch 1897:i-xvi).[10]

9 For Karageorgévitch see Pavlowitch 1978.
10 This foreword is not included in the English translation!

In contrast, Prince Bojidar sought what was still left of the original civilisation of the country. He saw the distinction between castes, which was so often criticised, as "a great force for maintaining the religion of the ancestors."[11]

Because of his aristocratic roots, Bojidar had easy access to the world of the native princes of India. That produced amusing anecdotes, such as the one about the *rājā* of Palitana, who brought him to the tennis court by elephant (Karageorgévitch 1897:122; 1899:83). Nevertheless, more important is the glimpse he could thus give of the past glory of the princely courts that had been robbed of their power but were still highly esteemed by the people. What is interesting here is that the prince mingled with equal ease among the princes and among the public on the street if there was an event to be watched.

Prince Bojidar was a remarkably sharp observer who also shared a number of details in his report that would probably have escaped the others. In a procession in Chennai (Madras), where an image of Rāma was being carried, it struck him that there were countless trinkets that were offered by the worshippers to the divinity. He recognised them as "innumerable gilt images, very suggestive of Jesuit influence—mincing, chubby angels, martyrs carrying palm-branches, and ecstatic virgins with clasped hands" (Karageorgévitch 1897:190; 1899:135).

He also had a good eye for aspects of popular religion that often went unnoticed. Thus, he describes an encounter with an old man at the coast, in Tuticorin, who told him how he had earned a great deal of money when he was young by bewitching the sharks so that the pearl divers would be safe in the water (Karageorgévitch 1897:173–74; 1899:123).[12] And Bojidar witnessed a kind of divine judgment in a temple, whereby a quarrel between two men about money that had disappeared was settled by an elephant who singled out the one as the thief without hesitation (Karageorgévitch 1897:171; 1899:121–22).

The greatest power of this writer, however, is his ability to empathise with people who experience something radical in their lives. That is clearly apparent from his description of the cremation rituals on the bank of the Ganges in Varanasi (Benares). The order and details of cremations had already been often described in the nineteenth century, but Bojidar made detailed reports on a number of burnings in which the differences between old and young as well as those between poor and rich come to the fore. He subtly describes the mood and feelings that struck him at the river:

---

11 Karageorgévitch 1897:xiii: "une grande force, ce maintien intact de la religion des ancêtres."

12 We encountered this practice of magic in connection with Marco Polo already in Ch. 1.

> A dome of smoke hangs like a vault over the fires, motionless, veiling the sun. The relations of the dead, sitting on their heels, gaze in the flames with an expression almost of indifference; no one weeps, and they converse calmly in no subdued tones.
> The pile of the girl with marigold wreaths and the shroud stained crimson and purple flung her ashes to the winds, reduced to mere atoms of bone and light cinder, and the servants of the place drowned a few still glowing sticks in the river; the family and friends slowly went up the yellow stone steps and disappeared through a gateway leading into the town.
>
> KARAGEORGÉVITCH 1897:230–37; 1899:168–69

Karageorgévitch's sensitivity—as is apparent from this citation—sometimes inclined towards sentimentality. This certainly stands out in his descriptions of the landscape. As an outsider, however, he managed to do what many an Englishman had failed at: to give in this decidedly literary travel account a striking image of the unbroken power of the Indian culture, including its own religion, Hinduism.

Bibliography

Sources

Carpenter, Mary (1868). *Six Months in India*. Two volumes. London: Longmans, Green, and Co.

Collins, Wilkie (1955). *The Moonstone*. Harmondsworth: Penguin Books. Originally published 1868.

Eden, Emily (1978). *Up the Country: Letters written to her Sister from the Upper Provinces of India*. London/Dublin: Curzon Press. Originally published 1866.

Eden, Emily (1844). *Portraits of the Princes & People of India*. London: J. Dickinson & Son.

Karageorgevitch, Bojidar (1899). *Enchanted India*. Transl. Clara Bell. New York/London: Harper and Brother.

Karageorgévitch, Bojidar (1897). *Notes sur l'Inde*. Paris: Calmann Lévy.

Moore, Thomas (n.y.). *The Poetical Works of Thomas Moore*. London: John Walker & Company. Originally published 1817.

Parvé, D.C. Steyn (1858–1859). *De Bijbel, de Koran en de Veda's: Tafereel van Britsch-Indië en van den opstand des Indischen legers aldaar.* Two volumes. Haarlem: J.J. Weeveringh.

Urwick, W. (1985). *India 100 Years Ago: The Beauty of Old India Illustrated*. London: Bracken Books.
Urwick, W. (1885). *Indian Pictures, Drawn with Pen and Pencil*. London: The Religious Tract Society.

Secondary Literature

Anonymous (1859). "Boekbeschouwing 'De Bijbel, de Koran en de Veda's'." *Vaderlandsche Letteroefeningen* 1859: 418–27.
Basham, A.L. (1975). *The Wonder that was India: A Survey of the History and Culture of the Indian Sub-Continent before the Coming of the Muslims*. Calcutta: Fontana Books.
Boyd, R.H.S. (1975). *An Introduction to Indian Christian Theology*. Rev. ed. Madras: The Christian Literature Society.
Fhlathúin, Máire Ní (2015). *British India and Victorian Literary Culture*. Edinburgh Critical Studies in Victorian Culture. Edinburgh: Edinburgh University Press.
Gottschalk, Peter (2013). *Religion, Science, and Empire: Classifying Hinduism and Islam in British India*. Oxford/New York: Oxford University Press.
Jürgens, Hanco (1994). *Ontdekkers en onderzoekers in de Oost: Britse reisverhalen gespiegeld, 1660–1830*. Utrecht: Vakgroep Geschiedenis der Universiteit Utrecht.
Kurin, Richard (2017). *Hope Diamond: The Legendary History of a Cursed Gem*. Washington DC: Smithsonian Books.
Pavlowitch, Stevan K. (1978). *Bijou d'art: Histoires de la vie, de l'œuvre et du milieu de Bojidar Karageorgévitch, artiste parisien et prince balkanique (1862–1908)*. Lausanne: L'Âge d'Homme.
Rietbergen, Peter (2007). *Europa's India: Fascinatie en cultureel imperialisme, circa 1750 - circa 2000*. Nijmegen: Uitgeverij Vantilt.
Said, Edward W. (1978). *Orientalism*. New York: Pantheon Books.
Schouten, Jan Peter (2008a) "Hindoeïsme." In: Meerten ter Borg et al. (eds.). *Handboek Religie in Nederland: Perspectief – overzicht – debat*. Zoetermeer: Uitgeverij Meinema. Pp. 253–64.
Schouten, Jan Peter (2008b). *Jesus as Guru: The Image of Christ among Hindus and Christians in India*. Transl. Henry and Lucy Jansen. Currents of Encounter 36. Amsterdam/New York: Rodopi.
Sharafuddin, Mohammed (1994). *Islam and Romantic Orientalism: Literary Encounters with the Orient*. London/New York: I.B. Tauris Publishers.
Tavernier, Jean Baptiste (1676). *Les six voyages de Jean Baptiste Tavernier*. Part 2. Paris: Gervais Clouzier/Claude Barbin.
Veer, P. van der (2001). *Imperial Encounters: Religion and Modernity in India and Britain*. Princeton/Oxford: Princeton University Press.

Online Resources

Vail, Jeffery W. (2005). "'The Standard of Revolt': Revolution and National Independence in Moore's Lalla Rookh." *Romanticism on the Net* 40. Accessed 10 November 2017. http://id.erudit.org/iderudit/012459ar.

CHAPTER 9

Missionaries from Switzerland: The Basel Mission in South India

1 A Minister Honoured

A special tribute was paid to the missionary Ferdinand Kittel (1832–1903) in 2001: a life-size bronze statue of him was unveiled on the Mahatma Gandhi Road, the main street of the city of Bengaluru (Bangalore). He is portrayed in full regalia, dressed in European minister's robes, with his hand on the Bible on the table next to him. But he was not being honoured as a preacher of the biblical message. The text on the pedestal draws primary attention to his services in the area of linguistics: he published classic Kannada literature, wrote an epic on Jesus Christ in that language and compiled a comprehensive Kannada-English dictionary that was considered to be "a perennial contribution to Kannada literature."

It is remarkable that a statue was erected for a European in a period in which Indians were more inclined to remove monuments of the colonial period. Ferdinand Kittel, however, did not play any role in British colonial policy, and, moreover, he was and is honoured not because of his activities as a missionary but because of his major contribution to the Indian cultural heritage. Thus, his statue played a role in the reinforcement of the sense of identity of the Karnataka state. Its own language, Kannada, is what binds the state together. It is remarkable that shortly before the statue was unveiled, Kittel's name became associated with one of the suburbs of the city: Austin Town, named after a British colonial administrator, became F. Kittel Nagar.

2 On the Road in a Mission Field

Georg Ferdinand Kittel was born in the parsonage of the small East Frisian village of Resterhafe on 7 April 1848.[1] Not only was his father a minister, but two of his brothers would also choose that profession while Ferdinand and two other brothers became missionaries. Ferdinand was admitted to the educational institute of the Basel Mission at the age of 18. Many south German young

1 See accounts of his life in Wendt 2006; Wendt 2008.

 | DOI:10.1163/9789004420076_011

FIGURE 14 The statue of Ferdinand Kittel in Bengaluru, decorated for Karnataka State Formation Day 2017

men from Württemburg continued their studies in the Swiss city of Basel, and the transition from the isolated coastal village in the extreme north of Germany to Basel was certainly a major one. The Basel Mission was founded in 1815 within the circles of the pietistic revival movements that arose in that time.[2]

2 For the history of the Basel Mission, see Christ-von Wedel and Kuhn 2015; Binder 2006a.

Kittel would certainly feel at home in this pious environment of hard-working serious people; he undoubtedly shared the idealism and urge for mission of the fellow students he associated with in Basel. Social factors did perhaps isolate him somewhat. East Frisians were very different from South Germans and the Swiss. Kittel was perhaps a dominant figure in Basel, both by background and disposition.[3]

In any case, the first period of Kittel's activity was marked by a great deal of tension and conflict. In 1853 he was sent out to the area that is now called Karnataka. For seven years he attempted to find his way into Indian society, church life, and the organisation of the Basel Mission. He was regularly transferred during this period, having to move again and again to another mission post because the organisation hoped that he would function better there. He started in North Karnataka (Dharwar, later Hubli and Betageri), then he was posted to the Nilgiris (northern Tamil Nadu), and then to the Coorg District (South Karnataka).

The problem with this young missionary was that he was obstinate and did not fit easily into existing ways of working. Driven by youthful enthusiasm, he felt called to take all kinds of initiatives and to spontaneously try things out to see what would work. He did not esteem collegiality very highly and thus quickly came into conflict with older missionaries who had developed fixed ways of working over the course of time. Moreover, the leaders of the organisation were not enthusiastic about experiments. Kittel's work reports regularly led to indignation and admonition.

What it came down to in the end was contact with the native population. At a certain moment, Kittel himself announced that he wanted to leave the mission post and move into a small house in a village, among the poorer members of the population. Some younger missionaries had made this move a few years earlier, and then as well there had been an intense response to such obstinacy (Stolz 2015:33). There was a strong reaction again: the executive Committee in Basel threatened to fire Kittel and told him to subject himself to the guidance of an older missionary (Wendt 2008:131).

To all appearances, this was a conflict between the lazy traditionalism of older staff members and the praiseworthy idealism of younger people. But it is not that black and white. Kittel did not give the impression that he was well acquainted with the sensitivities of the local culture that the older mission

3 Wendt emphasises both aspects. See Wendt 2008:125. Whether all Kittel's colleagues were simple men with a farming background is questionable. In any case, he was certainly not the only one to publish on a high level and on the basis of his extensive knowledge of languages.

staff could probably deal with better. Kittel was said to ignore social differences: he treated all people he met the same, spoke to everyone, visited people at home, and greeted them with a handshake, both men and women. In Hindu society, however, the differences among social groups and between men and women were felt much more than they were in Europe. Approaching both Brahmins and untouchables was simply not done. It was precisely for that reason that the older mission staff did have a point with their argument for a more distant relation to the population.

Kittel's starting point were the words of Paul, the same words that inspired John Muir: "I have become all things to all people" (1 Corinthians 9:22).[4] It is remarkable that Kittel, who did indeed want to take the culture of the Indians seriously, did not understand what the consequences of his actions were. For example, it was not wise to receive a woman who had a bad reputation in the mission house; the gossip of sexually impermissible behaviour that was to be expected began very quickly.

3 A New Beginning

A new phase in Kittel's Indian life began in 1860. His wife to be, Pauline Friederike Eyth, travelled to India and at the end of the year they married. Kittel was given different work. The Basel Mission had had printing facilities in Mangalore for years, where both English and Kannada could be printed. The executive Committee decided that this would be the best place to employ this man of letters. He was put in charge of preparing manuscripts for printing. This was indeed the best spot for him. In the many years that followed he produced a great many publications: edifying writings in the service of mission, schoolbooks, linguistic manuals, and academic works.

After three and a half years of marriage, however, Pauline died and left Ferdinand with two children. He was granted a leave of absence and spent some time in Germany, where he came into contact with Pauline's younger sister, Wilhelmine Julie. In 1867 they married and settled down together in Mangalore and had four additional children in the years following. Julie survived her husband; at his death on 19 December 1903, they had been married for 36 years.

4 He himself wrote in a travel account in 1856: "I felt very deeply that one had to be everything to all people." See Wendt 2008:25. On Muir, see Ch. 7 above.

FIGURE 15 Ferdinand and Julie Kittel-Eyth

4 Church in India—An Indian Church?

Ferdinand Kittel was a linguistic genius. Not only did he speak Kannada fluently, he was also able to write Kannada on a literary level. Most of the mission staff spoke the language reasonably and could also preach in Kannada and possibly write simple treatises. Kittel, however, had given himself the goal of studying the language thoroughly. During his whole life, he studied poetry intensely. And with that knowledge—rare among Europeans—he made his own contribution to mission work.

In Karnataka Kittel was known especially for a book of biblical stories, modest in size but written in a cultivated way.[5] This *Kathāmāle* (A Garland of Stories) was a reworking of a German children's Bible by the pietistic minister Christian Gottlob Barth (1799–1862). The choice for this book was not unexpected: Barth's version of the Bible story was used and translated in a number of countries where the Basel Mission was active. A translation of Barth's book had already been published twice in the Kannada-speaking part of India. Those, however, were prose translations, very close to the German original. But Kittel wanted something different.

5 Described in detail by Binder 2006b.

He had in the meantime become so acquainted with the native culture that he saw how important poetry and song were for people. A religious message was often conveyed in narrative verse: the *purāṇa* was the means par excellence for bringing people into contact with their religion. This had extra meaning because most people were illiterate; texts that had been written in verse could be memorised more easily. Kittel therefore made a new version of the classic German work in Kannada poetry, suitable for reciting or singing. A children's Bible was thus transformed into a *purāṇa*.

The content itself of the book is not very remarkable. It includes the most well-known episodes from the Gospel about Jesus, with a preference for Matthew's gospel. It begins in the middle of the infancy narrative: an angel announces the birth of the Saviour to shepherds in the field. The final story is Jesus' ascension into heaven. The verse form used is usually the classic *ṣaṭpadi*, and in some chapters a *rāga* and a *tāla* are indicated; these instructions indicate the way in which the verse can be sung. Here and there the author presents sermonic additions to the actual Bible stories, in which he draws the attention of the reader to a wise lesson or a learning moment. Moreover, there are countless footnotes that explain the biblical background.

With his *Kathāmāle*, Kittel gives a strong example of the inculturation of the biblical message. This was how the missionaries could reach the people in this country with the Christian message. He wanted to go even further than these Bible stories in Kannada. The musical notes, which would escape most European readers, indicate his intention: these biblical verses were not to be read but sung. This was a sensitive point at the Basel Mission. Up until then, German songs had been mainly used that had been—usually awkwardly—translated into Kannada. There was a prevailing mistrust of Indian music because it was thought that the music would recall heathen ideas and associations.

This led in 1870 to a serious conflict in the Basel Mission on Kittel's plans.[6] He had argued for using native music and instrumental music and had also expressed the desire that the Protestants, following the Roman Catholics, should make more use of festive rituals, processions, flags, and banners. That would, after all, speak to the people, and that would involve them in a more suitable way in the church culture. There was a fierce reaction from Basel to these proposals—in no way would Kittel be allowed to proceed further along this path. All his proposals were rejected and he was ordered not to introduce any changes in this area. Kittel was apparently far ahead of his time.[7]

6 Wendt 2006:70–76.

7 Thus correctly Wendt 2008:139–40.

A half-century later, such an adaptation to the Indian culture would take place everywhere, including the churches of the Basel Mission.

5 Mapping a Language

Kittel's greatest contribution to mission work was not in the area of new missionary and liturgical approaches. Although he regularly made his ideas known, he nevertheless only partly got the chance at some limited success. But he was the undisputed authority in another area and in the end was given free reign. In the dozens of years he stayed in India and afterwards, he made an even more thorough study of Kannada than anyone else. That led to a comprehensive dictionary and a solid descriptive grammar.

Even before it was published, the dictionary attracted the attention of the British colonial government, which even raised the possibility of Kittel coming to work for the government to complete the project. But he had no desire to do that: he was a missionary and wanted to remain one. The book was finally published in 1894: a hefty volume with at least 70,000 entries. He had worked on the book for more than twenty years. After more than a hundred years, the book is still the standard work on Kannada. The honorary doctorate that he received from Tübingen a year after its publication was thus completely justified.

6 Examining the Liṅgāyats

The dictionary and grammar were unique contributions by Kittel that no other colleague could have provided. In another area, in a series of articles from the mission in Karnataka, Kittel's studies do show the contribution of several others. An important study topic for missionaries in that area was constituted by the writings and institutions of the *vīraśaivas* or *liṅgāyats* (as they were then usually called). This Hindu tradition had a very prominent presence in North Karnataka at that time.[8]

When the director of the Basel Mission visited the missionary posts in this area in 1851 and 1852, he was struck by the dominant position held by the *liṅgāyats*. "As long as *liṅgāyatism* is not defeated, we cannot consider the victory of the Gospel either complete or guaranteed," he wrote combatively in his travel report (Josenhans 1854:139). He considered it absolutely necessary for

8 For this tradition, see Schouten 1991.

the missionaries to study the religious system of the Hindus as well, which the missionaries did indeed do.

At that time, the *Basava Purāṇa* and the *Cannabasava Purāṇa* were considered the most authoritative sacred books of the *liṅgāyats*. The Kannada text of both books—the latter very comprehensive—were published by Hermann Mögling (1811–1881) in his series *Bibliotheca Carnataca*.[9] It was another missionary, Gottlob Würth (1820–1869), who translated these texts and also wrote, using the *Basava Purāṇa* as his basis, the first treatment of this school (Würth 1865–1866a; Würth 1865–1866b; Würth 1853). The missionary Gottfried Weigle (1816–1855) described the funeral rites of the *liṅgāyats* (Weigle 1854).

Kittel added his works on the *liṅgāyats* to his colleagues' work. These had to do first of all with the most conspicuous characteristic of this group, the worship of the *liṅga* as the symbol par excellence of the divine. Kittel wrote a detailed brochure on this topic that shows his extensive knowledge of the history of India and of modern Indological research (Kittel 1876). In addition, he wrote articles about the literature of the *liṅgāyats* for his favourite journal, *The Indian Antiquary*.

7 In Search of a Point of Contact

The most important thing to clarify about Kittel's position concerning the encounter of religions is, however, his study on the concept of sacrifice in the Veda. The work was published in 1872 as a 'tract,' a simple work that would acquaint outsiders with the Christian message. The drift of the work is indeed a call to conversion, but it is much more than its title suggests. In fact, *A Tract on Sacrifice* is a solid discussion of the tradition of sacrifice in Hinduism since ancient times. Kittel had learned Sanskrit prior to writing this book, and that is obvious. Not only did he give Indian concepts in Sanskrit form, but he also translated numerous Christian terms into splendid Sanskrit. The number of notes with references to the Bible and Hindu texts border on the incredible: here and there are pages on which the actual text consists of only two or three lines and the rest of the page is taken up by footnotes.

As a whole, it is an ingenious argument along the lines of classical Protestant theology with a pietistic focus. In the old history of the religions, according to Kittel, sacrifice is the core concept. In particular, there had been a long

9 This series was published from 1852 on. The executive Committee in Basel had resisted such publications, but the financial support of a British government official made up for that. See Christ-von Wedel and Kuhn 2015:181.

development of the concept of sacrifice among the Aryans, among whom he included not only the Indian Brahmins but also the Parsis, the Germans, and the English. The sacrifice rituals were largely directed at the reconciliation of sin and guilt, with the goal of reaching heavenly bliss after death. This expressed a longing for the ultimate sacrifice by God that surpassed all human sacrifices. This sacrifice—for which the (Aryan) Hindus were also searching—has been fulfilled in the death of Jesus Christ.

It is a brave attempt to give the classic Hindu cultus from the Vedic period a place in Christian proclamation. From the point of view of the history of religion, there are certainly a few things of interest here. And we may certainly ask if there were many Brahmins who would have appreciated this work. But Kittel's sincere attempt to discover valuable elements in the Hindu tradition that could be given a place in Christian theology is indeed impressive. He himself wrote about the Brahmins:

> under the mass of wrong sacrificial notions [...] divine ones can be traced, [...] *especially* by referring to such notions among your ancestors, the ancient Indian Aryas. *Such right sacrificial notions are found with the non-Israelites, as it were, as pearls hidden in rubbish, which after having been found, frequently still want cleansing that their original beauty may appear.*
>
> KITTEL 1872:69–70

Kittel's biographer thus wrongly concluded that "positive standpoints regarding Hinduism cannot be found in his letters, reports, and writings" (Wendt 2008:123). He carried out his work within the framework of the Gospel: he always remained a missionary. It was certainly not his intention to arrive at a synthesis of Hinduism and Christianity. But he wanted to meet the Hindus part of the way by discussing what he saw as right and valuable in Hinduism. When he told the director in Basel about his plans to publish the tract on sacrifice, he wrote about the universal truths that he found in non-Christian religions such as the Vedic cultus of sacrifice. And he decided: "Well, such ideas can be points of contact, and sometimes that's worth much more than a harsh dispute."[10]

This was something he could take to his director, 'Inspector' Josenhans (1812–1884). However critical Josenhans might be about the 'immoral' situations he encountered in India, he was nevertheless certainly open to the positive ethics and edifying reflection that could sometimes be found in Hindu

10 Letter dated 23 February 1871: "Nun, an solche Gedanken läßt sich schon anknüpfen; und das ist manchmal viel lohnender als ein hartes Disputieren." See Wendt 2006:83.

writings. After his trip he wrote appreciatively of the *Cannabasava Purāṇa*, saying that it contained texts "in which moral awareness is articulated in a very splendid way and very strongly" (Josenhans 1854:134).

The Basel Mission is usually seen as a missionary organisation that took a strongly antithetical position in Indian society. Nevertheless, these missionaries could not avoid wondering how their message could find points of contact in the local culture and religion. This certainly obtained for Kittel who was so enthusiastic about understanding this culture—and certainly not in order to reject it as a whole. Kittel used the word *Anbequemung* (adaptation) in connection with the search for points of contact. In Latin, this is the classic term from missiology: *accomodatio* (Wendt 2006:38). He thus wanted to meet the Hindus part of the way. Many missionaries from the Basel Mission sought similar approaches to the Hindus, each in his own fashion.

8 An Exceptional French Swiss

Most missionaries from the Basel Mission came from the kingdom of Württemberg or from the German-speaking area of Switzerland. But there were also young men from other backgrounds who were trained as missionaries in Basel and were sent to mission fields. An exceptional example is Auguste Ali Bourquin (1848–1928). He was born on 8 April 1848 in the small farming village of Sonvilier in the French-speaking Swiss canton of Jura.[11]

Auguste Bourquin began training as a missionary in Basel already in his teens. He can be seen, 17 years old, in a photo from 1865, in the midst of a dozen classmates—and, judging by the names, the only French-speaking student. In 1871, when he was 23, he was ordained as a missionary and sent to India. There he worked for four years in Kannur (Cannanore), now the most northern part of the state of Kerala. The relations between the missionaries there were quite tense, however, and in 1875 he was transferred to Phalgat (Palakkad), somewhat to the south. But after a month and a half, things began to go wrong. Bourquin no longer felt at home in the strict hierarchical organisation of the Basel Mission. He could not see the surplus value of his work in his own station and complained to his colleagues that administrative tasks and teaching uninterested children could also best be done by someone else. Apparently, he was not on the same page as the others with respect to a number of principles.

11 His parents were Louis Alcide Bourquin, a teacher, and Zélie Chopard. The family were members of the state church, the Église Réformée (Reformed Church). The birth and baptism registry of Sonvilier are located in the state archives of the canton of Bern.

He thus resisted the inclination of the missionaries to pass on European culture with the Gospel: he did not think that native Christians had to dress like the missionaries. Bourquin drew the obvious conclusion and, on 1 July 1875 he broke with the Basel Mission.[12] He travelled to Mumbai where he was given a new chance with the mission of the Church of Scotland.

Bourquin worked for the Scottish mission in Mumbai until 1882. In many respects, these were fruitful years. He had a special position as the only clergyman in the mission of the Scottish church in Mumbai. The yearly reports present him as a very appreciated missionary: "Mr Bourquin has hitherto fully justified the favourable anticipations formed of his character and fitness for the important work on which he has entered in connection with the Mission" (Church of Scotland General Assembly 1877:116; see also 151–53). That work consisted of the usual preaching on the street, Christian education, and building up the church. In connection with this missionary, it is also striking here that the work required extensive knowledge of the Indian languages: the church services in Mumbai on Sunday were in Tamil in the morning and in Marathi in the afternoon; the home visits and street preaching also required knowledge of these languages (Church of Scotland General Assembly 1878:153). In one of the yearly reports Bourquin laments the fact that he could not preach, but Marathi proved to be a hindrance for some months. There was some improvement, however: "Since I have become somewhat surer in the way of expressing my thoughts, I have tried several times to preach in the streets" (Church of Scotland General Assembly 1877:152).

Life in a large city, one with university institutions, presented him with many opportunities. He studied the religious traditions he saw around him intensely. He learned Sanskrit and built up valuable contacts with Hindu scholars. In these years he laid the foundation for the academic work that would seal his reputation in Europe. It slowly became clear that he would take a different direction in life. He would return to the West with a stack of preparatory work for publications. Even when he was still in Mumbai, he joined some reputable academic institutions as a member: the Deutsche Morgenländische Gesellschaft and the Société asiatique.[13] The young man who left as a missionary returned as an academic.

12 The conflict is extensively described in the quarterly report of the mission post Palghuat, July 1875. See also Bourquin's resignation letter, dated 22 June, 1875 (Basler Mission Archives, Basel).

13 See the yearly membership lists in the *Zeitschrift der Deutschen Morgenländischen Gesellschaft* and the *Journal asiatique*. He appears in both from 1882 on: 'le Rév. A. Bourquin, à Bombay.'

FIGURE 16 Auguste Bourquin in 1871

9 Back in Europe

After eleven years of missionary work, Bourquin went back to Europe in 1882. He did not, however, return to the country of his birth but settled in France, becoming a minister in a village in the Ardèche, Vals-les-Bains. Apparently, pastoral work in the small congregation left him enough time for study, for while he lived there he published a great deal. The basis for these publications had been laid during his time in Mumbai. In 1883 he made a contribution to an Indologists' conference in Leiden on the Vedic calendar. He would certainly have been an exception in this learned society: at that time he had no academic degree at all. In 1884 he published two extensive translations of Sanskrit works, and in 1885 he defended a thesis on pantheism in the Vedas at the Protestant Theological Faculty in Paris. That gained him a bachelor's degree in theology.[14]

Although he had in the meantime acquired a certain fame as an Indologist, after a number of years Bourquin chose to go in a different direction. It is not known why he left both the study of Hinduism and France behind him. In any case, from 1890 on, he focused on classical theology and returned to Switzerland where he wrote a thesis for the University of Geneva on the authenticity

14 For Bourquin's publications, see Karttunen, website *Persons of Indian Studies*, ad 'Bourquin, Auguste Ali.'

of Paul's pastoral letters. In 1891 he was appointed assistant minister of the state church, the National Church of Vaud (Église National de Vaud) in Vevey near Lausanne. This position became a full-time ministerial position sometime later.

10 To America

But this was not yet the end of Bourquin's wanderings. He was already long past 50 when he emigrated to the United States in 1902. He bought a ranch in Denver, Colorado and was also given a diplomatic role: he was appointed consular agent in Denver for the French Republic. Bourquin had never married and made the trip to the American west alone. He lived in this new country for more than a quarter of a century and died in Denver in 1928, where few would have known about his colourful career. His diplomatic position is emphatically inscribed on his imposing gravestone in Fairmount Cemetery. Above the name on the gravestone is a large cross with the Freemason emblem according to the Scottish rite underneath. Auguste Bourquin was, in any event, not narrow-minded.

11 The Brahmanical Culture

In his Indological period, during his time in the Ardeche, Auguste Bourquin concentrated primarily on the classic Brahmanical version of Hinduism. This is apparent from two translations of ritual books in particular that he published in 1884. The first translation concerns an 18th-century work that was attributed to a certain Kāśīnātha. The title is *Dharmasindhu*, or 'Ocean of Teachings' and contains an encyclopaedic overview of the ritual system on the basis of classic manuals. Bourquin had already published part of this work in an English translation in the *Journal of the Bombay Branch of the Royal Asiatic Society* (1881–1882, three articles). Now the French version appeared in a journal from Paris, the *Annales du Musée Guimet*. A separate book edition was also published.

The discussion contains extremely specialised information on the calendar of the Brahmanical priests. The book dealt more with the times at which rituals had to be performed than with the content of those rituals as such. It informs the reader as to which gods sacrifices and vows can be brought every day (*tithi*) in the favourable half of the month. It is not a brilliant work as far as the translation from Sanskrit is concerned, for the text is enumerative in nature

FIGURE 17 Bourquin's Grave in Fairmount Cemetery in Denver

and includes a lot of repetitions. Nonetheless, the project required a special knowledge from the translator concerning the complex astronomical and astrological ideas in Brahmanical circles. A few hundred footnotes show how thoroughly Bourquin approached his work.

The second work is more interesting for the reader, a work that was also published in the *Annales du Musée Guimet*, as well as issued separately as a book. It is called *Brahmakarma* (The Service of the Brahmins) and concerns the most prominent daily rituals that the Brahmanical priests carried out, complete with the texts that were recited at these rituals. In the nineteenth century, this book, whose complete title was *Brahmakarmapustaka*, became the manual par excellence for the Brahmins of the traditional schools. A printed edition of the anonymous work was published in Alibag, somewhat to the south of Mumbai, in 1876.[15] Bourquin offers a translation in French but also includes the Sanskrit text of the original work, along with an introduction in Marathi.

The book describes in detail the rituals of the Brahmins, beginning with the bath at sunrise. After that, the other ritual baths are described, along with the sacrificial rituals for gods, sacred objects and ancestors, the worship of the sun, and finally fastening the sacred thread that had to be repeated daily. What is noteworthy about this book is that it cites a number of Vedic texts that are given in their ritual context. In Bourquin's time, there were already translations of such proverbs, particularly of the Ṛg-Veda, but it was not widely known that these ancient texts were still used by the Brahmins in their rituals.

Bourquin reproduces striking mantras that are coloured by the ritual they turn out to be connected with. That obtains for well-known proverbs like the *Gāyatrī-mantra* as well as, for example, for less well-known texts like the text that is recited during the morning bath, before rinsing one's mouth.

> That the Sun, the Furies, and the leaders of the Furies
> may save me from those who wish me harm,
> as well as from the sins I committed in the night,
> either by my thoughts or my words,
> by my hands, my feet, my belly, or my penis;
> that the disappearing night takes with it everything that is bad in me.
> It is myself that I offer as sacrifice
> to the source of the nectar, to the light of the rising sun. Honour![16]

In his foreword, Bourquin makes a connection between his translation work and his stay in India. He describes how he stayed in India for eleven years, seven of which were in constant contact with learned Brahmins of the old school who had not yet been influenced by Western culture. He was convinced that "no European who had not seen the Brahmanical cultus with his own eyes

15 Other nineteenth-century writers confirm that this book was a very authoritative manual on Brahmins; see, for example, Monier Williams 1891:401.

16 Bourquin reports in a note that he could not find this text in the Ṛg-veda. Monier-Williams (1891:404) does report the source however: Taittirīya Āraṇyaka X:25.

and heard it with his own ears [could] understand and correctly report on the holy rites of the Brahmins" (Bourquin 1884:4). His activities for the Scottish mission in Mumbai did achieve something in this area at any rate.

12 Pantheism and the Vedas

On 26 November 1885 Auguste Bourquin defended his thesis *Le panthéisme dans les Védas* at the Paris Faculty of Protestant Theology. Because of his years in India, the faculty exempted him from classes and exams: he could earn the bachelor's degree by writing a thesis (Robert 1978:300; cf. also 584).

This book discusses the concept of God in the oldest Hindu writings. Not only the Vedas themselves but the works connected with that, such as the Brāhmaṇas and the Upaniṣads, were also searched for texts that gave a picture of the belief in God in the earliest Hindu traditions. Bourquin's central thesis is that, despite the appearance of polytheism in these writings, they present a pure pantheism. The mythological form with many divine figures that represent natural phenomena and powers seems to point to the separate existence of many gods. It is apparent from many texts, however, that it concerns one and the same divine power that manifests itself in different shapes.

This is a materialistic pantheism. The Vedas do not depict an ideal that exists behind existing reality, such as Plato later proposed. In the Vedic presentation, it concerns a unity of the existing, visible phenomena itself. That unity is seen as a divine appearance and can be called by various divine names. According to the oldest tradition, what the Hindu worships in the end is this divine power. And these are the same Vedic writings that provide orientation for India: "Materialistic pantheism has its source in the hymns of the Veda, and for India it has no other basis than the Veda" (Bourquin 1885:42).

Bourquin does have an inclination to oversystematise. In addition to the materialistic pantheism he exhaustively discusses, he also talks of an ontological pantheism, a cosmological pantheism, a psychological pantheism, and a mystical pantheism. All can be found in the Vedic writings, although materialistic pantheism is dominant. It is important, however, that Bourquin asks that attention be paid to the idea of unity that would be elaborated later in Hindu philosophy but can already be found right at the beginning.

This also has practical importance, according to Bourquin. The missionaries' usual approach to their work was wrong since they always aimed their arrows at polytheism. They should have directed their efforts, however, at combatting pantheism, for that is, in his view, where the battle between the two worldviews was to be fought (Bourquin 1885:116–17).

When Bourquin wrote his work, pantheism was not only an important spiritual force in India but was also gaining in popularity in Europe. Bourquin indicated that the influence of Spinoza in the materialistic philosophy of his time was great. And pantheism was also a popular theme in more popular literature. The English writer Constance Plumptre (1848–1929) published a voluminous book on the history of pantheism that devoted a great deal of attention to the Vedic scriptures (Plumptre 2011:I, 29–83). It is striking how well Bourquin, from his experience as a missionary in India, could capitalise on what was popular in Europe.

Bibliography

Archival Records

State Archives of the Canton of Bern.

Régistre des Naissances et Baptêmes de la Paroisse de Sonvillier (1832–1853) inv.no. K Sonvilier 1.

Basler Mission Archives, Basel.

Correspondence of A.A. Bourquin with the Basler Mission, 1875.

Quarterly report of the Mission Post Palghaut July 1875.

Sources

Bourquin, A. (1885). *Le panthéisme dans les Védas*. Paris: Fischbacher.

Bourquin, A. (1884a). *Brahmakarma ou rites sacrés des brahmanes*. Extrait des annales du Musée Guimet VII. Paris: Ernest Leroux.

Bourquin, A. (1884b). *Dharmasindhu ou océan des rites religieux Par le Prêtre Kāshinātha*. Transl. L. de Milloué. Extrait des annales du Musée Guimet VII.2. Paris: Ernest Leroux.

Josenhans, [J.F.] (1854). "Die ostindische Visitationsreise des Inspector Josenhans im Jahr 1851–1852 (von ihm selbst beschrieben)." *Magazin für die neueste Geschichte der evangelischen Missions- und Bibel-Gesellschaften* 1854/2: 60–163.

Kittel, F. (1982). *A Grammar of the Kannaḍa Language Comprising the Three Dialects of the Language (Ancient, Medieval and Modern)*. New Delhi: Asian Educational Services. Originally published 1908.

Kittel, F. (1968–1977). *Kittel's Kannaḍa-English Dictionary in 4 Volumes*. Ed. M. Mariappa Bhat. Madras: University of Madras. Originally published 1894.

Kittel, F. (1876). *Ueber den Ursprung des Lingakultus in Indien.* Mangalore: Basel Mission Book & Tract Depository.

Kittel, F. (1875a). "Old Kanarese Literature." *The Indian Antiquary* IV: 15–21.

Kittel, F. (1875b). "Seven Liṅgâyta Legends." *The Indian Antiquary* IV: 211–18.

Kittel, F. (1874). *Kāvyamāle: Canarese Poetical Anthology.* 3rd rev. ed. Mangalore: Basel Mission Book & Tract Depository.

Kittel, F. (1872). *A Tract on Sacrifice (Yajnasudhānidhi).* Mangalore: Stolz & Reuter.

Kittel, F. (1862). *Kathāmāle: A Selection of Scripture Stories in Hindu Metre, New Testament.* Mangalore: Basel Mission Book and Tract Depository.

Weigle, G. (1854). "Die Leichenceremonien der Lingaiten." *Magazin für die neueste Geschichte der evangelischen Missions- und Bibel-Gesellschaften* 1854/1: 102–08.

Würth, G. (1865–1866a). "The Basava Purâna of the Lingaits." *Journal of the Bombay Branch of the Royal Asiatic Society* VIII/24: 65–97.

Würth, G. (1865–1866b). "Channa-Basava Purâṇa of the Lingaits." *Journal of the Bombay Branch of the Royal Asiatic Society* VIII/24: 98–221.

Würth, G. (1853). "Ueber das Religionssystem der Lingaiten." *Magazin für die neueste Geschichte der evangelischen Missions- und Bibel-Gesellschaften* 1853/1: 86–149.

Secondary Literature

Badley, B.H. (1881). *Indian Missionary Directory and Memorial Volume.* Rev. ed. Lucknow/New York: Methodist Episcopal Church Press/Phillips and Hunt.

Binder, Katrin (2006a) "Die Basler Mission in Karnataka und Kerala." In: Michael Mann (ed.). *Europäische Aufklärung und protestantische Mission in Indien.* Heidelberg: Draupadi Verlag. Pp. 203–24.

Binder, Katrin (2006b). "A Garland of Stories: Kathāmāle." In: Reinhard Wendt (ed.). *An Indian to the Indians? On the Initial Failure and the Posthumous Success of the Missionary Ferdinand Kittel (1832–1903).* Studien zur außereuropäischen Christentumsgeschichte 9. Wiesbaden: Otto Harrassowitz Verlag. Pp. 231–53.

Christ-von Wedel, Christine, and Thomas K. Kuhn (eds.) (2015). *Basler Mission. Menschen, Geschichte, Perspektiven 1815–2015.* Basel: Schwabe Verlag.

Church of Scotland General Assembly (1878). *Reports on the Schemes of the Church of Scotland for the Year 1878.* Edinburgh: William Blackwood and Sons.

Church of Scotland General Assembly (1877). *Reports on the Schemes of the Church of Scotland for the Year 1877.* Edinburgh: William Blackwood and Sons.

Faltin, Thomas (2000). *Heil und Heilung: Geschichte der Laienheilkundigen und Struktur antimodernistischer Weltanschauungen in Kaiserreich und Weimarer Republik am Beispiel von Eugen Wenz (1856–1945).* Medizin, Gesellschaft und Geschichte: Beiheft 15. Stuttgart: Franz Steiner Verlag.

Jürgens, Hanco (2014). *Roeping India: Religie, Verlichting en koloniale expansie. Duitse zendingsberichten 1750–1810.* Nijmegen: Radboud University.

Monier-Williams, Monier (1891). *Brāhmanism and Hindūism or, Religious Thought and Life in India.* 4th ed. London: Murray.

Plumptre, Constance E. (2011). *General Sketch of the History of Pantheism.* Cambridge Library Collection – Religion. Cambridge: Cambridge University Press. Originally published 1878.

Robert, Daniel (1978). "Les diplômes décernés par la faculté protestante de théologie de Paris (1877–1906)." *Bulletin de la société de l'Histoire du Protestantisme Français* 124: 282–309, 424–45, 552–84.

Schouten, Jan Peter (1991). *Revolution of the Mystics: On the Social Aspects of Vīraśaivism.* Kampen: Kok Pharos.

Stolz, C. (2015). *Die Basler Mission in Indien: Zugleich als Festschrift zum 50jährigen Jubiläum der Kanara-Mission.* Treuchtlingen: Literaricon. Originally published 1884.

Wendt, Reinhard (2008). "Visionärer Missionsstratege oder praxisferner Schreibstubengelehrter? Ferdinand Kittel und seine Studien zum südindischen Kannada." In: Michael Mann (ed.). *Aufgeklärter Geist und evangelische Missionen in Indien.* Heidelberg: Draupadi Verlag. Pp. 119–42.

Wendt, Reinhard (ed.) (2006). *An Indian to the Indians? On the Initial Failure and the Posthumous Success of the Missionary Ferdinand Kittel (1832–1903).* Studien zur außereuropäischen Christentumsgeschichte 9. Wiesbaden: Otto Harrassowitz Verlag.

Online Resources

Karttunen, Klaus. *Persons of Indian Studies.* www.whowaswho-indology.info. Accessed 23 October 2017.

Le temps: Rechercher dans les archives de la Gazette de Lausanne et du Journal de Genève. www.letempsarchives.ch. Accessed 17 November 2017.

Scriptorium, Bibliotèque cantonale et universitaire BCU Lausanne. https://scriptorium.bcu-lausanne.ch. Accessed 17 November 2017.

CHAPTER 10

Reflections

1 A Fascinating Country

The wondrous land beyond the Indus has held a special attraction for Europeans throughout the centuries. Merchants knew the fame of the region that was the source of precious trading goods that reached some European cities via the Levant. And however inaccessible the area was, adventuresome spirits dreamed of travels in which they could obtain gemstones and silk, ivory and spices. It is thus no surprise that the first travel reports were those by traders. The Venetian Marco Polo started a trend, and many a merchant followed in his footsteps, even though there were few that put their experiences down on paper like he did.

In general, people had hardly any real idea of Indian culture. But they did know that people there lived differently than in the familiar world of Europe. Writers from antiquity had already shared some things about cultural and religious peculiarities about the country. For instance, it was known that there were wise people living there called 'Brahmins,' of whom it was said that they travelled through the country completely naked. Their knowledge of that religion was limited, however, not going much beyond the fact that numerous gods, or rather personifications of natural forces, were worshipped, as had also been done in the Western world before Christ.

The reports from antiquity remained the standard for centuries. The scarce knowledge about India was seen as authoritative and was not questioned. For centuries, there was the inclination to start with what people knew from the ancient Greeks and Romans when it came to the description of cultural phenomena. A true humanist like Poggio Bracciolini, who was very well versed in the ancient writers, then also eagerly sought for new information that could supplement the existing canon of classical knowledge. But the idea that those celebrated writers from antiquity should be corrected did not emerge quickly.

Phenomena were sometimes found in other cultures that were already known from antiquity, and it was concluded with remarkable ease that the one culture had adopted it from the other. Thus, at the end of the sixteenth century, Jan Huygen van Linschoten saw the ancient ideas of Pythagoras in the Hindu doctrine of reincarnation: Pythagoras' influence had apparently reached other

 | DOI:10.1163/9789004420076_012

continents. The not illogical idea that this Greek philosopher would have borrowed his ideas from Eastern wisdom did not dawn on anyone at that time.

The view of non-Christian religions was also generally determined by the way in which people viewed the Greek-Roman religion: a repugnant idolatrous religion from an era prior to the Christian revelation. There were apparently areas in which this heathenism had managed to survive. Idolatry was thus expressed in the same way everywhere, just as, for that matter, the gods of other peoples were usually equated in ancient times with Zeus and the Greek pantheon. Aside from their own religion and Judaism, Islam was the only religion Christian writers actually recognised as a different religion: everything else was just simply collected under one unspecified category: 'heathenism.'

2 Wondrous Phenomena

Fact and fiction were entirely mixed in the reports from antiquity. For example, the legendary story that some people in India had dogs' heads was ineradicable, and many of the earliest travellers were searching out of curiosity for such a variant of the human race. The stubbornness of such clear fables could surprise us. But we do well to remember that similar stories about the inaccessible city of Mecca were still being circulated at the end of the nineteenth century: the city was reputed to have people living there with tails (Dröge 2017:11, 311).

The few reports about peculiarities in the nature or culture of India were easily filled in by means of well-known European narrative traditions. Was there an animal in India that had a single horn on its head? What else could it be than the legendary unicorn that played such a large role both in narratives and in art? Marco Polo, who had seen this rhinoceros himself, described the animal in all its plumpness—this was certainly not the graceful unicorn that would submissively nestle up with a virgin. It is remarkable, by the way, that the European legend of the shy, slender unicorn probably goes back to a Hindu myth.[1] Thus, there is a connection, but it is more complicated than people think.

Even though they did not have much of an idea of the religion of this strange country, visitors were impressed by the radicality of the adherents of this religion. Very quickly, the vast repertoire of stories about India included stories about believers who did not recognise any restraint in their religious devotion. The fourteenth-century monk Odoric already reported on processions in

1 The myth of the hermit Ṛśyaśṛṅga; see Gerritsen 2007.

which spectators threw themselves under the wheels of the temple wagon so they could be crushed by the image being carted around.

That participants in religious festivities let themselves be hoisted up by means of metal hooks in their backs for the greater glory of the divinity was also astonishing. This hook-swinging was something that people still survived in any case. Nicolò de' Conti made his European audience shudder with his stories of machines resembling a guillotine whereby people, driven by religious belief, could behead themselves. Technological curiosity and revulsion at the sin of suicide struggled for the upper hand when people heard such stories.

Throughout the centuries, the ascetics also drew attention through their extreme penitential practices. The fakir on his bed of nails has become almost the prototype of the Indian ascetic, even though, strictly speaking, the word *faqīr* refers not to a Hindu but to an Islamic mendicant. The idea behind this is the same, however, for both Muslims and Hindus: a harsh ascetic exercise can help one cope with what happens in life. *Sādhūs*, holy men who were skilled in such ascetic practices can be found in all branches of Hindu spirituality. For the earliest visitors, it would not have been a strange sight, for in the fourteenth and fifteenth centuries Europe was overrun with flagellants who matched the Indians when it came to self-castigation. The pretentions of Indian ascetics were, however, often much greater: some claimed to have supernatural powers. There were those who claimed to be able to fly through the air, while others let themselves be buried alive and dug up again after some time unharmed. Such stories strengthened the view of this culture as magical, mysterious, a land that people in Europe could only marvel at.

This image of an unfathomable culture in which supernatural phenomena were never far away persisted until far into the nineteenth century. Especially at the time when Romantic Orientalism was at its peak, Europeans poets and writers indulged themselves in imagining a world that, in contrast to the Western rationalistic attitude, was still caught in the spell of magic and divine powers. If it was true anywhere in the world that there was more in heaven and in earth than was dreamt of in rationalistic philosophy, that place was India.

3 A Major Stumbling Block

There were also religious-cultural phenomena in India, however, that evoked general disapproval and repugnance. That was the case with the custom of burning a man's widow along with him at his cremation. *Satī* (virtuous wife) was the classic name for a woman who sacrificed her life in such a way after the death of her husband. In the West, this term has also been used since the seventeenth century for the phenomenon itself. It is this ritual suicide that can be found in almost all descriptions of Indian culture from antiquity on.[2]

The condemnation and disgust that *satī* evoked among visitors from Europe is almost universal. The outburst of indignation that the VOC minister Rogerius—who was usually very restrained in his descriptions of this foreign culture—gave vent to at the "inhuman cruelty" that this custom expressed was typical. Whereas authors in antiquity, such as Propertius, could display some admiration for the widow's willingness to sacrifice herself, Christian authors outdid each other in their indignation and revulsion. Undoubtedly, this had to do with the rejection of suicide of any kind in Christian morality. The idea that such a sacrifice of one's own life could be meritorious and entail the forgiveness of sins that had been committed was difficult to reconcile with the teachings of Christianity.

An exception to this attitude of condemnation found among so many Christian preachers was Roberto de Nobili. This Jesuit missionary witnessed the cremation of a ruler in which no less than four hundred women from his harem were burned with him. De Nobili was not shocked at this but deeply impressed by such a heroic proof of marital fidelity. He had, apparently, so appropriated the native culture that his values were also determined by it.

The practice of burning widows was ultimately forbidden in 1829 by the colonial government after joint protests by liberal Hindus and missionaries from Baptist circles.[3] For the missionaries, it was the crowning achievement of a centuries-long battle against what they had always considered to be completely unacceptable.

4 Minor Stumbling Blocks

Other elements from the religious culture of India that irritated the visitors had to do with eroticism and sexuality. But unlike the case of *satī*, this did not lead to a unanimous condemnation that carried the same weight in all periods. Eroticism is not shunned in Hindu myths. This also fits into the image that the Hindus have of the gods: nothing human is strange to them. That is why the gods also have partners, make love, and have children. Various European writers eagerly passed on the mythological stories, but it could go too far. Philippus

---

2 For an overview of references, see the article "Suttee" in Yule and Burnell 1986.

3 The Hindus were led in this by Rammohan Roy and the Christians by William Carey. See Schouten 2008:9–14.

Baldaeus, for example, was not at all edified by the *liṅga* that depicted the presence of Śiva in the temples. With holy indignation he raged against this phallic cultus in which people "scandalously display their bestial lust."

The depictions of erotic scenes that can be found here and there on the temples in India evoked many responses. It is, however, striking that it was primarily in the nineteenth century that people were offended by this candid portrayal of sexual techniques and positions. This is obviously connected with the proverbial Victorian prudishness that even saw classical sculptures as extraordinarily shocking. Visitors at this time expressed themselves in particularly sharp ways when they described such scenes for their readers: "a mass of obscenity cut in stone, such as one could hardly imagine depravity itself capable of inventing"—this was the judgment of Rev. Urwick who, as a rule, showed openness towards the Indian civilisation.

The temple complex in Khajuraho (Madhya Pradesh), where a relatively large amount of erotic sculpture can be found, was gradually seen as the standard example of this kind of art.[4] The discussions about the accessibility of such art even went too far when Indians—under the influence of British sensitivities—began to be preoccupied with these aspects of their cultural heritage. Mahatma Gandhi called for protests against these unwholesome depictions and even wanted to go so far as to destroy the sculptures or at least remove them from view. Rabindranath Tagore took a stand against these protests and asked for understanding for what was previously considered normal and was even viewed as sacred.[5]

A comparable sensitivity can be observed in the phenomenon of the temple dancers, the *devadāsīs*. Ziegenbalg and those like him displayed great indignation when they described how the dancers were also hired by Europeans in the Danish colony Tharangambadi (Tranquebar) for private performances. Their prostitutes' trade nevertheless remained an insurmountable stumbling block for the missionaries. The Danish and German inhabitants of the colony turned out to be considerably more relaxed about this. And Ziegenbalg's native informants had done their best to show the finer and artistic sides of the existence of these women, as is apparent from the Malabar Correspondence.

It was difficult to present positive reports of the temple dancers in the strict, Puritanical milieu of the pietists in Halle. Missionaries from other organisations did have more freedom. Rogerius saw temple dancers in Paliacatta as well, but he was much more positive. He placed all the emphasis on the unique but consistent morality that these women imposed on themselves: in their

4 On these temples see Krishna Deva 1990.

5 Sibnarayan Roy in Singh and Sundaram 1996:288.

relations with their lovers, faithfulness and devotion were primary after all. In that way, their way of life could be approved, despite the free sexual relations.

5 Languages

The greatest challenge for travellers from Europe right from the start was dealing with the foreign languages. Traders could make themselves understood in general in Persian; this language functioned as a *lingua franca*. Interpreters could also make it possible to arrive at acceptable communication in negotiations on goods and prices. This was different for missionaries, however, Francis Xavier's complaint that he could not understand his dialogue partners, "as I spoke Castilian and they Malabar" was characteristic. Although he did eventually succeed with the help of interpreters to clarify his intentions, it was more than clear that a religious message could be communicated only if the missionaries thoroughly learned the local language.

It was therefore the missionaries who, during the whole history of the encounter with Hindus, were at the forefront in learning the languages. Among the preachers of the Gospel in India were a number of exceptional men who succeeded in completely mastering the native languages. Roberto de Nobili should be mentioned first of all; he managed to learn to speak Tamil so well that it seemed as if it was his mother tongue. He also mastered Telugu and Sanskrit. That he had learned this sacred language, thanks to the willing help of a Brahmin, is particularly worthy of mention. The knowledge he had acquired made it also possible for him to become thoroughly familiar with Sanskrit literature. Modern Indologists still argue that it was the academics of the eighteenth century who opened up Sanskrit for the West and that, though the missionaries themselves knew the language somewhat, they did not study the literature.[6] The case of Roberto de Nobili already proves the opposite.

Bartholomäus Ziegenbalg was the linguistic virtuoso of the older Protestants. After arriving in Tharangambadi, he took lessons from an interpreter who had worked for the Danish administration. His very intensive instruction resulted in him being able to speak the language already after eight months and to understand the people. During the next year he also learned to preach in Tamil, first from a text completely written out beforehand but very quickly learned to do so extemporaneously. Ziegenbalg also built up a library of palm leaf manuscripts and became very familiar with literature in Tamil. He even

6 Bodewitz 2002:9: "Some missionaries were perhaps not inferior with respect to linguistics [compared to Jones and his associates], but they had little interest in literature."

made a contribution to literature by translating a number of Christian works into Tamil.

Classic Hindu religious literature was written in Sanskrit, and this language was only slowly deciphered by Europeans. That was partly because Sanskrit was less used in the southern part of the subcontinent where most missionary activity took place. The fact that traditional Brahmanical scholars were very hesitant to share their sacred language with Westerners who did, after all, lack the required ritual purity, also played a role. Through his far-reaching adaptation to Indian life, De Nobili had gained sufficient trust to be allowed to learn Sanskrit, but he was an exception. In the second half of the eighteenth century, some government officials were eventually able to be taught by Sanskrit scholars and learn the sacred language. The pioneer was William Jones, who translated classic works from Sanskrit. European universities continued the work of translating the sacred texts that were written in Sanskrit.

The missionaries continued to be active, however, in opening up the Hindu heritage. The Baptists in the Danish colony Serampore translated writings from Sanskrit and Bengali, and it was a missionary from the Basel Mission in southwest India, Ferdinand Kittel, who laid the foundation for the study of a less well-known Dravidian language, Kannada. His very extensive dictionary has continued to be a standard work right up to the present, and the first translations from this language were provided by him and his colleagues.

Thus, the missionaries and government officials took up the study of the languages and cultures of India. Sometimes the boundaries between both groups became blurred. John Muir had an acceptable civil service career in the British East India company but, because of his evangelical background, he also felt strongly drawn to play a role in the spread of Christianity as well. He mastered Sanskrit so well that he could write in that language and even in classic Sanskrit verse. Many discussions testify to his talent and his passion for spreading the Christian faith among learned Hindus.

6 A Broad Interest

The missionaries did not limit themselves to the tasks that they were traditionally given: public preaching, education, and building up the community. Many who spent a great deal of their lives in India also attempted to chart the culture and religion of India in all kinds of ways. Among the Catholics, the Jesuits were the ones who usually recorded many aspects of life in India. Later, other missionaries also continued this work. For instance, Abbé Dubois became well known because of his large manual on Indian culture, for which the foundation was laid by the eighteenth-century Jesuits. The abbé followed in De Nobili's steps in more respects than one. In his way of life as well, he also attempted to adapt as much as possible to what Hindus expected from a spiritual guide. His continually expanding report on the Hindu culture shows a very broad interest and a phenomenal knowledge of the writings and of morals and customs.

The situation was no different among the Protestants. At the end of the eighteenth century, more and more missionaries became interested in studying nature in India. Immense shell collections were started, thousands of plants, birds, and insects were systematically described, and even fish were named after the missionary staff doing the research (Jürgens 2014:185–90, 336). Even missionaries from pietistic circles, such as those associated with Halle, sought to combine mission work and research in natural history. One of them wrote that he wanted to propagate both religion and the Enlightenment in India (Christoph Samuel John [1746–1813], cited in: Jürgens 2014:186).

More was discovered during the course of the nineteenth century on the origins of the various population groups. Linguistic studies made some things clear about the differences between the Aryan invaders and the original Dravidian inhabitants. German missionaries from the Leipzig Mission helped with the development of various theories about race and caste that was based on this distinction between the Aryans and the Dravidian inhabitants. Modern ethnological methods, including the measurement of skulls, also helped the missionaries in elaborating on theories that often had more to do with questionable ideologies than with reliable science (Nehring 2003:137–52; see also 5).

The question of what led the missionary staff to devote so much attention to areas that were outside their purview is an interesting one. What lay behind Abbé Dubois' drive is clear: he was very disappointed in missionary work as such and gradually concluded that the missionisation of India was an impossible task. With his cultural anthropological studies, however, he made a very valuable contribution for both scientists and administrators. The linguistic achievements of Ferdinand Kittel seem to have had a similar background. The more he came to know the surrounding culture, the less motivated he was to remove people from that environment. His descendants have preserved a statement by him to the effect that he was grateful to God for not having converted anyone because then he would have taken something from a human being (cited by Majan Mulla in Wendt 2006:118). The study of Kannada, which resulted in his voluminous dictionary, was his passion, however, and thus also his contribution to missionary work.

7 Another Religious Structure and Culture

Missionaries and administrators, visitors and scholars—all attempted to draw a picture of the culture of the region in which they found themselves. And all saw the socio-religious structure there as determinative. The division of the population into castes, determined by birth and hierarchically structured, was the most prominent characteristic of Hindu society.

The first visitors in the Middle Ages had already observed this remarkable structure. In those cases, it was primarily the Brahmins who, as the highest in the religious pyramid, drew the most attention. Marco Polo came to know them via the object that characteristically distinguished them: the sacred thread. And he also saw something of the doctrine of the different phases of life in real life: he distinguished between the Brahmins who were socially active and the Brahmins who had withdrawn from society to live a 'homeless' life, the *sannyāsīs*. It is remarkable that this Venetian merchant was very impressed by the moral sense he saw in the Brahmins. He described them as very virtuous: good, trustworthy merchants who never told lies or engaged in deceit. And he was also aware of the principles that they painstakingly lived by: purity rules, vegetarianism, and marital faithfulness.

This dealt only with the top of the pyramid, however. It would be some time yet before Western travellers saw the whole of the structure. Jan Huygen van Linschoten, who published his work *Itinerario* shortly before 1600, was the first to provide insight into the complete structure as he observed it in Goa. It turned out that there was a wide variety of castes, each with its own professions, its own norms and lifestyle, and its own place in the hierarchy. For the first time, the lowest groups, who lived in abject poverty and were treated with contempt by the higher caste groups, were also described.

With respect to religion, the Brahmins claimed the right, on the basis of their inherited position, to define religious belief and rules for conduct. After all, they were traditionally the teachers of the religion. That did not mean, however, that the lower castes experienced religion in the same way. Although the Brahmins had ultimate control over the literature in Sanskrit that had been passed on, other caste groups, right down to the lowest, also had their own cults, rituals, and beliefs. On the one hand, Hinduism—as Europeans gradually came to understand it—consisted of a comprehensive system in which Brahmins had the highest position. On the other hand, the lower castes were subservient to the Brahmins, but they did have their own group experience.

It was a long time before this stratification of Hindu society was recognised. In the seventeenth century, Roberto de Nobili managed to build a bridge to Hinduism by adapting himself completely to the Brahmins and endorsing their supremacy in full. Because of that, church communities consisting of Hindus did form and acquired a respectable place in society. This stood in the way of the acceptance of the Christian faith for castes below the Brahmins, however. It is understandable and not incorrect that contemporary Christians from a *Dalit* background strongly resist the Brahmin-oriented church that arose.

Later missionaries allowed more room for the lower castes. Dubois conquered all his disgust in order to visit the shabby and filthy huts of the poorest of his parishioners. After all, the poor did constitute the largest group of Hindus who had become Christians. That was no different for the Protestant missionaries who also found a response to their message among the lowest castes. In particular, those who, as 'untouchables,' had no status at all in Hindu society were open to the Gospel. Acceptance of the Gospel probably entailed some steps up the social ladder for them (Fernando and Gispert-Sauch 2004:179–200; see also Bauman 2008).

Ziegenbalg and his colleagues deliberately attempted to provide a picture of whole breadth of Hindu culture in Tharangambadi. Of course, the learned Brahmins were the first to be asked about the religious literature and customs. They were also the ones most used to preparing letters and explanations. In addition, the correspondence with people from the lower castes is striking. Information about the cultus of the village gods and the life and industriousness of the less prominent people was also discussed.

8 Idols and Monotheism

What kind of religion did the travellers from Europe come to know? For the first visitors from the thirteenth and fourteenth centuries, it was clear: "These people worship idols" was the characteristic refrain from Odoric and his fellow Franciscans. That judgment is not all surprising. And it is no more surprising that people—given the beliefs at the time—viewed this idolatry as a local variant of a 'heathenism' that was present everywhere in the world. It is indeed striking that the idea quite quickly developed that there was one God behind the plurality of divine figures—or, more accurately, that the God whom the Christians worshipped was ultimately the same as the one behind the strange religiosity of India.

This idea can be found already in the middle of the fifteenth century. It was the Venetian merchant Nicolò de' Conti who speculates about a monotheistic basis when he presents a morning prayer said by people in East India (or Indochina) that emphatically calls on a "triune God." De' Conti is probably confusing this with the Hindu threefold figure of the Trimūrti, but an association with the Christian concept of God could arise from this example.

The case is very direct in Jan Huygen van Linschoten's major work from 1596, *Itinerario*. He notes various times that, though the native inhabitants of Goa did worship all kinds of idols, they all believed that in the end there was one God who created and governs everything. The same idea was also advanced by the VOC minister Abraham Rogerius. He vehemently disputed the popular view that the indigenous peoples had no concept of God whatsoever.[7] To the contrary, he argued that they not only recognise the existence of gods but also that there is a supreme God, who is 'one' and that there is no other equal to him.

The first to look deeply at the concept of God in the Hindu and Christian traditions was Roberto de Nobili. His incentive was the notion of *accomodatio*, the adaptation of the Christian faith to the Hindu culture in order to be able to appeal to the Brahmins. In this undertaking, De Nobili was followed by the church authorities in an extremely critical way. We know of no positive explanations of Hinduism from his hand. He could not permit himself to give any credit to the religion that he was thought to be combatting. But some things can be derived from his choices in formulating the Christian message. It is telling that he initially wanted to use the name *Śiva* to refer to God in Christianity. Here the adaptation to Hindu culture went quite far: it suggested without any reservation that Christians and Hindus worshipped the same God. When De Nobili began to recognise the objections of mythological connotations, he opted in the end for a neologism: *Carvēcuraṉ*, 'Master of everything.' Although this was a newly coined term, it was a bridge between the two traditions, for it could also function well in Hinduism as a reference to a godhead.

In the following century, Ziegenbalg followed De Nobili. He also wanted to do justice to the monotheism that he saw in Hinduism behind the plurality of divine figures (Tiliander 1974:91–94). It is striking that Ziegenbalg, whose orthodox pietistic background made him extremely critical of everything that could refer to polytheism, made a choice here that was intended to honour what Hindus believed.

It was a step forward in the encounter with Hindus that Christians learned to recognise that the idea of a supreme divinity, on which everything that

7 Rogerius 1915:85: "No one should think that this people are simply like animals, with no knowledge of God or religion." Sweetman understands the Dutch word for 'religion' (*Godsdienst*) in this quote to be the same as the German word *Gottesdienst* (liturgy, worship) and translates it as 'divine service,' which gives a completely wrong idea. See Sweetman 2003:96.

existed depended could be found in Hinduism as well. For modern Hindus, monotheism as the most profound truth is obvious, whether or not it lies behind the plurality of divine figures. Nevertheless, the question whether this did not give too Christian a view of Hinduism remained. In the experience of many Hindus, after all, the notion of a creator and chief god had never been as central throughout the centuries as Christians expected. It is, for example, typical that there are hardly any temples dedicated to Brahmā as creator.

The question of the Hindu concept of God has justifiably been raised repeatedly. When the missionary Auguste Bourquin argued at the end of the nineteenth century for a pantheistic interpretation of the oldest literature of Hinduism, he was certainly not exempt from a certain trendy one-sidedness. But he was right in his critical questioning: a classic Christian dichotomy of monotheism versus polytheism did not offer the best approach to Hinduism.

9 Plurality and Colourfulness

The umbrella term *Hinduism* covers a plurality of religious differences. More so than is the case with Christianity and Islam, differing interpretations can be found that can exist alongside each other, even though they sometimes contradict each other. The Hinduism of the one is not the Hinduism of the other.

Not until the nineteenth century did people slowly begin to see this remarkable pluriformity. On the one hand, the Hindu tradition could be described as a uniform whole through the opening up of Sanskrit literature, with authoritative sources and a long history of explanation and elaboration. On the other hand, mission workers, visitors, and government officials showed more than ever how enormously different the religious and cultural worlds of castes, tribes, and regions were.

The impact of these developments can be found in the monumental manual written by Abbé Dubois. This book contains a comprehensive description of the belief system of the Brahmins, with all the distinctions between life phases and directions that people had come to understand. But the book also contains descriptions of the other, lower castes with their own peculiarities with respect to way of life and cultus. Reading between the lines clearly shows that Dubois felt more connected with the less privileged Hindus. He had come to know them very well through his pastoral work, and he had been struck by their appalling living conditions and their dependence on the Brahmins and members of other higher castes. Dubois was thus the first to pay attention to the lot of these who were called *Dalits* (the broken ones) at the end of the twentieth century.

Dubois' work is certainly not a value-free and neutral description from the sidelines. Much of his resistance to the Brahmanical rigour comes out of a sincere engagement with the majority of the population that suffered under the supremacy of the Brahmins. The disillusioned missionary saw no possibility for motivating the Brahmins, who held so tightly to their ancestral traditions, to engage in Christian humanitarianism. And that was ultimately what stimulated him.

Visitors in this period also came face to face with the persistence and conservativism of the top religious and social layer. Mary Carpenter came to learn that the social changes that she fought for on behalf of women and girls had received little chance in the rigid world of classical Hinduism. But she discovered hopeful signs of another dynamic in that same Hinduism in the reform movements that arose in the nineteenth century.

The missionaries of the Basel Mission attempted to portray Hinduism in its pluriformity. Kittel not only described the classic doctrine of sacrifice in order to find points of contact for the Gospel; with some of his colleagues, he also helped open up the literary heritage of liṅgāyatism that had arisen centuries ago in Karnataka as an alternative to the Brahmanical system. It was obviously worthwhile to follow different directions in the encounter with Hinduism.

10 Nascent Dialogue

Various positions can be distinguished in the history of the encounter of Europeans with Hinduism. Among Portuguese Jesuits and French missionaries, Caland found primarily "critique that seemed to be unpleasant," while viewing Rogerius, in contrast—because of his great objectivity—as the opposite extreme. He placed Ziegenbalg in the middle between these two extremes: Ziegenbalg did speak of the blindness of the heathens, but he did note at the same time the good that was found among them and could appreciate their knowledge (Caland 1924:11–12).

It did indeed take a long time before the biased critique disappeared from the encounter with Hindus and appreciation grew for what this religion had to contribute. Only then could a dialogue between adherents of the different religious traditions arise. For Europeans, the wisdom literature of the Indians played an important role in this. Rogerius was already impressed by the proverbs of Bhartṛhari, which he added to his book on "hidden heathenism." Ziegenbalg also found wisdom for life in the ethical tractates of the Hindus he translated he could approve of. And John Muir, who once started with a self-evident rejection of Hinduism, searched for wisdom texts from India at the end of his life that would also appeal to Christians.

From the other side, from the beginning of the 19th century, there was a sincere interest in the proclamation of Jesus Christ among progressive Hindus. Raja Rammohan Roy was the first Hindu to publish a book on Jesus' teachings, and that book evoked a great deal of response among Hindus and Christians (Schouten 2008:5–34). From then on, Hindus also had to justify their attitude towards the beliefs of the Christians.

In many ways, the dialogue between Hindus and Christians was carried on in both India and other countries. But that dialogue would never have been possible without the history that has been described in this book: this was a becoming acquainted that took centuries, as Europeans slowly became familiar with a culture and a religion that was so different from theirs but continued to fascinate them.

Bibliography

Secondary Literature

Bauman, Chad M. (2008). *Christian Identity and Dalit Religion in Hindu India, 1868–1947*. Studies in the History of Christian Missions. Grand Rapids/Cambridge: William B. Eerdmans Publishing Company.

Bodewitz, H.W. (2002). *De late 'ontdekking' van het Sanskrit en de Oudindische cultuur in Europa.* Farewell Lecture. Leiden: Leiden University.

Caland, W. (1924). "Over Ziegenbalg's Malabarisches Heidenthum." *Mededeelingen der Koninklijke Akademie van Wetenschappen Amsterdam*, Afd. Letterkunde, Deel 57, Serie A, No. 4: 73–89.

Dröge, Philip (2017). *Pelgrim: Leven en reizen van Christiaan Snouck Hurgronje.* Houten: Uitgeverij Unieboek/Het Spectrum.

Fernando, Leonard, and G. Gispert-Sauch (2004). *Christianity in India: Two Thousand Years of Faith.* New Delhi: Penguin-Viking.

Gäbler, Ulrich (2018). *Ein Missionarsleben: Hermann Gäbler und die Leipziger Mission in Südindien (1891–1916).* Leipzig: Evangelische Verlagsanstalt.

Gerritsen, W.P. (2007). "De eenhoorn, de Bijbel en de *Physiologus*: De metamorfose van een Oud-Indische mythe." *Queeste. Tijdschrift over middeleeuwse letterkunde in de Nederlanden* 14: 78–87.

Jürgens, Hanco (2014). *Roeping India: Religie, Verlichting en koloniale expansie. Duitse zendingsberichten 1750–1810.* Nijmegen: Radboud University.

Krishna Deva (1990). *Temples of Khajuraho.* 2 parts. New Delhi: Archaeological Survey of India.

Nehring, Andreas (2003). *Orientalismus und Mission: Die Repräsentation der tamilischen Gesellschaft und Religion durch Leipziger Missionare 1840–1940*. Studien zur außereuropäischen Christentumsgeschichte 7. Wiesbaden: Otto Harrassowitz Verlag.

Rogerius, Abraham (1915). *De Open-Deure tot het Verborgen Heydendom*. Ed. W. Caland. 's-Gravenhage: Martinus Nijhoff. Originally published 1651.

Schouten, Jan Peter (2008). *Jesus as Guru: The Image of Christ among Hindus and Christians in India*. Transl. Henry and Lucy Jansen. Currents of Encounter 36. Amsterdam/New York: Rodopi.

Singh, Ramjee, and S. Sundaram (eds.) (1996). *Gandhi and The World Order*. New Delhi: APH Publishing Corp.

Sweetman, Will (2003). *Mapping Hinduism: 'Hinduism' and the Study of Indian Religions, 1600–1776*. Neue Hallesche Berichte 4. Halle: Verlag der Franckeschen Stiftungen.

Tiliander, Bror (1974). *Christian and Hindu Terminology: A Study in Their Mutual Relations with Special Reference to the Tamil* Area. Skrifter utgivna av Religionshistoriska Institutionen i Uppsala (Hum. Fak.) 12. Uppsala: Almqvist & Wiksell.

Wendt, Reinhard (ed.) (2006). *An Indian to the Indians? On the Initial Failure and the Posthumous Success of the Missionary Ferdinand Kittel (1832–1903)*. Studien zur außereuropäischen Christentumsgeschichte 9. Wiesbaden: Otto Harrassowitz Verlag.

Yule, Henry and A.C. Burnell (1986). *Hobson-Jobson: A Glossary of Colloquial Anglo-Indian Words and Phrases*. 2nd ed. London/New York: Routledge & Kegan Paul.

Glossary

accomodatio adaptation of Christian forms of expression to the culture of India in line with the project of Roberto de Nobili

ādivāsī someone who belongs to one of the tribal communities outside of the classical caste system

Agni the divine personification of the sacrificial fire in Hinduism

aiyar a Hindu scholar, teacher

Anbequemung Kittel's term for the adaptation of the Christian message to the local culture

anuṣṭubh a specific metre that is used in Sanskrit poetry, based on four-line stanzas

avarṇa term for castes considered so unclean that they are not included in the classical four social classes (*varṇa*)

avatāra incarnation, descent of a divinity in human form, especially of the god Viṣṇu

bachali term that Nicolò de' Conti used for Brahmins who carry out priestly functions, probably derived from *baqqāl*, dealers in grain

Baniyā name of a caste of merchants from Gujarat

Basava Purāṇa sacred text in Kannada of the *Liṅgāyatas* on the founder of their movement

bautismu bastardised Portuguese word for 'baptism'

Bengali language spoken in eastern India and in Bangladesh, part of the Indo-European family of languages

Bhadrakālī śaivistic divinity

Bhagavad Gītā "Song of the Lord," a sacred Hindu text in which Kṛṣṇa gives instruction; part of the *Mahābhārata*

Bhāgavata Purāṇa sacred Hindu text with mythological stories, primarily about Kṛṣṇa

bhakti the path to God through loving devotion

Brahmā god to whom the origin of the world and humanity is primarily attributed

brahmacarya first of the four life phases according to the *varṇāśramadharma*, devoted to study and characterised by renouncing sex

Brahmakarmapustaka "Service of the Brahmins," nineteenth-century book of rituals, translated by A. Bourquin

Brāhma Samāj "Society of Worshippers of God," a religious monotheistic society founded by Rammohan Roy

Brāhmaṇa Vedic scriptures, especially devoted to the interpretation of ritual

Brahmin (Brāhmaṇa) a member of the highest group in the Hindu caste system to whom priestly functions are entrusted

Candra divinity in Hinduism, personification of the moon, often equated with Soma

Cannabasava Purāṇa sacred text in the Kannada language of the *Liṅgāyatas* on one of the first leaders of their movement

Carvēcuraṉ neologism coined by De Nobili for God in accordance with the Christian concept of God: 'Master of all'; Sanskrit: *Sarveśvara*

cattiyavētam 'the true knowledge,' a Tamil term that De Nobili coined for the Christian faith: *satyaveda*

cynocephali people with dogs' heads who, according to ancient tradition, are said to live in India

Dakṣiṇā name of a caste of dealers in textiles who come from the Deccan plateau

Dalits 'the broken ones,' a term given to themselves by the lowest castes in the hierarchy since the middle of the twentieth century; they were traditionally viewed as unclean

Dasahrā a Hindu feast that closes the Navarātri season of feasts, celebrated especially in the city of Mysore

devadāsī a woman whose life is devoted to service in the temple and as a temple dancer

devanāgari the script that is traditionally used for Sanskrit and related languages

Devī general name for a goddess, used in particular for Pārvatī

dharma religious teachting, religion, spiritual merit

dharmaśāstra science that gives a description of ethics according to Brahmin principles

Dharmasindhu "Ocean of Teachings," book of rituals in Sanskrit written by Kāśīnātha and translated by A. Bourquin

Dīvālī a Hindu feast in the fall, whereby numerous oil lamps are lit in honour of Lakṣmī

Doḍḍa svāmiyavaru 'Great Lord' in Kannada, honourary title given to Abbé Dubois

evidential theology theological school of thought in which reason was seen as supplementary to revelation; this was a position defended by William Paley

faqīr term for ascetic mendicants, primarily Islamic

fidalgos European nobility; the Portuguese used the term for the *Nāyars*

Gajendramokṣa mythological story in which Viṣṇu rescues a king who had been changed into an elephant (recorded in the eighth book of the *Bhāgavata Purāṇa*)

Gaṇeśa god of wisdom in Hinduism, characteristically depicted with an elephant's head, son of Śiva and Pārvatī

Gaṅgā lesser divinity in Hinduism, a personification of the river Ganges

garbhagṛha the innermost, most sacred space in a Hindu temple where a divine image stands; literally: womb chamber

Garuḍa lesser divinity in Hinduism in the form of a bird that serves as transportation for Viṣṇu

Gavi old designation of a caste in which beef was eaten

Gāyatrī-mantra one of the most sacred mantras in Hinduism (Ṛg-Veda 3: 62, 10)

gopuram large decorated towers that serve as entrances to temples in South India

gṛhastha second of the four life phases according to the *varṇāśramadharma*, devoted to family life

Gujarātī name of a caste from Gujarat

guru a spiritual teacher, in particular a Brahmin who initiates young boys into the teaching and rituals of the religion

Hallesche Berichte usual name for the journal that was published by the pietistic mission organisation in Halle (official title: *Der Königl. Dänischen Missionarien aus Ost-Indien eingesandter Ausführlichen Berichten…*)

Hanumān Hindu divinity in the form of a monkey; important in the *Rāmāyaṇa*

Hiraṇyakaśipu tyrannical figure in a mythological story who was killed by Viṣṇu in his incarnation as *Narasiṃha*

Holī a Hindu feast in spring in which people throw coloured powder at each other

hook-swinging a devotional act whereby people are elevated after having hooks inserted into their back muscles

Indra a divinity who was already worshipped in the Vedas and was called the 'king of the gods.'

Jagannātha 'Lord of the world,' a form of Kṛṣṇa who is worshipped especially in the great temple of Puri (Orissa)

jñāna-snāna 'bath of knowledge'; neologism for 'baptism'

jñānī a wise man, someone who attempts to reach God via the way of knowledge

Kailāsa heaven, home of the gods, especially Śiva and Pārvatī

Kanara name of a caste of dealers in textiles, from the Deccan Plateau

Kannada language in South India, particularly in Karnataka, from the family of Dravidian languages

Kannaḍiyan name of a low caste of small farmers in Goa

karma the positive and negative balance of someone's actions during his life that determine his or her next life

Kathāmāle "A Garland of Stories," a work by Ferdinand Kittel in Kannada

kāvi classic attire of the Hindu ascetic, consisting of three ochre-coloured pieces of cloth with raw edges

Konkani language in South India, especially in Goa, part of the Indo-European family of languages

Koṉṟaivēntaṉ "The king with the cassia flowers"; classic Tamil textbook with precepts for one's life, attributed to the poetess Auvaiyār

Kristapurāṇa epic in Marathi on Christ, written by Thomas Stephens

Kristu Svāmī 'Lord Christ,' neologism in Marathi

Kṛṣṇa most famous incarnation of Viṣṇu, according to Hindu mythology, a central figure in the mysticism of love

Kṣatriya the second class in the classic fourfold division of the castes: after the Brahmins and before the *Vaiśyas* and the *Śūdras*

kuḍumi the traditional lock of hair that the Brahmins left on their heads after shaving off the rest; also called *cūḍā*

Kuṭumbī name of a low caste in Goa

Lakṣmī goddess of prosperity and wealth, consort of Viṣṇu

Lalla Rookh 'tulip-cheeked,' legendary Islamic princess, the main character in the poem of the same name by Thomas Moore

Lambāḍi a nomadic tribe in the middle of India

Lawbook of Manu officially called *Mānavadharmaśāstra*, the classic collection of rights and duties according to Brahmin principles

Lettres édifiantes et curieuses a Jesuit journal on mission and non-European culture and religions

liṅga symbol of the god Śiva, originally a phallic representation

Liṅgāyatism a religious movement in South India whose adherents practise devotion to Śiva and wear a small *liṅga*; literally: *liṅga* bearer; also known as Vīraśaivism

Mahābhārata "The Great Epic of the Descendants of Bharata," a very long poem in Sanskrit from the beginning of the Christian calendar

Mahāśivarātri a Hindu feast in honour of the god Śiva, celebrated early in the year

"Malabar Correspondence" (Malabarische Korrespondenz) name of a project whereby Indians provided written information to the missionaries in Tharangambadi (Tranquebar) about their religion and culture

Malabar Rites Controversy church conflict on the permissibility of rituals and customs from Hindu sources

Malayalam language in South India, particularly in Kerala, part of the family of Dravidian languages

Malay widespread language in Southeast Asia, including Indonesia, part of the family of Austronesian languages

Mānavadharmaśāstra see Lawbook of Manu

Marathi language of the state of Maharashtra, part of the family of Indo-European languages

Mataparīkṣā "An Examination of Religions," work by John Muir

Mataparīkṣāśikṣā "A Study in the Examination of Religions," work by Somanath Vyas as a response to John Muir

Mataparīkṣottara "A Response to the Writer of An Examination of Religions," a work by Harachandra Tarkapanchanana as a response to John Muir

maṭha a holy place, especially a monastery

mesquita Portuguese term for a mosque, an Islamic house of prayer

mīsai bastardised Portuguese word for 'Holy Mass,' which means 'moustache' in Tamil

mohadharma Hindu idea that certain doctrines have been designed by a divinity to mislead people

Nandī mount of the god Śiva, a bull

nāraka one of several hells where people with a bad karma are punished after death

Narasiṃha divine appearance in the form of a man-lion, the fourth incarnation of Viṣṇu

Navarātri a Hindu feast in the fall that continues for nine nights

Nāyar name of a prominent caste of warriors in Kerala who practised polyandry

nīti the art of living, ethics; a category in the work of Bhartṛhari

Nītiveṇpā "Verses in the Veṇpa Metre on Morality," a Tamil book with proverbs on ethics

ovi metre in Marathi poetry, with four-line stanzas, of which the last line is shorter and does not rhyme with the previous three

Padma-Purāṇa a sacred book of the Hindus with mythological stories

padroado Papal ruling whereby Portugal was made responsible for the government and missionisation of India (and Spain would concern itself with the American continent)

pagoda a old term for a temple in China or India; also used to refer to an image of a god in a temple

pañcagavya a mixture of the five products of the cow (milk, buttermilk, butter, urine, and excrement) that is said to have a beneficial effect

Pañcatantra a collection of stories, mostly fables, in Sanskrit, compiled in the first centuries CE

paṇḍit customary term for a Hindu scholar, in particular someone who has mastered Sanskrit

paṇṭāracāmi priest for non-Brahmin Hindus; Sanskrit: *paṇḍāra-svāmī*

Paṟaiyar pariah, name of a very low caste whose members are viewed by others as very unclean

paraṅgi term used by the Indians for Europeans; literally: 'Frank,' from which it is derived

paraṅgi mārkkam term used by the Indians for the religion of the Europeans

Parāparavastu God, as the all-encompassing; a Hindu term in Tamil for the divine, highlighted by Ziegenbalg

Parava name of a caste of fishermen in Tamil Nadu

Parsi adherent of Zoroastrianism

Pārvatī Hindu mother goddess, consort of Śiva

Patarenes a movement in twelfth-century Italy viewed as heretical, similar to the Cathars

peri a supernatural figure in the Persian mythology of Zoroastrianism, 'angel'

Poṅkal harvest festival that is celebrated in January in Tamilnadu in which cooking new rice is central

Prahlāda a mythological figure, son of Hiraṇyakaśipu who, despite his father's resistance, remains faithful in his devotion to Viṣṇu

prasād food that is offered to the gods and then shared with believers

pūjā sacrifice; especially in the worship of a divinity before an image of the god

Puliyar name of a low caste in Kerala

purāṇa Hindu sacred texts, usually in poetic form, in which mythological narratives are central

rāga musical notation of Indian music in which the scale and range are set

the Raj the direct government of India by the English crown without any role for the East Indian Company, from 1858 to 1947

Rājā prince, title of an Indian monarch; also the name of a caste from which the princes came, part of the *kṣatriya* class

Rāmā divine avatar, one of the incarnations of Viṣṇu

Rāmāyaṇa "The Life of Rāma," a long epic in Sanskrit on the incarnation of Viṣṇu as Rāmā, from the beginning of the Christian calendar

Ṛg-Veda the oldest and most sacred book in the Hindu canon, going back to the second millennium BCE

Romanae sedis antistes literally: "The Bishop on the Seat of Rome," title of an apostolic constitution issued by Pope Gregory XV in 1623

roteiros detailed shipping routes to Asia, used by the Portuguese as strictly confidential information

Ṛśyaśṛṅga a mythological figure, a hermit who wears a single horn on his head

sacrifiçiu bastardised Portuguese word for 'sacrifice'

sādhū holy man, ascetic

śaiva worshipper of the god Śiva

Sakkili name of a very low ranked caste, shoemakers

Śakuntalā a play in Sanskrit on the legend of Śakuntalā who grew up in the forest and married the king, written by Kālidāsa, fifth century CE

saṃsāra the continuing cycle of birth, death, and rebirth

sanātana dharma eternal teaching, classical Indian designation of Hinduism

sannyāsī fourth of the four life phases according to the *varṇāśramadharma*: life as a wandering ascetic

Sanskrit Indo-European language in which most sacred texts of Hinduism are written; previously closed by the Brahmins to all who did not belong to their caste

Sarasvatī Hindu goddess of knowledge and art; consort of Brahmā

Sarveśvara see *Carvēcuraṉ*

Śāstratattvavinirṇaya "The Proof of the Truth of the Scriptures," work by Nilakantha Goreh, a response to John Muir

Śatapatha-Brāhmaṇa sacred Hindu text that further explains rituals, from the middle of the first millennium BCE

satī a woman who sacrifices her life at her husband's cremation; later also the term for such a ritual suicide

ṣaṭpadi a metre in Kannada poetry, with stanzas of six-lines each

Seminarium Indicum the educational institute for theologians who wanted a career in the VOC (Dutch East Indian Company)

sepoy Indian soldier, Muslim or Hindu, in the British army

Śiva god who is associated primarily with asceticism and the decline of all that exists

Soma divinity who appears in all Vedic writings as the personification of the sacrificial drink, later equated with Candra

śṛṅgāra love, category in the work of Bhartṛhari

Subrahmaṇya Hindu divinity, son of Śiva and Pārvatī; in Tamil: Murukaṉ

Śūdra the fourth class in the classical fourfold division of the castes; after the Brahmins, *Kṣatriyas*, and *Vaiśyas*

svarga one of several heavens in which people with a good karma are rewarded after their death

Taittirīya-āraṇyaka a sacred Hindu text, concerned primarily with ritual and mysticism

tāla musical notation of Indian music in which a rhythmic cycle is set

Tamil language in South India, part of the family of Dravidian languages

Tampirāṉ classic Tamil term for the supreme God: 'lord with no lord above him'

Telugu language in South India, part of the family of Dravidian languages

ṭhag member of a gang who joined visitors on their travels with the intention of robbing them by surprise and strangling them

tilaka sign made with dye on the forehead worn by, for example, Brahmin scholars

tithi a day in the lunar cycle

Trimūrti doctrine of the three chief gods (Brahmā, Viṣṇu, and Śiva) as one divine entity with creation, preservation, and destruction as its functions

Tūṣaṇat Tikkāram "Refutation of Calumnies," work by Roberto de Nobili in Tamil

Ulakanīti "Precepts"; Tamil manual with ethical proverbs

upanayana ritual in which the sacred thread is hung on a Brahmin boy for the first time

Upaniṣad Hindu works from the first millennium BCE, that contained secret instructions about worldview and mysticism

vairāgya renunciation of the world; category in the work of Bhartṛhari

vaiṣṇava worshipper of the god Viṣṇu

Vaiśya the third class in the classical fourfold division of the castes; after the Brahmins and *Kṣatriyas*, before *Śūdras*

vanaprastha forest dweller, third of the four life phases according to the *varṇāśramadharma*

varṇa classic division of the castes into four classes: Brahmins, *Kṣatriyas*, *Vaiśyas*, and *Śūdras*

varṇāśramadharma the classic Hindu division into four caste groups and four life phases

Veda the oldest and most sacred books of Hinduism, the oldest of which go back to the second millennium BCE

Veda Samāj group that broke away from the Brāhma Samāj, a more positive attitude towards Christ

Vīraśaivism a reform movement in Hinduism whereby the *liṅga* is central to the cultus; also called Liṅgāyatism

Viṣṇu one of the most important gods in Hinduism who is believed to have appeared on earth ten times

yajña sacrifice, as brought by the Brahmins

yajñopavīta sacred thread, a cord worn by male members of the Brahmin and other high castes on the upper body

Yajur-Veda one of the four sacred texts of the Veda

yogī ascetic, practitioner of yoga

yoni female genitals, vulva

yuga one of the four very long cosmic ages according to Hindu mythology

Zoroastrianism Persian religion, going back to the preaching of the prophet Zarathustra; religion of the Parsis

Bibliography

Anonymous (1859). "Boekbeschouwing 'De Bijbel, de Koran en de Veda's'." *Vaderlandsche Letteroefeningen* 1859: 418–27.

Arasaratnam, S. (1960). "Reverend Philippus Baldaeus: His Pastoral Work in Ceylon, 1656–1665." *Nederlands Theologisch Tijdschrift* 14: 350–60.

Arokiasamy, Soosai (1986). *Dharma, Hindu and Christian, according to Roberto de Nobili: Analysis of its Meaning and its Use in Hinduism and Christianity*. Documenta missionalia 19. Rome: Editrice Pontificia Università Gregoriana.

Arokiasamy, Soosai (1985). "De Nobili on Non-Christians and Non-Christian Religions." *Neue Zeitschrift für Missionswissenschaft* 41: 288–93.

Atkinson, George F. (1859). *Curry & Rice (on Forty Plates) or the Ingredients of Social Life at 'Our' Station in India*. London: Day & Son.

Bachmann, Peter R. (1972), *Roberto Nobili 1577–1656: Ein missionsgeschichtlicher Beitrag zum christlichen Dialog mit Hinduismus*. Bibliotheca Instituti Historici S.I. 32. Rome: Institutum Historicum S.I.

Badley, B.H. (1881). *Indian Missionary Directory and Memorial Volume*. Rev. ed. Lucknow/New York: Methodist Episcopal Church Press/Phillips and Hunt.

Bakker, Hans T. (1997). *De Schaamteloosheid tot het Uiterste Gedreven*. Amsterdam: Koninklijke Nederlandse Akademie van Wetenschappen.

Bakker, Hans T. (1988). "De culturele ontdekking van India: Romantische Geestdrift en de Opkomst der Oriëntalistiek." In: Hans Bakker and Martin Gosman (eds.). *De Oriënt: droom of dreiging?* Kampen: Kok Agora. Pp. 94–112.

Baldaeus, Philip (2000). *A Description of the East India Coasts of Malabar and Coromandel and also of the Isle of Ceylon with Their Adjacent Kingdoms and Provinces*. New Delhi/Madras: Asian Educational Services. https://archive.org/details/trueexactdescripoobald.

Baldaeus, Philip (1917). *Afgoderye der Oost-Indische Heydenen*. Ed. A.J. de Jong. 's-Gravenhage: Martinus Nijhoff.

Baldaeus, Philip (1672). *Naauwkeurige Beschryvinge van Malabar en Choromandel, Der zelver aangrenzende Ryken, En het machtige Eyland Ceylon, Nevens een omstandige en grondigh doorzochte ontdekking en wederlegginge van de Afgoderye der Oost-Indische Heydenen*. Amsterdam: Janssonius van Waasberge en Van Someren.

Barbosa, Duarte (1946). *Livro em que dá relação do que viu e ouviu no Oriente*. Ed. Augusto Reis Machado. Lisbon: Agência Geral das Colónias.

Barbosa, Duarte (1866). *A Description of the Coasts of East Africa and Malabar in the Beginning of the Sixteenth Century*. Transl. Henry E.J. Stanley. London: Hakluyt Society.

Basham, A.L. (1975). *The Wonder that was India: A Survey of the History and Culture of the Indian Sub-Continent before the Coming of the Muslims*. Calcutta: Fontana Books.

Bauman, Chad M. (2008). *Christian Identity and Dalit Religion in Hindu India, 1868–1947*. Studies in the History of Christian Missions. Grand Rapids/Cambridge: William B. Eerdmans Publishing Company.

Beumer, Mieke (1999). "Philippus Baldaeus en Gerrit Mosopatam: een buitengewoon portret." *Bulletin van het Rijksmuseum* 47: 144–73.

Binder, Katrin (2006a) "Die Basler Mission in Karnataka und Kerala." In: Michael Mann (ed.). *Europäische Aufklärung und protestantische Mission in Indien*. Heidelberg: Draupadi Verlag. Pp. 203–24.

Binder, Katrin (2006b). "A Garland of Stories: Kathāmāle." In: Reinhard Wendt (ed.). *An Indian to the Indians? On the Initial Failure and the Posthumous Success of the Missionary Ferdinand Kittel (1832–1903)*. Studien zur außereuropäischen Christentumsgeschichte 9. Wiesbaden: Otto Harrassowitz Verlag. Pp. 231–53.

Bodewitz, H.W. (2002). *De late 'ontdekking' van het Sanskrit en de Oudindische cultuur in Europa*. Farewell Lecture. Leiden: Leiden University.

Boogaart, Ernst van den(2000). *Het verheven en verdorven Azië: Woord en beeld in het* Itinerario *en de* Icones *van Jan Huygen van Linschoten*. Amsterdam/Leiden: Het Spinhuis/KITLV Uitgeverij.

Bornet, Philippe (2017). "Review of N. Falcao, Father Thomas Stephens' Kristapurana I & II." *Exchange* 46: 73–77.

Bourquin, A. (1885). *Le panthéisme dans les Védas*. Paris: Fischbacher.

Bourquin, A. (1884a). *Brahmakarma ou rites sacrés des brahmanes*. Extrait des annales du Musée Guimet VII. Paris: Ernest Leroux.

Bourquin, A. (1884b). *Dharmasindhu ou océan des rites religieux Par le Prêtre Kāshinātha*. Transl. L. de Milloué. Extrait des annales du Musée Guimet VII.2. Paris: Ernest Leroux.

Boyd, R.H.S. (1975). *An Introduction to Indian Christian Theology*. Rev. ed. Madras: The Christian Literature Society.

Bracciolini, Poggio (1723). *Historiae de varietate fortunae*. Vol. IV. Lutetiae Parisiorum: Typis Antonii Urbani Coustelier. Pp. 126–52.

Brockington, J.L. (1993). *The Sacred Thread: Hinduism in its Continuity and Diversity*. 4th ed. Edinburgh: Edinburgh University Press.

Burnell, A.C. (1879). "On Some Early References to the Vedas by European Writers." *The Indian Antiquary* VIII: 98–100.

Caesar, Gaius Iulius (1958). *Commentarii de bello gallico*. Ed. P.K. Huibregtse. Groningen: J.B. Wolters.

Caland, W. (1924a). "Over Ziegenbalg's Malabarisches Heidenthum." *Mededeelingen der Koninklijke Akademie van Wetenschappen Amsterdam*, Afd. Letterkunde, Deel 57, Serie A, No. 4: 73–89.

Caland, W. (1924b). "Roberto de Nobili and the Sanskrit Language and Literature." *Acta Orientalia* III: 38–51.

Cannon, Garland and Kevin R. Brine (eds.) (1995). *Objects of Enquiry: The Life, Contributions, and Influences of Sir William Jones (1746–1794)*. New York/London: New York University Press.

Canter Visscher, Jacobus (2008). *Mallabaarse Brieven: De brieven van de Friese predikant Jacobus Canter Visscher (1717–1723)*. Ed. Bauke van der Pol. Zutphen: Walburg Pers.

Canter Visscher, Jacobus (1743). *Mallabaarse Brieven: Behelzende eene Naukeurige Beschryving van de Kust van Mallabaar, Den Aardt des Landts, de Zeden en Gewoontens der Inwoneren, en al het voornaamste dat in dit Gewest van Indië valt aan te merken.* Leeuwarden: Abraham Ferwerda.

Carey, William, and Joshua Marshman (1806–1810). *The Ramayuna of Valmeeki, in the Original Sungskrit, with a Prose Translation.* Three volumes. Serampore: s.n.

Carpenter, Mary (1868). *Six Months in India.* Two volumes. London: Longmans, Green, and Co.

Chakravarthy, Ananya (2014). "The Many Faces of Baltasar da Costa: Imitatio and Accomodatio in the Seventeenth Century Madurai Mission." *Etnográfica* 18: 135–58.

Charpentier, Jarl (1924). "The Brit. Mus. Ms. Sloane 3290, the Common Source of Baldaeus and Dapper." *Bulletin of the School of Oriental Studies* 3: 413–20.

Charpentier, Jarl (1923). "Preliminary Report on the 'Livro da Seita dos Indios Orientais' (Brit. Mus. Sloane, 1820)." *Bulletin of the School of Oriental Studies* 2: 731–54.

Christ-von Wedel, Christine, and Thomas K. Kuhn (eds.) (2015). *Basler Mission. Menschen, Geschichte, Perspektiven 1815–2015*. Basel: Schwabe Verlag.

Church of Scotland General Assembly (1878). *Reports on the Schemes of the Church of Scotland for the Year 1878*. Edinburgh: William Blackwood and Sons.

Church of Scotland General Assembly (1877). *Reports on the Schemes of the Church of Scotland for the Year 1877*. Edinburgh: William Blackwood and Sons.

Clooney, Francis X. (1990). "Roberto de Nobili, Adaptation and the Reasonable Interpretation of Religion." *Missiology* XVIII: 25–36.

Cœurdoux, G.-L. (1987). *Mœurs et coutumes des Indiens: Un inédit du Père G.-L. Cœurdoux s.j. dans la version de N.-J. Desvaulx*. Ed. Sylvia Murr. L'inde philosophique entre Bossuet et Voltaire 1. Paris: École française d'Extrême-Orient.

Coleridge, Henry James (1881). *The Life and Letters of St. Francis Xavier*. Volume I. London: Burns and Oates.

Collins, Wilkie (1955). *The Moonstone.* Harmondsworth: Penguin Books. Originally published 1868.

Cornille, Catherine (2008). "Missionary Views of Hinduism." *Journal of Hindu-Christian Studies* 21: 28–32.

Cronin, Vincent (1959). *A Pearl to India: The Life of Roberto de Nobili.* London: Hart-Davis.

Dahmen, Pierre (1931). *Robert de Nobili, l'apôtre des Brahmes: Première apologie,* 1610. Paris: Spes.

Deppermann, Klaus (1992). *Protestantische Profile von Luther bis Francke: Sozialgeschichtliche Aspekte.* Göttingen: Vandenhoeck & Ruprecht.

DeSmet, Richard (1991). "R. de Nobili as Forerunner of Hindu-Christian Dialogue." *Journal of Hindu-Christian Studies* 4: 1–9.

DeSmet, Richard (1990). "Review of Sylvie Murr, Moeurs et Coutumes des Indiens/L'Indologie du Père Coeurdoux." *Indian Theological Studies* 27: 371–73.

Dharampal-Frick, Gita (2006). "'...ausgesandt, das Heidenthum in Indien auszurotten, nicht aber den heidnischen Unsinn in Europa zu verbreiten': Bartholomäus Ziegenbalg und die Hallesche Tranquebar-Mission zwischen pietistischem Sendungsbewusstsein und ethnologischer Aufklärung." In: Michael Mann (ed.). *Europäische Aufklärung und protestantische Mission in Indien.* Heidelberg: Draupadi Verlag. Pp. 143–63.

Dharampal, Gita (1982), *La religion des malabars: Tessier de Quéralay et la contribution des missionaires européens à la naissance de l'indianisme.* Supplementa Nouvelle Revue de science missionnaire XXIX. Immensee: Nouvelle Revue de science mission naire.

Dröge, Philip (2017). *Pelgrim: Leven en reizen van Christiaan Snouck Hurgronje.* Houten: Uitgeverij Unieboek/Het Spectrum.

Dubois, J.A. (1985). *Hindu Manners, Customs and Ceremonies.* Ed. Henry K. Beauchamp. 3rd ed. 5th impression. Delhi: Oxford University Press.

Dubois, J.A. (1826). *Le Pantcha-Tantra ou les cinq ruses: Fables du Brahme Vichnou-Sarme, aventures de Paramarta, et autres contes.* Paris: J.-S. Merlin.

Dubois, J.A. (1823). *Letters on the State of Christianity in India: In which the Conversion of the Hindoos is Considered as Impracticable.* London: Longman, Hurst, Rees, Orme, Brown, and Green.

Dumont, Louis (1980). *Homo Hierarchicus: The Caste System and Its Implications.* Transl. Mark Sainsbury, Louis Dumont, and Basia Gulati. Chicago/London: University of Chicago Press.

Eden, Emily (1978). *Up the Country: Letters written to her Sister from the Upper Provinces of India.* London/Dublin: Curzon Press. Originally published 1866.

Eden, Emily (1844). *Portraits of the Princes & People of India.* London: J. Dickinson & Son.

Eteriano, Hugh (2004). *Contra Patarenos.* Ed. Bernard Hamilton et al. The Medieval Mediterranean 55. Leiden/Boston: Brill.

Falcao, Nelson (2003). *Kristapurāṇa: A Christian-Hindu Encounter. A Study of Inculturation in the Kristapurāṇa of Thomas Stephens, S.J. (1549–1619).* Pune/Anand: Snehasadan Studies.

Faltin, Thomas (2000). *Heil und Heilung: Geschichte der Laienheilkundigen und Struktur antimodernistischer Weltanschauungen in Kaiserreich und Weimarer Republik am Beispiel von Eugen Wenz (1856–1945)*. Medizin, Gesellschaft und Geschichte: Beiheft 15. Stuttgart: Franz Steiner Verlag.

Fenger, J. Ferd. (1845). *Geschichte der Trankebarschen Mission nach den Quellen bearbeitet*. Grimma: J.M. Gebhardt.

Fernando, Leonard, and G. Gispert-Sauch (2004). *Christianity in India: Two Thousand Years of Faith*. New Delhi: Penguin-Viking.

Fhlathúin, Máire Ní (2015). *British India and Victorian Literary Culture*. Edinburgh Critical Studies in Victorian Culture. Edinburgh: Edinburgh University Press.

Filliozat, Jean (1953). "Les premières étapes de l'indianisme." *Bulletin de l'Association Guillaume Budé* 3/3: 80–96.

Franklin, Michael J. (2011). *'Orientalist Jones': Sir William Jones, Poet, Lawyer, and Linguist (1746–1794)*. Oxford /New York: Oxford University Press.

Frasch, Tilman (2008). "'Deliver their land from error's chain': Mission und Kolonialherrschaft in Indien, 1793–1857." In: Michael Mann (ed.). *Aufgeklärter Geist und evangelische Missionen in Indien*. Heidelberg: Draupadi Verlag. Pp. 103–16.

Gäbler, Ulrich (2018). *Ein Missionarsleben: Hermann Gäbler und die Leipziger Mission in Südindien (1891–1916)*. Leipzig: Evangelische Verlagsanstalt.

Gelder, Roelof van, Jan Parmentier, and Vibeke Roeper (eds.) (1998). *Souffrir pour parvenir: De wereld van Jan Huygen van Linschoten*. Haarlem: Uitgeverij Arcadia.

Georgi, Lotte (1958). *Maria Dorothea Ziegenbalg: Tatsachenberichte aus dem Leben der ersten deutschen evangelischen Missionarsfrau in Süd-Indien*. Berlin: Evangelische Verlagsanstalt.

Gerritsen, W.P. (2007). "De eenhoorn, de Bijbel en de *Physiologus*: De metamorfose van een Oud-Indische mythe." *Queeste. Tijdschrift over middeleeuwse letterkunde in de Nederlanden* 14: 78–87.

Gispert-Sauch, George (2012). "Hinduism and Christianity." In: Knut A. Jacobsen (ed.). *Brill's Encyclopedia of Hinduism IV*. Leiden/Boston: Brill. Pp. 505–20.

Glasenapp, Helmuth von (1961). *Die Literaturen Indiens von ihren Anfängen bis zur Gegenwart*. Stuttgart: Alfred Kröner Verlag.

Gottschalk, Peter (2013). *Religion, Science, and Empire: Classifying Hinduism and Islam in British India*. Oxford /New York: Oxford University Press.

Groot, Hugo de (1622). *Bewys van den Waren Godsdienst*. S.l.

Gross, Andreas, Y. Vincent Kumaradoss, and Heike Liebau (2006). *Halle and the Beginning of Protestant Christianity in India*. Three volumes. Halle: Verlag der Franckeschen Stiftungen.

Gründler, Johann, and Bartholomäus Ziegenbalg (1998). *Die Malabarische Korrespondenz: Tamilische Briefe an deutsche Missionare*. Ed. Kurt Liebau. Fremde Kulturen in alten Berichten 5. Sigmaringen: Jan Thorbecke Verlag.

Halbfass, Wilhelm (1981). *Indien und Europa: Perspektiven ihrer geistigen Begegnung.* Basel/Stuttgart: Schwabe.

Havart, Daniël (1693). *Op- en ondergang van Cormandel, In zijn binnenste geheel open, en ten toon gesteld.* Three volumes. Amsterdam: Jan ten Hoorn.

Hoeberichts, J. (1994). *Franciscus en de Islam.* Scripta Franciscana 1. Assen: Van Gorcum.

Hoole, Elijah (1844). *Madras, Mysore, and the South of India: Or, A Personal Narrative.* 2nd ed. London: Longman, Brown, Green, and Longmans.

Hough, James (1824). *A Reply to the Letters of the Abbé Dubois on the State of Christianity in India.* London: L.B. Seeley & Son.

Irschick, Eugene F. (2003). "Conversations in Tarangambadi: Caring for the Self in Early Eighteenth Century South India." *Comparative Studies of South Asia, Africa and the Middle East* 23: 254–70.

Jeyaraj, Daniel (2006). *Bartholomäus Ziegenbalg: The Father of Modern Protestant Mission. An Indian Assessment.* New Delhi/Chennai: Indian Society for Promoting Christian Knowledge/Gurukul Lutheran Theological College and Research Institute.

John of Montecorvino (Johannes de Monte Corvino) (1929). "Epistolae." In: Anastasius van den Wyngaert (ed.). *Itinera et relationes fratrum minorum saeculi XIII et XIV.* Vol. I. Ad Claras Aquas Quaracchi-Firenze: apud Collegium S. Bonaventurae. Pp. 333–55.

Jones, William (1796). *Institutes of Hindu Law; or, the Ordinances of Menu, according to the Gloss of Cullúca.* Calcutta/London: Government/J. Sewell and J. Debrett.

Jongeneel, J. (2015). *Nederlandse zendingsgeschiedenis: Ontmoeting van protestantse christenen met andere godsdiensten en geloven (1601–1917).* Zoetermeer: Boekencentrum Academic.

Joosse, L.J. (2001a). "Baldaeus, Philippus." In: C. Houtman et al. (eds.). *Biografisch Lexicon voor de geschiedenis van het Nederlandse Protestantisme 5.* Kampen: Kok. Pp. 35–36.

Joosse, L.J. (2001b). "Rogerius, Abraham." In: C. Houtman et al. (eds.). *Biografisch Lexicon voor de geschiedenis van het Nederlandse Protestantisme 5.* Kampen: Kok. Pp. 433–34.

Joosse, L.J. (1992). *'Scoone dingen sijn swaere dingen': Een onderzoek naar de motieven en activiteiten in de Nederlanden tot verbreiding van de gereformeerde religie gedurende de eerste helft van de zeventiende eeuw.* Leiden: Groen.

Josenhans, [J.F.] (1854). "Die ostindische Visitationsreise des Inspector Josenhans im Jahr 1851–1852 (von ihm selbst beschrieben)." *Magazin für die neueste Geschichte der evangelischen Missions- und Bibel-Gesellschaften* 1854/2: 60–163.

Jürgens, Hanco (2014). *Roeping India: Religie, Verlichting en koloniale expansie. Duitse zendingsberichten 1750–1810.* Nijmegen: Radboud University.

Jürgens, Hanco (1994). *Ontdekkers en onderzoekers in de Oost: Britse reisverhalen gespiegeld, 1660–1830.* Utrecht: Vakgroep Geschiedenis der Universiteit Utrecht.

Karageorgévitch, Bojidar (1899). *Enchanted India*. Transl. Clara Bell. New York/London: Harper and Brother.

Karageorgévitch, Bojidar (1897). *Notes sur l'Inde*. Paris: Calmann Lévy.

Kersenboom, Saskia Cornelia (1984). *Nityasumaṅgalī: Towards the Semiosis of the Devadasi Tradition of South India*. Utrecht: Rijksuniversiteit.

Kittel, F. (1982). *A Grammar of the Kannaḍa Language Comprising the Three Dialects of the Language (Ancient, Medieval and Modern)*. New Delhi: Asian Educational Services. Originally published 1908.

Kittel, F. (1968–1977). *Kittel's Kannaḍa-English Dictionary in 4 Volumes*. Ed. M. Mariappa Bhat. Madras: University of Madras. Originally published 1894.

Kittel, F. (1876). *Ueber den Ursprung des Lingakultus in Indien*. Mangalore: Basel Mission Book & Tract Depository.

Kittel, F. (1875a). "Old Kanarese Literature." *The Indian Antiquary* IV: 15–21.

Kittel, F. (1875b). "Seven Liṅgâyta Legends." *The Indian Antiquary* IV: 211–18.

Kittel, F.(1874). *Kāvyamāle: Canarese Poetical Anthology*. 3rd rev. ed. Mangalore: Basel Mission Book & Tract Depository.

Kittel, F. (1872). *A Tract on Sacrifice (Yajnasudhānidhi)*. Mangalore: Stolz & Reuter.

Kittel, F. (1862). *Kathāmāle: A Selection of Scripture Stories in Hindu Metre, New Testament*. Mangalore: Basel Mission Book and Tract Depository.

Klerk, Cornelis Johannes Maria de (1951). *Cultus en ritueel van het orthodoxe Hindoeïsme in Suriname*. Amsterdam: Urbi et Orbi.

Klerk, Jan de, and Hanno Wijsman (2008). *Marco Polo's boek over de wonderen van de wereld: Toelichtingen bij de miniaturen, de tekst en de historische achtergronden aan de hand van 86 folio's van het handschrift van het Livre des merveilles van Marco Polo bewaard in de Bibliothèque nationale de France te Parijs (manuscrit français 2810)*. 's-Hertogenbosch: Stichting Erasmus Festival.

Koeman, C. (1985). "Jan Huygen van Linschoten." *Revista da Universidade de Coimbra* XXXII: 27–47.

Kolff, D.H.A. (1993). "Een Brits-Indische omwandeling." *De Gids* 156: 635–45.

Krishna Deva (1990). *Temples of Khajuraho*. 2 parts. New Delhi: Archaeological Survey of India.

Kurin, Richard (2017). *Hope Diamond: The Legendary History of a Cursed Gem*. Washington DC: Smithsonian Books.

Lach, Donald F., and Edwin J. van Kley (1993). *Asia in the Making of Europe*. Volume III. Books 1 and 2. Chicago/London: University of Chicago Press.

Lach, Donald F. (1965). *Asia in the Making of Europe*. Vol. I. Book 1. Chicago /London: University of Chicago Press.

Launay, Adrien (1898). *Histoire des Missions de l'Inde. Pondichéry, Maïssour, Coïmbatour. Five volumes*. Paris: Ancienne maison Charles Douniol.

Lee, Ton van der(2016). *Jan Huygen: Het gedroomde leven van de grondlegger van de VOC*. Amsterdam: Uitgeverij Balans.

Liebau, Heike (2008). *Die indischen Mitarbeiter der Tranquebarmission (1706–1845). Katecheten, Schulmeister, Übersetzer*. Hallesche Forschungen 26. Tübingen: Verlag der Franckeschen Stiftungen Halle im Max Niemeyer Verlag.

Lind van Wijngaarden, Jan Daniël de (1891). *Antonius Walaeus*. Leiden: Los.

Linschoten, Jan Huygen van (1955–1957). *Itinerario: Voyage ofte schipvaert van Jan Huygen van Linschoten naer Oost ofte Portugaels* Indien. Ed. H. Kern and H. Terpstra. 2nd ed. Three parts. 's-Gravenhage: Martinus Nijhoff.

Linschoten, Jan Huygen van (1596). *Itinerario: Voyage ofte Schipvaert van Jan Huygen van Linschoten naer Oost ofte Portugaels Indien*. Amstelredam (Amsterdam): Cornelis Claesz.

Llewellyn, J.E. (ed.) (2014). *Defining Hinduism: A Reader*. London /New York: Routledge.

Lorenzen, David N. (2014). "Who Invented Hinduism?" In: J.E. Llewellyn (ed.) *Defining Hinduism: A Reader*. London/New York: Routledge. Pp. 52–80.

McKew Parr, Charles (1964). *Jan van Linschoten: The Dutch Marco Polo*. New York: Crowell.

Mazon, A. (1899). "L'abbé Dubois, de St-Remèze." *Revue Historique, Archéologique, Littéraire et Pittoresque du Vivarais Illustrée* 7: 49–57, 97–109, 145–62, 193–210, 241–59.

Mehta, Ved (1982). *Mahatma Gandhi and His Apostles*. Harmondsworth: Penguin Books.

Ménard, Diane, and Anne-Laure Amilhat-Szary (2004). *Le voyage aux Indes de Nicolò de' Conti (1414–1439)*. Collection magellane. Paris: Éditions Chandeigne.

Mitter, Partha (1977). *Much Maligned Monsters: A History of European Reactions to Indian Art*. Oxford: Clarendon Press.

Mohan, Jyoti (2004). "British and French Ethnographies of India: Dubois and his English Commentators." *French Colonial History* 5: 229–46.

Monier-Williams, Monier (1891). *Brāhmanism and Hindūism or, Religious Thought and Life in India*. 4th ed. London: Murray.

Moore, Thomas (n.y.). *The Poetical Works of Thomas Moore*. London: John Walker & Company. Originally published 1817.

Mooij, J. (1927–1931). *Bouwstoffen voor de geschiedenis der Protestantsche Kerk in Nederlandsch-Indië*. Three volumes. Weltevreden: Landsdrukkerij.

Muir, J. (1874). *Religious and Moral Sentiments Freely Translated from Indian Writers*. Edinburgh.

Muir, J. (1860–1872). *Original Sanskrit Texts on the Origin and History of the People of India, their Religion and Institutions*. Five volumes. London: Trübner & Co.

Muir, J. (1852–1854). *Mataparīkṣā: An Examination of Religions*. Two volumes. Mirzapore/Calcutta: Orphan Press/Bishop's College Press.

Muir, J. (1839). *Mataparīkṣā: A Sketch of the Argument for Christianity and against Hinduism, In Sanskrit Verse*. Calcutta: Bishop's College Press.

Murr, Sylvia (1987). *L'indologie du Père Cœurdoux: Stratégies, apologétique et scientificité*. L'inde philosophique entre Bossuet et Voltaire 2. Paris: École française d'Extrême-Orient.

Murr, Sylvia (1977). "Nicolas Jacques Desvaulx (1745–1823), véritable auteur des 'Mœurs, institutions et cérémonies des peuples de l'Inde,' de l'Abbé Dubois." *Puruṣārtha* III: 245–58.

Muusses, Martha Adriana (1920). *Koecultus bij de Hindoes*. Purmerend: J. Muusses.

Nagel, Jürgen C. (2006). "Predikanten und Ziekentrooster: Der Protestantismus in der Welt der Verenigden Oostindischen Compagnie." In: Michael Mann (ed.). *Europäische Aufklärung und protestantische Mission in Indien*. Heidelberg: Draupadi Verlag. Pp. 101–21.

Nehring, Andreas (2003). *Orientalismus und Mission: Die Repräsentation der tamilischen Gesellschaft und Religion durch Leipziger Missionare 1840–1940*. Studien zur außereuropäischen Christentumsgeschichte 7. Wiesbaden: Otto Harrassowitz Verlag.

Neill, Stephen (1985). *A History of Christianity in India 1707–1858*. Cambridge: Cambridge University Press.

Nichols, Andrew (2011). *Ctesias: On India, and Fragments of his Minor Work: Introduction, Translation and Commentary*. London: Bristol Classical Press.

Nilakanta Sastri, K.A. (1957). "Marco Polo on India." In: É. Balazs et al. (eds.). *Oriente Poliano: Studi e conferenze tenute all'Is. M.E.O. in occasione del VII centenario della nascita di Marco Polo (1254–1954)*. Rome: Istituto Italiano per il Medio ed Estremo Oriente. Pp. 111–20.

Noak, Bettina (2012). "Kennistransfer en culturele differentie. Abraham Rogerius en zijn *Open deure tot het verborgen heydendom* (1651)." *Tijdschrift voor Nederlandse Taal- en Letterkunde* 128: 350–64.

Nørgaard, Anders (1988). *Mission und Obrigkeit: Die Dänisch-hallische Mission in Tranquebar 1706–1845*. Transl. Eberhard Harbsmeier. Missionswissenschaftliche Forschungen 22. Gütersloh: Gerd Mohn.

Odoric of Pordenone (Odoric of Friuli) (2008). *Mijn reis naar het verre oosten: Een verslag uit het begin van de veertiende eeuw*. Transl. Vincent Hunink and Mark Nieuwenhuis. Amsterdam: Athenaeum-Polak & Van Gennep.

(Odorich von Pordenone) (1987). *Die Reise des seligen Odorich von Pordenone nach Indien und China (1314/18–1330)*. Transl. Folker Reichert. Heidelberg: Manutius Verlag.

(Odoricus de Portu Naonis) (1929). "Relatio." In: Anastasius van den Wyngaert (ed.). *Itinera et relationes fratrum minorum saeculi XIII et XIV*. Vol. I. Ad Claras Aquas Quaracchi-Firenze: apud Collegium S. Bonaventurae. Pp. 379–495.

Orta, Garcia de(1895). *Coloquios dos simples e drogas da India*. Vol. II. Ed. Conde de Ficalho. Lisbon: Imprensa Nacional.

Ost-Indisches Gespräch (1732a). *Ost-Indisches Gespräch, In dem Reiche der Todten, Zwischen Bartholomäo Ziegenbalg, Königl. Dänischen Missionario, und Evangelisch-Lutherischen Prediger, zu Tranquebar auf der Küste Coromandel in Ost-Indien, und Johann Cocceo, Einen Holländischen Schiff-Prediger*. Franckfurt.

Ost-Indisches Gespräch (1732b). *Continuatio oder Fortsetzung Des Ost-Indianischen Gesprächs in dem Reiche der Todten, Zwischen Bartholomäo Ziegenbalg, Königl. Dänischen Mißionarien zu Tranquebar auf der Küste Coromandel, Und Einem Heydnisch-Malabarischen Priester, Aleppa Kuru*. Franckfurt.

Parvé, D.C. Steyn (1858–1859). *De Bijbel, de Koran en de Veda's: Tafereel van Britsch-Indië en van den opstand des Indischen legers aldaar*. Two volumes. Haarlem: J.J. Weeveringh.

Pavlowitch, Stevan K. (1978). *Bijou d'art: Histoires de la vie, de l'œuvre et du milieu de Bojidar Karageorgévitch, artiste parisien et prince balkanique (1862–1908)*. Lausanne: L'Âge d'Homme.

Peters, Marion (2002). *In steen geschreven: Leven en sterven van VOC-dienaren op de Kust van Coromandel in India*. Amsterdam: Stichting Historisch Onderzoek in Woord en Beeld/Bas Lubberhuizen.

Phillips, Kim M. (2014). *Before Orientalism: Asian Peoples and Cultures in European Travel Writing, 1245–1510*. The Middle Ages Series. Philadelphia: University of Pennsylvania Press.

Plattner, Felix A. (1955). *Pfeffer und Seelen: Die Entdeckung des See- und Landweges nach Asien*. Einsiedeln: Benziger.

Plumptre, Constance E. (2011). *General Sketch of the History of Pantheism*. Cambridge Library Collection—Religion. Cambridge: Cambridge University Press. Originally published 1878.

Pol, Bauke van der(2011). *De VOC in India: Een reis langs Nederlands erfgoed in Gujarat, Malabar, Coromandel en Bengalen*. Zutphen: Walburg Pers.

Polo, Marco (2008). De wonderen van de Oriënt: Il Milione. Transl. Anton Haakman. 2nd ed. Amsterdam: Athenaeum-Polak & Van Gennep.

Polo, Marco (1994). *Milione: Versione toscana del Trecento*. Ed. Valeria Bertolucci Pizzorusso and Giorgio R. Cardona. Milano: Adelphi.

Polo, Marco (1993). *The Travels of Marco Polo: The Complete Yule-Cordier Edition, including the Unabridged Third Edition (1903) of Henry Yule's Annotated Translation, as Revised by Henri Cordier, Together with Cordier's Later Volume of Notes and Addenda (1920)*. Two volumes. New York: Dover Publications.

Powell, A.A. (2010). *Scottish Orientalists and India: The Muir Brothers, Religion, Education and Empire*. Worlds of the East India Company 4. Woodbridge: Boydell Press.

Prasad, Ram Chandra (1980). *Early English Travellers in India: A Study in the Travel Literature of the Elizabethan and Jacobean Periods with Particular Reference to India*. Delhi: Motilal Banarsidass.

Prins, Yvonne (2002). "Leidse vrouwen naar de Oost." *Jaarboek van het Centraal Bureau voor Genealogie* 56. The Hague: Centraal Bureau voor Genealogie. Pp. 179–216.

Rajaiah, Jeyaraj (2016). *Dalit Humanization: A Quest Based on M.M. Thomas' Theology of Salvation and Humanization*. Utrecht: Utrecht University.

Rajamanickam, S. (1972a). *Roberto de Nobili on Indian Customs: Informatio de quibusdam moribus nationis Indicae*. Palayamkottai: De Nobili Research Institute.

Rajamanickam, S. (1972b). *The First Oriental Scholar*. Tirunelveli: De Nobili Research Institute.

Rajkumar, Peniel (2016). *Dalit Theology and Dalit Liberation: Problems, Paradigms and Possibilities*. London /New York: Routledge.

Rietbergen, Peter (2007). *Europa's India: Fascinatie en cultureel imperialisme, circa 1750–circa 2000*. Nijmegen: Uitgeverij Vantilt.

Ristuccia, Nathan J. (2013). "Eastern Religions and the West: The Making of an Image." *History of Religions* 53: 170–204.

Robert, Daniel (1978). "Les diplômes décernés par la faculté protestante de théologie de Paris (1877–1906)." *Bulletin de la société de l'Histoire du Protestantisme Français* 124: 282–309, 424–45, 552–84.

Rocaries, André (1967). *Robert de Nobili s.j. ou le "sannyasi" chrétien*. Toulouse: Prière.

Rogerius, Abraham (1915). *De Open-Deure tot het Verborgen Heydendom*. Ed. W. Caland. 's-Gravenhage: Martinus Nijhoff.

Rogerius, Abraham (1651). *De Open-Deure Tot het Verborgen Heydendom Ofte Waerachtigh vertoog van het Leven ende Zeden, mitsgaders de Religie, ende Gods-dienst der Bramines, op de Cust Chormandel ende de Landen daar ontrent*. Leyden: Françoys Hackes.

Rubiés, Joan-Pau (2000). *Travel and Ethnology in the Renaissance: South India through European Eyes, 1250–1625*. Cambridge: Cambridge University Press.

Said, Edward W. (1978). *Orientalism*. New York: Pantheon Books.

Saldanha, Joseph L. (1907). *The Christian Puranna of Father Thomas Stephens of the Society of Jesus*. Mangalore: Simon Alvares.

Scharfe, Hartmut (2002). *Education in Ancient India*. Handbuch der Orientalistik Indien 16. Leiden/Boston: Brill.

Schmidt, Yvonne (2006). "Tranquebar unter dem Danebrog: Die Rolle der Dänen im multikulturellen Handelsnetz an der Koromandel-Küste." In: Michael Mann (ed.). *Europäische Aufklärung und protestantische Mission in Indien*. Heidelberg: Draupadi Verlag. Pp. 81–99.

Schouten, Jan Peter (2010). "Piëtistische propaganda in een heidens jasje: Een onbekend geschrift over het zendingswerk van Ziegenbalg." *Kerk en Theologie* 61: 143–55.

Schouten, Jan Peter (2008a) "Hindoeïsme." In: Meerten ter Borg et al. (eds.). *Handboek Religie in Nederland: Perspectief—overzicht—debat*. Zoetermeer: Uitgeverij Meinema. Pp. 253–64.

Schouten, Jan Peter (2008b). *Jesus as Guru: The Image of Christ among Hindus and Christians in India*. Transl. Henry and Lucy Jansen. Currents of Encounter 36. Amsterdam/New York: Rodopi.

Schouten, Jan Peter (1996). *Goddelijke vergezichten: Mystiek uit India voor westerse lezers*. Baarn: Ten Have.

Schouten, Jan Peter (1991). *Revolution of the Mystics: On the Social Aspects of Vīraśaivism*. Kampen: Kok Pharos.

Schurhammer, Georg (1957). "Der Marathidichter Thomas Stephens S.I. Neue Dokumente." *Archivum historicum Societatis Iesu* 26: 67–82.

Schurhammer, Georg (1955–1973), *Franz Xaver: Sein Leben und seine Zeit*. Four parts. Freiburg: Herder.

Sewell, Robert (1900). *A Forgotten Empire (Vijayanagar): A Contribution to the History of India*. London: Swan Sonnenschein.

Sharafuddin, Mohammed (1994). *Islam and Romantic Orientalism: Literary Encounters with the Orient*. London/New York: I.B. Tauris Publishers.

Singh, Ramjee, and S. Sundaram (eds.) (1996). *Gandhi and The World Order*. New Delhi: APH Publishing Corp.

Sivapriyananda, Swami (1995). *Mysore Royal Dasara*. New Delhi: Abhinav Publications.

Smith, George (1913). *The Life of William Carey: Shoemaker and Missionary*. 2nd ed. London/New York: J.M. Dent/Dutton.

Starža-Majewski, Olgierd Maria Ludwik (1983). *The Jagannātha Temple at Puri and its Deities*. Amsterdam: University of Amsterdam.

Stolz, C. (2015). *Die Basler Mission in Indien: Zugleich als Festschrift zum 50jährigen Jubiläum der Kanara-Mission*. Treuchtlingen: Literaricon. Originally published 1884.

Sweetman, Will (2004). "The Prehistory of Orientalism: Colonialism and the Textual Basis for Bartholomäus Ziegenbalg's Account of Hinduism." *New Zealand Journal of Asian Studies* 6: 12–38.

Sweetman, Will (2003). *Mapping Hinduism: 'Hinduism' and the Study of Indian Religions, 1600–1776*. Neue Hallesche Berichte 4. Halle: Verlag der Franckeschen Stiftungen.

Tafur, Pero (1874). *Andanças é viajes de Pero Tafur por diversas partes del mundo avidos (1435–1439)*. Madrid: Ginesta.

Tavernier, Jean Baptiste (1676). *Les six voyages de Jean Baptiste Tavernier.* Part 2. Paris: Gervais Clouzier/Claude Barbin.

Terpstra, H. (1946). "Tropische levenskunst in de XVIIe eeuw." *Cultureel Indië* 8: 199–210.

Tertullian (1952). *Apologeticum: Verteidigung des Christentums.* Ed. Carl Becker. Munich: Kösel-Verlag.

Thurston, Edgar, and K. Rangachari (1975). *Castes and Tribes of Southern India.* Seven volumes. Delhi: Cosmo Publications.

Tiliander, Bror (1974). *Christian and Hindu Terminology: A Study in Their Mutual Relations with Special Reference to the Tamil Area.* Skrifter utgivna av Religionshistoriska Institutionen i Uppsala (Hum. Fak.) 12. Uppsala: Almqvist & Wiksell.

Troostenburg de Bruijn, C.A.L. van(1893). *Biographisch Woordenboek van Oost-Indische Predikanten.* Nijmegen: Milborn.

Troostenburg de Bruijn, C.A.L. van (1884). *De Hervormde Kerk in Nederlandsch Oost-Indië onder de Oost-Indische Compagnie (1602–1795).* Arnhem: Tjeenk Willink.

Urwick, W. (1985). *India 100 Years Ago: The Beauty of Old India Illustrated.* London: Bracken Books.

Urwick, W.(1885). *Indian Pictures, Drawn with Pen and Pencil.* London: The Religious Tract Society.

Valentijn, François (1724–1726). *Oud en Nieuw Oost-Indiën: Vervattende Een Naaukeurige en Uitvoerige Verhandelinge van Nederlands Mogentheyd In die Gewesten.* Five volumes. Dordrecht/Amsterdam: Joannes van Braam/Gerard onder de Linden.

Vaudeville, Charlotte (1993). *A Weaver Named Kabir: Selected Verses, With a Detailed Biographical and Historical Introduction.* Delhi: Oxford University Press.

Veer, P. van der(2001). *Imperial Encounters: Religion and Modernity in India and Britain.* Princeton/Oxford: Princeton University Press.

Veth, P.J. (1884). *Ontdekkers en onderzoekers: Zevental levensschetsen.* 2nd ed. Leiden: Brill.

Weigle, G. (1854). "Die Leichenceremonien der Lingaiten." *Magazin für die neueste Geschichte der evangelischen Missions- und Bibel-Gesellschaften* 1854/1: 102–08.

Wendt, Reinhard (2008). "Visionärer Missionsstratege oder praxisferner Schreibstubengelehrter? Ferdinand Kittel und seine Studien zum südindischen Kannada." In: Michael Mann (ed.). *Aufgeklärter Geist und evangelische Missionen in Indien.* Heidelberg: Draupadi Verlag. Pp. 119–42.

Wendt, Reinhard (ed.) (2006). *An Indian to the Indians? On the Initial Failure and the Posthumous Success of the Missionary Ferdinand Kittel (1832–1903).* Studien zur außereuropäischen Christentumsgeschichte 9. Wiesbaden: Otto Harrassowitz Verlag.

Wessels, C. (1935). "De verzwegen bronnen van Philippus Baldaeus' 'Afgoderije der Oost-Indische Heydenen'." *Studiën* 67: 482–85.

Wilkins, Charles (1785). *The Bhăgvăt-Gēētā, or Dialogues of Krēēshnă and Ărjŏŏn*. London: C. Nourse.

Winter Jones, J. (1857). "The Travels of Nicolò Conti in the East in the Early Part of the Fifteenth Century." In: R.H. Major (ed.). *India in the Fifteenth Century*. London: Hakluyt Society.

Wittkower, R. (1957). "Marco Polo and the Pictorial Tradition of the Marvels of the East." In: É. Balazs et al. (eds.). *Oriente Poliano: Studi e conferenze tenute all'Is. M.E.O. in occasione del VII centenario della nascita di Marco Polo (1254–1954)*. Rome: Istituto Italiano per il Medio ed Estremo Oriente. Pp. 155–72.

Würth, G. (1865–1866a). "The Basava Purâna of the Lingaits." *Journal of the Bombay Branch of the Royal Asiatic Society* VIII/24: 65–97.

Würth, G. (1865–1866b). "Channa-Basava Puráṇa of the Lingaits." *Journal of the Bombay Branch of the Royal Asiatic Society* VIII/24: 98–221.

Würth, G. (1853). "Ueber das Religionssystem der Lingaiten." *Magazin für die neueste Geschichte der evangelischen Missions- und Bibel-Gesellschaften* 1853/1: 86–149.

Wyss-Giacosa, Paola von, and Andreas Isler (2006). "Die 'Offne Thür zu dem Verborgenen Heydenthum': Frühe Titelkupfer zu Indien." *Librarium* 49: 58–68.

Xavier, Ângela Barreto, and Ines G. Županov (2015). *Catholic Orientalism: Portuguese Empire, Indian Knowledge (16th–18th Centuries)*. New Delhi: Oxford UniversityPress.

Young, Richard Fox (2008). "Can Christians Be Bhaktas?" *Journal of Hindu-Christian Studies* 21: 56–62.

Young, Richard Fox (1981). *Resistant Hinduism: Sanskrit Sources on Anti-Christian Apologetics in Early Nineteenth-Century India*. Publications of the De Nobili Research Library VIII. Vienna: Indological Institute University of Vienna.

Yule, Henry, and Henri Cordier (1913–1916). *Cathay and the Way Thither: Being a Collection of Medieval Notices of China*. New ed. Four volumes. London: Hakluyt Society.

Yule, Henry, and A.C. Burnell (1986). *Hobson-Jobson: A Glossary of Colloquial Anglo-Indian Words and Phrases*. 2nd ed. London/New York: Routledge & Kegan Paul.

Ziegenbalg, Bartholomaeus (2006). *A German Exploration of Indian Society: Ziegenbalg's "Malabarian Heathenism." An Annotated English Translation with an Introduction and a Glossary*. Transl. Daniel Jeyaraj. Chennai/New Delhi: Mylapore Institute for Indigenous Studies/Indian Society for Promoting Christian Knowledge.

Ziegenbalg, Bartholomaeus (2005). *Genealogy of the South Indian Deities: An English Translation of Bartholomäus Ziegenbalg's Original German Manuscript with a Textual Analysis and Glossary*. Transl. Daniel Jeyaraj. RoutledgeCurzon Studies in Asian Religions. London/New York: RoutledgeCurzon.

Ziegenbalg, Bartholomaeus (1930). *Kleinere Schriften: Nītiveṇpā, Koṉṟaivēntaṉ, Ulakanīti.* Ed. W. Caland. Verhandelingen der Koninklijke Akademie van Wetenschappen te Amsterdam, Afd. Letterkunde, Nieuwe reeks XXIX/2. Amsterdam: Koninklijke Akademie van Wetenschappen.

Ziegenbalg, Bartholomaeus (1926). *Ziegenbalg's Malabarisches Heidenthums.* Ed. W. Caland. Verhandelingen der Koninklijke Akademie van Wetenschappen te Amsterdam, Afd. Letterkunde, Nieuwe reeks XXV/3. Amsterdam: Koninklijke Akademie van Wetenschappen.

Ziegenbalg, Bartholomaeus (1867). *Genealogie der malabarishen* [sic] *Götter.* Ed. Wilhelm Germann. Madras: Christian Knowledge Society's Presse.

Zubkova, Luba (2004). "Pioneers of Orientalism at the VOC." *IIAS Newsletter* 35: 14.

Županov, Ines G. (2001), *Disputed Mission: Jesuit Experiments and Brahmanical Knowledge in Seventeenth-Century India.* New Delhi: Oxford University Press.

Online Resources

Der Königl. Dänischen Missionarien aus Ost-Indien eingesandter Ausführlichen Berichten, Von dem Werck ihres Amts unter den Heyden, angerichteten Schulen und Gemeinen, ereigneten Hindernissen und schweren Umständen; Beschaffenheit des Malabarischen Heydenthums, gepflogenen brieflichen Correspondentz und mündlichen Unterredungen mit selbigen Heyden ... Teil 1–9 (Continuation 1–108) (Halle 1710–1772) [the 'Hallesche Berichte']. Accessed 6 July 2017. http://192.124.243.55/digbib/hb.htm.

Karttunen, Klaus. *Persons of Indian Studies.* www.whowaswho-indology.info. Accessed 23 October 2017.

Le temps: Rechercher dans les archives de la Gazette de Lausanne et du Journal de Genève. www.letempsarchives.ch. Accessed 17 November 2017.

Scriptorium, Bibliotèque cantonale et universitaire BCU Lausanne. https://scriptorium.bcu-lausanne.ch. Accessed 17 November 2017.

Vail, Jeffery W. (2005). "'The Standard of Revolt': Revolution and National Independence in Moore's Lalla Rookh." *Romanticism on the Net* 40. Accessed 10 November 2017. http://id.erudit.org/iderudit/012459ar.

Archival Records

Basel

Basler Mission Archives

Correspondence of A.A. Bourquin with the Basler Mission, 1875.

Quarterly report of the Mission Post Palghaut July 1875.

Bern

State Archives of the Canton of Bern

Régistre des Naissances et Baptêmes de la Paroisse de Sonvillier (1832–1853). inv.no. K Sonvilier 1.

Leiden

Regional Archives Leiden (Erfgoed Leiden en omstreken)

Kerkelijke huwelijksproclamaties der gereformeerden deel 1626–1633, inv. no. 1004/10.

Leiden University, Special Collections

Correspondence of John Muir with Abraham Kuenen 1869–1881 (BPL 3028).

Index

accomodatio 49, 156, 176, 181
ādivāsī 109, 181
Agni 49, 181
aiyar 45, 181
Aleppa Kuru (ca. 1660–1730) 84, 86, 87
Anbequemung 156, 181
anuṣṭubh 122, 181
Aurangzeb, Mogul emperor (1618–1707) 131, 134
avarṇa 108, 181
avatāra 51, 66, 73, 74, 181

bachali 28, 181
Baldaeus, Philippus (1632–1671) IV, 60, 72–77, 101, 170
Baniyā 32, 181
Barbosa, Duarte (ca. 1480–1521) 33
Barth, Christian Gottlob (1799–1862) 151
Basava Purāṇa 73, 154, 181
bautismu 56, 181
Beauchamp, Henry King (1866–1907) 109
Bengali 115, 118, 119, 172, 181
Bentinck, Lord William (1774–1839) 100
Bhadrakālī 73, 181
Bhagavad Gītā 114, 115, 116, 130, 137, 181
Bhāgavata Purāṇa 73, 111, 181
bhakti 4, 94, 181
Bhartṛhari (seventh century CE) 70, 178
Bouchet, Jean Venant (1655–1732) 99
Bourquin, Auguste Ali (1848–1928) 156–163, 177
Bracciolini, Poggio (1380–1459) 24–30, 166
Brahmā 28, 73, 77, 99, 124, 177, 181
Brahmin (Brāhmaṇa) passim
Brahmacarya 17, 181
Brahmakarmapustaka 161, 181
Brāhma Samāj 139, 181
Burnell, Arthur C. (1840–1882) 60

Caland, Willem (1859–1932) 60, 178
Candra 133, 181
Cannabasava Purāṇa 154, 156, 182
Canter Visscher, Jacobus (1692–1735) 77, 78
Carey, William (1761–1834) 118, 119, 121, 169
Carpenter, Mary (1807–1877) 137–139, 178
Carvēcuraṉ (Sarveśvara) 50, 110, 176, 182
cattiyavētam (satyaveda) 43, 182
Charpentier, Jarl (1884–1935) 74
Clement of Rome (first century CE) 127
Coccejus, Johannes (1603–1669) 86
Cœrdoux, Gaston-Laurent (1691–1779) 99, 101
Collins, Wilkie (1824–1889) 133–135
Confucius (551–479 BCE) 41
Conti, Nicolò de' (1395–1469) 24–30, 168, 175
Ctesias of Cnidos (ca. 400 BCE) 10
Cynocephali 11, 12, 182
Cyprian (third century CE) 126

Dakṣiṇā 32, 182
Dalits 53, 106, 175, 177, 182
Damersa (mentioned 1642) 65, 66
Dasahrā 29, 182
Desvaulx, Nicolas-Jacques (1745–1817) 101
Deussen, Paul (1845–1919) 126
devadāsī 14, 17, 69, 90, 170, 182
devanāgari 119, 182
Devī 29, 182
Dharampal-Frick, Gita (* 1952) 95
dharmaśāstra 48, 124, 182
Dharmasindhu 159, 182
Dickens, Charles J.H. (1812–1870) 133
Diderot, Denis (1713–1784) 72
Dīvālī 29, 182
Doḍḍa svāmiyavaru 103, 182
Doetechum, Baptista van (ca. 1560–1611) 35
Doetechum, Joannes van (ca. 1560–1630) 35
Dubois, Jean-Antoine (1766–1848) 99–112, 114, 172, 173, 175, 177, 178

Eden, Emily (1797–1869) 134, 135–137
Eden, George, Earl of Auckland (1784–1849) 135
Eknāth (sixteenth century) 54
Eusebius of Caesarea (ca. 260–ca. 340) 127
evidential theology 122, 182
Eyth, Pauline Friederike (1833–1864) 150
Eyth, Wilhelmine Julie (1844–1927) 150, 151

faqīr 168, 182
Fenicio, Jacobo (ca. 1558–ca. 1632) 74
Fernandez, Gonçalo (1541–1619) 42, 43, 46, 47, 48
fidalgos 33, 182
Francis of Assisi (1181/2–1226) 8
Francisco, Pero (1564–1615) 47
Francke, August Hermann (1663–1727) 83, 88
Frederick IV, king of Denmark (1671–1730) 82

Gajendramokṣa 68, 182
Gama, Vasco da (1460/9–1524) 40
Gandhi, Mohandas (Mahatma) (1869–1948) 17, 170
Gaṇeśa 71, 73, 182
Gaṅgā 72, 182
garbhagṛha 34, 182
Garuḍa 69, 182
Gavi 13, 182
Gāyatrī-mantra 49, 161, 182
Genghis Khan, ruler of Mongolia (1162–1227) 7, 8
Goethe, Johann Wolfgang von (1749–1832) 69
gopuram 141, 183
Goreh, Nilakantha (Nehemiah) (1825–1885) 126
Gregory XV, Pope (1554–1623) 47
gṛhastha 15, 183
Groot, Hugo de (1583–1645) 21
Gujarātī 32, 183
guru 44, 110, 183

Hackes, Françoys (1605–1669) 64
Hallesche Berichte 86, 88, 90, 91, 92, 99, 183
Hanumān 69, 71, 183
Harachandra Tarkapanchanana (nineteenth century) 125, 126
Hastings, Warren (1732–1818) 114, 115, 116
Herodotus of Halicarnassus (ca. 485–425/420 BCE) 7
Hiraṇyakaśipu 73, 75, 183
Holī 29, 183
hook-swinging 30, 65, 72, 168, 183
Hoole, Elijah (1798–1872) 107
Humboldt, Wilhelm Freiherr von (1767–1835) 117

Indra 69, 183

Jagannātha 19, 133, 134, 183
Jahangir, Mogul emperor (1569–1627) 132
Jenner, Edward (1749–1823) 105
jñāna-snāna 56, 183
Jñāneśvar (1275–1296) 54
jñānī 94, 183
John of Montecorvino (1246–1338) 8, 11, 17, 18, 21
John of Plano Carpini (ca. 1185–1252) 8
John the Fearless, duke of Burgundy (1371–1419) 11, 17
John, Christoph Samuel (1746–1813) 173
Jones, William (1746–1794) 116, 117, 171, 172
Jong, Albert Johannes de (1880–1961) 74, 75
Josenhans, Joseph Friedrich (1812–1884) 153, 155, 156
Junius, Robertus (1606–1655) 64

Kabīr (fifteenth century) 4, 5
Kailāsa 67, 183
Kālidāsa (fifth century CE) 117
Kanara 32, 183
Kannada 107, 147, 150, 151, 152, 153, 154, 172, 173, 183
Kannaḍiyan 33, 183
Karageorgévitch, Prince Bojidar (Božidar Karađorđević) (1862–1908) 142–144
karma 51, 57, 126, 183
Kāśīnātha (eighteenth century) 159
Kathāmāle 151, 152, 183
kāvi 44, 183
Kittel, Georg Ferdinand (1832–1903) 147–156, 172, 173, 178
Konkani 54, 183
Koṉṟaivēntaṉ 93, 183
Kristapurāṇa 55, 56, 183
Kristu Svāmī 57, 183
Kṛṣṇa 132, 133, 137, 183
Kṣatriya 43, 108, 183
Kublai Khan, ruler of Mongolia (1215–1294) 9

kuḍumi (cūḍā) 47, 184
Kuenen, Abraham (1828–1891) 120
kuṭumbī 33, 184

Laerzio, Alberto (1557–1630) 42, 47, 49
Lakṣmī 29, 184
Lalla Rookh 130, 131, 132, 133, 184
Lambāḍi 109, 184
Lawbook of Manu (Mānavadharmaśāstra) 48, 117, 184
Lettres édifiantes et curieuses 99, 100, 184
liṅga 12, 66, 67, 73, 76, 91, 154, 170, 184
Liṅgāyatism 12, 13, 153, 154, 178, 184
Linschoten, Jan Huygen van (1562/3–1611) 24–38, 166, 174, 176
Lütkens, Franz Julius (1650–1712) 83

Mahābhārata 115, 117, 128, 184
Mahāśivarātri 28, 184
Mahmud of Ghazni, Muslim ruler (971–1030) 133
"Malabar Correspondence" (Malabarische Korrespondenz) 86, 88, 89, 90, 91, 92, 93, 170, 184
Malabar Rites Controversy 47, 184
Malayalam 77, 78, 184
Malay 61, 63, 184
Mānavadharmaśāstra *see* Lawbook of Manu
Mandeville, John (fourteenth century) 11
Māṇikka Vācakar (ninth century) 50
Marathi 54, 55, 157, 161, 184
Marshman, Joshua (1768–1837) 118, 119
Mataparīkṣā 122, 123, 124, 125, 126, 127, 184
Mataparīkṣāśikṣā 125, 184
Mataparīkṣottara 125, 126, 184
maṭha 45, 184
mesquita 35, 184
mīsai 50, 184
Mögling, Hermann Friedrich (1811–1881) 154
mohadharma 126, 184
Molinaeus, Nicolaus († 1640) 62
Moore, Thomas (1779–1852) 130–133
Muir, John (1810–1882) 114, 119–128, 150, 172, 178
Müller, Friedrich Max (1823–1900) 100, 101, 118
Murr, Sylvia (1947–2002) 101

Nandī 12, 34, 185
nāraka 111, 185
nārasiṃha 19, 66, 73, 185
Navarātri 29, 185
Nāyar 33, 34, 78, 185
nīti 70, 185
Nītiveṇpā 93, 185
Nobili, Roberto de (1577–1656) 41–53, 54, 56, 57, 99, 103, 110, 169, 171, 172, 173, 174, 176

Odoric of Pordenone; also: of Friuli († 1331) 8, 11, 12, 18–20, 167, 175
Otto III, emperor of the Holy Roman Empire (980–1002) 43
ovi 55, 185

Padmanābha (mentioned 1642) 65, 66, 70
Padma-Purāṇa 67, 73, 111, 185
padroado 40, 42, 185
pagoda 31, 34, 132, 185
Paley, William (1743–1805) 122, 123
pañcagavya 19, 185
Pañcatantra 107, 185
paṇḍit 116, 122, 185
paṇṭāracāmi (paṇḍāra-svāmī) 52, 53, 185
Paṟaiyar 13, 43, 53, 68, 107, 108, 109, 141, 185
paraṅgi 42, 43, 46, 47, 99, 185
paraṅgi mārkkam 43, 185
Parāparavastu 94, 185
Parava 41, 42, 185
Parsi 155, 185
Pārvatī 66, 67, 73, 185
Parvé, Daniël Couperus Steyn (1812–1882) 139–140
Patarenes 13, 185
Paul of Tarsus (first century CE) 49, 122, 150, 159
peri 132, 185
Persant, Laurentius (mentioned 1643) 64
Peter I, king of Serbia (1844–1921) 142
Plato (ca. 427–347 BCE) 111, 162
Pliny the Elder (23/4–79) 7
Plumptre, Constance E. (1848–1929) 163
Plütschau, Heinrich († 1752) 82, 83, 84, 86

Polo, Marco (1254–1324) 7–21, 24, 28, 143, 166, 167, 174
Poṅkal 50, 51, 185
Pools, Emmerentia (mentioned 1647) 63, 64
Prahlāda 73, 76, 185
prasād 69, 186
Propertius, Sextus (ca. 47–14 BCE) 169
pūjā 50, 56, 57, 141, 142, 186
Puliyar 33, 186
purāṇa 48, 55, 56, 57, 124, 152, 186
Pythagoras (sixth century BCE) 32, 111, 166

rāga 152, 186
the Raj 140, 141, 186
Rājā 43, 143, 186
Rāmā 143, 186
Ramalocana Kanthavarna (eighteenth century) 116
Rāmāyaṇa 118, 119, 186
Rammohan Roy, Raja (1772–1833) 137, 138, 139, 169, 179
Ranjit Singh, Sikh ruler (1780–1839) 134
Ṛg-Veda 118, 161, 186
Ricci, Matteo (1552–1610) 41
Rogerius, Abraham († 1649) 60–78, 169, 170, 176, 178
Romanae sedis antistes 47, 186
roteiros 25, 186
Ṛśyaśṛṅga 167, 186
Rustichello da Pisa (thirteenth century) 10

sacrifiçiu 56, 186
sādhū 168, 186
Said, Edward W. (1935–2003) 4, 131
śaiva 50, 53, 73, 90, 186
sakkili 108, 186
Śakuntalā 117, 186
saṃsāra 57, 186
sannyāsī 15, 16, 43, 44, 45, 46, 48, 51, 52, 53, 66, 99, 105, 174, 186
Sanskrit 1, 4, 45, 49, 50, 55, 56, 60, 70, 74, 77, 78, 100, 115, 116, 117, 118, 119, 120, 121, 122, 124, 127, 130, 154, 157, 158, 159, 161, 171, 172, 174, 177, 186
Sarasvatī 99, 186
Sarveśvara *see* Carvēcuraṉ
Śāstratattvavinirṇaya 126, 186
Śatapatha-Brāhmaṇa 67, 186
satī 13, 14, 29, 31, 52, 65, 69, 72, 77, 168, 169, 186
ṣaṭpadi 152, 187
Sceperus, Jacobus (1607–1677) 61
Schlegel, Friedrich von (1772–1829) 117
Seminarium Indicum 60, 187
Sen, Keshab Chandra (1838–1884) 139
sepoy 139, 187
Shore, Frederick John (1799–1837) 119, 120
Śiva 28, 50, 66, 67, 69, 71, 73, 76, 77, 124, 170, 176, 187
Soma 133, 187
Somanath Vyas (1807–1885) 125
Spinoza, Baruch (1632–1677) 163
śṛṅgāra 70, 187
Stephens, Thomas (1549–1619) 40, 54–57
Subrahmaṇya 73, 187
śūdra 108, 187
svarga 111, 187

Tafur, Pero (ca. 1410–1484) 25, 29
Tagore, Rabindranath (1861–1941) 170
Taittirīya-āraṇyaka 49, 161, 187
tāla 152, 187
Tamil 1, 13, 41, 42, 45, 46, 48, 50, 51, 63, 73, 77, 84, 85, 86, 88, 91, 93, 94, 95, 100, 107, 157, 171, 172, 187
Tampirāṉ 50, 187
Tavernier, Jean-Baptiste (1605–1689) 133
Telugu 45, 107, 171, 187
Tertullian (ca. 160–ca. 230) 15, 16
ṭhag 140, 187
Tijmans, Maria (married 1630, † before 1636) 61
tilaka 47, 187
Tipu Sultan, ruler of Mysore (1750–1799) 102, 134
tithi 159, 187
Trimūrti 28, 176, 187
Tūṣaṇat Tikkāram 51, 187

Ulakanīti 93, 187
upanayana 49, 187
Upaniṣad 36, 118, 162, 187
Urwick, William, the Younger (1826–1905) 140–142, 170

vairāgya 70, 187
vaiṣṇava 73, 187

vaiśya 108, 187
Valentijn, François (1666–1727) 77
vanaprastha 15, 187
varṇa 68, 108, 187
varṇāśramadharma 15, 188
Veda 4, 5, 45, 48, 49, 68, 77, 115, 118, 124, 126, 127, 140, 154, 155, 158, 161, 162, 163, 188
Veda Samāj 139, 188
Veth, Pieter Johannes (1814–1895) 139
Vīraśaivism 153, 188
Viṣṇu 19, 28, 66, 68, 69, 73, 74, 92, 124, 188
Vlamingh, Arnoldus (mentioned 1643) 64

Walaeus, Antonius (1573–1639) 61
Ward, William (1769–1823) 118, 119
Weigle, Gottfried Hartmann (1816–1855) 154
Wilkins, Charles (1749–1836) 114, 115, 116
Wilks, Mark (1759–1831) 100, 103
William of Rubruck (thirteenth century) 8
William of Solagna (fourteenth century) 18
Würth, Gottlob (1820–1869) 154

Xavier, Francis (1506–1552) 41, 42, 57, 171

yajña 68, 188
yajñopavīta 15, 45, 47, 49, 188
Yajur-Veda 48, 188
yogī 15, 188
yoni 67, 188
yuga 69, 188

Ziegenbalg, Bartholomäus (1682–1719) 82–96, 106, 170, 171, 175, 176, 178
Ziegenbalg-Saltzmann, Maria Dorothea (1693–1776) 96
Zoroastrianism 131, 132, 188

Printed in the United States
By Bookmasters